GNU MP - Multiple Precision Arithmetic Library

A catalogue record for this book is available from the Hong Kong Public Libraries.

Published in Hong Kong by Samurai Media Limited.

Email: info@samuraimedia.org

ISBN 978-988-8381-96-8

Table of Contents

GNU MP Copying Conditions

This library is *free*; this means that everyone is free to use it and free to redistribute it on a free basis. The library is not in the public domain; it is copyrighted and there are restrictions on its distribution, but these restrictions are designed to permit everything that a good cooperating citizen would want to do. What is not allowed is to try to prevent others from further sharing any version of this library that they might get from you.

Specifically, we want to make sure that you have the right to give away copies of the library, that you receive source code or else can get it if you want it, that you can change this library or use pieces of it in new free programs, and that you know you can do these things.

To make sure that everyone has such rights, we have to forbid you to deprive anyone else of these rights. For example, if you distribute copies of the GNU MP library, you must give the recipients all the rights that you have. You must make sure that they, too, receive or can get the source code. And you must tell them their rights.

Also, for our own protection, we must make certain that everyone finds out that there is no warranty for the GNU MP library. If it is modified by someone else and passed on, we want their recipients to know that what they have is not what we distributed, so that any problems introduced by others will not reflect on our reputation.

More precisely, the GNU MP library is dual licensed, under the conditions of the GNU Lesser General Public License version 3 (see `COPYING.LESSERv3`), or the GNU General Public License version 2 (see `COPYINGv2`). This is the recipient's choice, and the recipient also has the additional option of applying later versions of these licenses. (The reason for this dual licensing is to make it possible to use the library with programs which are licensed under GPL version 2, but which for historical or other reasons do not allow use under later versions of the GPL).

Programs which are not part of the library itself, such as demonstration programs and the GMP testsuite, are licensed under the terms of the GNU General Public License version 3 (see `COPYINGv3`), or any later version.

1 Introduction to GNU MP

GNU MP is a portable library written in C for arbitrary precision arithmetic on integers, rational numbers, and floating-point numbers. It aims to provide the fastest possible arithmetic for all applications that need higher precision than is directly supported by the basic C types.

Many applications use just a few hundred bits of precision; but some applications may need thousands or even millions of bits. GMP is designed to give good performance for both, by choosing algorithms based on the sizes of the operands, and by carefully keeping the overhead at a minimum.

The speed of GMP is achieved by using fullwords as the basic arithmetic type, by using sophisticated algorithms, by including carefully optimized assembly code for the most common inner loops for many different CPUs, and by a general emphasis on speed (as opposed to simplicity or elegance).

There is assembly code for these CPUs: ARM Cortex-A9, Cortex-A15, and generic ARM, DEC Alpha 21064, 21164, and 21264, AMD K8 and K10 (sold under many brands, e.g. Athlon64, Phenom, Opteron) Bulldozer, and Bobcat, Intel Pentium, Pentium Pro/II/III, Pentium 4, Core2, Nehalem, Sandy bridge, Haswell, generic x86, Intel IA-64, Motorola/IBM PowerPC 32 and 64 such as POWER970, POWER5, POWER6, and POWER7, MIPS 32-bit and 64-bit, SPARC 32-bit ad 64-bit with special support for all UltraSPARC models. There is also assembly code for many obsolete CPUs.

For up-to-date information on GMP, please see the GMP web pages at

    https://gmplib.org/

The latest version of the library is available at

    https://ftp.gnu.org/gnu/gmp/

Many sites around the world mirror 'ftp.gnu.org', please use a mirror near you, see https://www.gnu.org/order/ftp.html for a full list.

There are three public mailing lists of interest. One for release announcements, one for general questions and discussions about usage of the GMP library and one for bug reports. For more information, see

    https://gmplib.org/mailman/listinfo/.

The proper place for bug reports is gmp-bugs@gmplib.org. See Chapter 4 [Reporting Bugs], page 29 for information about reporting bugs.

1.1 How to use this Manual

Everyone should read Chapter 3 [GMP Basics], page 17. If you need to install the library yourself, then read Chapter 2 [Installing GMP], page 3. If you have a system with multiple ABIs, then read Section 2.2 [ABI and ISA], page 8, for the compiler options that must be used on applications.

The rest of the manual can be used for later reference, although it is probably a good idea to glance through it.

2 Installing GMP

GMP has an autoconf/automake/libtool based configuration system. On a Unix-like system a basic build can be done with

```
./configure
make
```

Some self-tests can be run with

```
make check
```

And you can install (under `/usr/local` by default) with

```
make install
```

If you experience problems, please report them to gmp-bugs@gmplib.org. See Chapter 4 [Reporting Bugs], page 29, for information on what to include in useful bug reports.

2.1 Build Options

All the usual autoconf configure options are available, run '`./configure --help`' for a summary. The file `INSTALL.autoconf` has some generic installation information too.

Tools   '`configure`' requires various Unix-like tools. See Section 2.4 [Notes for Particular Systems], page 12, for some options on non-Unix systems.

It might be possible to build without the help of '`configure`', certainly all the code is there, but unfortunately you'll be on your own.

Build Directory
To compile in a separate build directory, `cd` to that directory, and prefix the configure command with the path to the GMP source directory. For example

```
cd /my/build/dir
/my/sources/gmp-6.0.0/configure
```

Not all '`make`' programs have the necessary features (`VPATH`) to support this. In particular, SunOS and Slowaris `make` have bugs that make them unable to build in a separate directory. Use GNU `make` instead.

`--prefix` and `--exec-prefix`
The `--prefix` option can be used in the normal way to direct GMP to install under a particular tree. The default is '`/usr/local`'.

`--exec-prefix` can be used to direct architecture-dependent files like `libgmp.a` to a different location. This can be used to share architecture-independent parts like the documentation, but separate the dependent parts. Note however that `gmp.h` and `mp.h` are architecture-dependent since they encode certain aspects of `libgmp`, so it will be necessary to ensure both `$prefix/include` and `$exec_prefix/include` are available to the compiler.

`--disable-shared`, `--disable-static`
By default both shared and static libraries are built (where possible), but one or other can be disabled. Shared libraries result in smaller executables and permit code sharing between separate running processes, but on some CPUs are slightly slower, having a small cost on each function call.

Native Compilation, `--build=CPU-VENDOR-OS`
For normal native compilation, the system can be specified with '`--build`'. By default '`./configure`' uses the output from running '`./config.guess`'. On some

systems '`./config.guess`' can determine the exact CPU type, on others it will be necessary to give it explicitly. For example,

>   ./configure --build=ultrasparc-sun-solaris2.7

In all cases the '`OS`' part is important, since it controls how libtool generates shared libraries. Running '`./config.guess`' is the simplest way to see what it should be, if you don't know already.

Cross Compilation, `--host=CPU-VENDOR-OS`

When cross-compiling, the system used for compiling is given by '`--build`' and the system where the library will run is given by '`--host`'. For example when using a FreeBSD Athlon system to build GNU/Linux m68k binaries,

>   ./configure --build=athlon-pc-freebsd3.5 --host=m68k-mac-linux-gnu

Compiler tools are sought first with the host system type as a prefix. For example `m68k-mac-linux-gnu-ranlib` is tried, then plain `ranlib`. This makes it possible for a set of cross-compiling tools to co-exist with native tools. The prefix is the argument to '`--host`', and this can be an alias, such as '`m68k-linux`'. But note that tools don't have to be setup this way, it's enough to just have a `PATH` with a suitable cross-compiling `cc` etc.

Compiling for a different CPU in the same family as the build system is a form of cross-compilation, though very possibly this would merely be special options on a native compiler. In any case '`./configure`' avoids depending on being able to run code on the build system, which is important when creating binaries for a newer CPU since they very possibly won't run on the build system.

In all cases the compiler must be able to produce an executable (of whatever format) from a standard C `main`. Although only object files will go to make up `libgmp`, '`./configure`' uses linking tests for various purposes, such as determining what functions are available on the host system.

Currently a warning is given unless an explicit '`--build`' is used when cross-compiling, because it may not be possible to correctly guess the build system type if the `PATH` has only a cross-compiling `cc`.

Note that the '`--target`' option is not appropriate for GMP. It's for use when building compiler tools, with '`--host`' being where they will run, and '`--target`' what they'll produce code for. Ordinary programs or libraries like GMP are only interested in the '`--host`' part, being where they'll run. (Some past versions of GMP used '`--target`' incorrectly.)

CPU types

In general, if you want a library that runs as fast as possible, you should configure GMP for the exact CPU type your system uses. However, this may mean the binaries won't run on older members of the family, and might run slower on other members, older or newer. The best idea is always to build GMP for the exact machine type you intend to run it on.

The following CPUs have specific support. See `configure.ac` for details of what code and compiler options they select.

- Alpha: '`alpha`', '`alphaev5`', '`alphaev56`', '`alphapca56`', '`alphapca57`', '`alphaev6`', '`alphaev67`', '`alphaev68`' '`alphaev7`'

- Cray: '`c90`', '`j90`', '`t90`', '`sv1`'

- HPPA: '`hppa1.0`', '`hppa1.1`', '`hppa2.0`', '`hppa2.0n`', '`hppa2.0w`', '`hppa64`'

- IA-64:   '`ia64`', '`itanium`', '`itanium2`'

- MIPS: '`mips`', '`mips3`', '`mips64`'

- Motorola: 'm68k', 'm68000', 'm68010', 'm68020', 'm68030', 'm68040', 'm68060', 'm68302', 'm68360', 'm88k', 'm88110'
- POWER: 'power', 'power1', 'power2', 'power2sc'
- PowerPC: 'powerpc', 'powerpc64', 'powerpc401', 'powerpc403', 'powerpc405', 'powerpc505', 'powerpc601', 'powerpc602', 'powerpc603', 'powerpc603e', 'powerpc604', 'powerpc604e', 'powerpc620', 'powerpc630', 'powerpc740', 'powerpc7400', 'powerpc7450', 'powerpc750', 'powerpc801', 'powerpc821', 'powerpc823', 'powerpc860', 'powerpc970'
- SPARC: 'sparc', 'sparcv8', 'microsparc', 'supersparc', 'sparcv9', 'ultrasparc', 'ultrasparc2', 'ultrasparc2i', 'ultrasparc3', 'sparc64'
- x86 family: 'i386', 'i486', 'i586', 'pentium', 'pentiummmx', 'pentiumpro', 'pentium2', 'pentium3', 'pentium4', 'k6', 'k62', 'k63', 'athlon', 'amd64', 'viac3', 'viac32'
- Other: 'arm', 'sh', 'sh2', 'vax',

CPUs not listed will use generic C code.

Generic C Build

If some of the assembly code causes problems, or if otherwise desired, the generic C code can be selected with the configure `--disable-assembly`.

Note that this will run quite slowly, but it should be portable and should at least make it possible to get something running if all else fails.

Fat binary, `--enable-fat`

Using `--enable-fat` selects a "fat binary" build on x86, where optimized low level subroutines are chosen at runtime according to the CPU detected. This means more code, but gives good performance on all x86 chips. (This option might become available for more architectures in the future.)

ABI   On some systems GMP supports multiple ABIs (application binary interfaces), meaning data type sizes and calling conventions. By default GMP chooses the best ABI available, but a particular ABI can be selected. For example

```
./configure --host=mips64-sgi-irix6 ABI=n32
```

See Section 2.2 [ABI and ISA], page 8, for the available choices on relevant CPUs, and what applications need to do.

CC, CFLAGS

By default the C compiler used is chosen from among some likely candidates, with gcc normally preferred if it's present. The usual 'CC=whatever' can be passed to './configure' to choose something different.

For various systems, default compiler flags are set based on the CPU and compiler. The usual 'CFLAGS="-whatever"' can be passed to './configure' to use something different or to set good flags for systems GMP doesn't otherwise know.

The 'CC' and 'CFLAGS' used are printed during './configure', and can be found in each generated Makefile. This is the easiest way to check the defaults when considering changing or adding something.

Note that when 'CC' and 'CFLAGS' are specified on a system supporting multiple ABIs it's important to give an explicit 'ABI=whatever', since GMP can't determine the ABI just from the flags and won't be able to select the correct assembly code.

If just 'CC' is selected then normal default 'CFLAGS' for that compiler will be used (if GMP recognises it). For example 'CC=gcc' can be used to force the use of GCC, with default flags (and default ABI).

CPPFLAGS   Any flags like '-D' defines or '-I' includes required by the preprocessor should be set in 'CPPFLAGS' rather than 'CFLAGS'. Compiling is done with both 'CPPFLAGS' and 'CFLAGS', but preprocessing uses just 'CPPFLAGS'. This distinction is because most preprocessors won't accept all the flags the compiler does. Preprocessing is done separately in some configure tests.

CC_FOR_BUILD
              Some build-time programs are compiled and run to generate host-specific data tables. 'CC_FOR_BUILD' is the compiler used for this. It doesn't need to be in any particular ABI or mode, it merely needs to generate executables that can run. The default is to try the selected 'CC' and some likely candidates such as 'cc' and 'gcc', looking for something that works.

              No flags are used with 'CC_FOR_BUILD' because a simple invocation like 'cc foo.c' should be enough. If some particular options are required they can be included as for instance 'CC_FOR_BUILD="cc -whatever"'.

C++ Support, --enable-cxx
              C++ support in GMP can be enabled with '--enable-cxx', in which case a C++ compiler will be required. As a convenience '--enable-cxx=detect' can be used to enable C++ support only if a compiler can be found. The C++ support consists of a library libgmpxx.la and header file gmpxx.h (see Section 3.1 [Headers and Libraries], page 17).

              A separate libgmpxx.la has been adopted rather than having C++ objects within libgmp.la in order to ensure dynamic linked C programs aren't bloated by a dependency on the C++ standard library, and to avoid any chance that the C++ compiler could be required when linking plain C programs.

              libgmpxx.la will use certain internals from libgmp.la and can only be expected to work with libgmp.la from the same GMP version. Future changes to the relevant internals will be accompanied by renaming, so a mismatch will cause unresolved symbols rather than perhaps mysterious misbehaviour.

              In general libgmpxx.la will be usable only with the C++ compiler that built it, since name mangling and runtime support are usually incompatible between different compilers.

CXX, CXXFLAGS
              When C++ support is enabled, the C++ compiler and its flags can be set with variables 'CXX' and 'CXXFLAGS' in the usual way. The default for 'CXX' is the first compiler that works from a list of likely candidates, with g++ normally preferred when available. The default for 'CXXFLAGS' is to try 'CFLAGS', 'CFLAGS' without '-g', then for g++ either '-g -O2' or '-O2', or for other compilers '-g' or nothing. Trying 'CFLAGS' this way is convenient when using 'gcc' and 'g++' together, since the flags for 'gcc' will usually suit 'g++'.

              It's important that the C and C++ compilers match, meaning their startup and runtime support routines are compatible and that they generate code in the same ABI (if there's a choice of ABIs on the system). './configure' isn't currently able to check these things very well itself, so for that reason '--disable-cxx' is the default, to avoid a build failure due to a compiler mismatch. Perhaps this will change in the future.

              Incidentally, it's normally not good enough to set 'CXX' to the same as 'CC'. Although gcc for instance recognises foo.cc as C++ code, only g++ will invoke the linker the right way when building an executable or shared library from C++ object files.

Temporary Memory, `--enable-alloca=<choice>`

GMP allocates temporary workspace using one of the following three methods, which can be selected with for instance '`--enable-alloca=malloc-reentrant`'.

- '`alloca`' - C library or compiler builtin.
- '`malloc-reentrant`' - the heap, in a re-entrant fashion.
- '`malloc-notreentrant`' - the heap, with global variables.

For convenience, the following choices are also available. '`--disable-alloca`' is the same as '`no`'.

- '`yes`' - a synonym for '`alloca`'.
- '`no`' - a synonym for '`malloc-reentrant`'.
- '`reentrant`' - `alloca` if available, otherwise '`malloc-reentrant`'. This is the default.
- '`notreentrant`' - `alloca` if available, otherwise '`malloc-notreentrant`'.

`alloca` is reentrant and fast, and is recommended. It actually allocates just small blocks on the stack; larger ones use malloc-reentrant.

'`malloc-reentrant`' is, as the name suggests, reentrant and thread safe, but '`malloc-notreentrant`' is faster and should be used if reentrancy is not required.

The two malloc methods in fact use the memory allocation functions selected by `mp_set_memory_functions`, these being `malloc` and friends by default. See Chapter 13 [Custom Allocation], page 89.

An additional choice '`--enable-alloca=debug`' is available, to help when debugging memory related problems (see Section 3.12 [Debugging], page 24).

FFT Multiplication, `--disable-fft`

By default multiplications are done using Karatsuba, 3-way Toom, higher degree Toom, and Fermat FFT. The FFT is only used on large to very large operands and can be disabled to save code size if desired.

Assertion Checking, `--enable-assert`

This option enables some consistency checking within the library. This can be of use while debugging, see Section 3.12 [Debugging], page 24.

Execution Profiling, `--enable-profiling=prof/gprof/instrument`

Enable profiling support, in one of various styles, see Section 3.13 [Profiling], page 26.

MPN_PATH Various assembly versions of each mpn subroutines are provided. For a given CPU, a search is made though a path to choose a version of each. For example '`sparcv8`' has

```
MPN_PATH="sparc32/v8 sparc32 generic"
```

which means look first for v8 code, then plain sparc32 (which is v7), and finally fall back on generic C. Knowledgeable users with special requirements can specify a different path. Normally this is completely unnecessary.

Documentation

The source for the document you're now reading is `doc/gmp.texi`, in Texinfo format, see *Texinfo*.

Info format '`doc/gmp.info`' is included in the distribution. The usual automake targets are available to make PostScript, DVI, PDF and HTML (these will require various TEX and Texinfo tools).

DocBook and XML can be generated by the Texinfo `makeinfo` program too, see Section "Options for `makeinfo`" in *Texinfo*.

Some supplementary notes can also be found in the `doc` subdirectory.

2.2 ABI and ISA

ABI (Application Binary Interface) refers to the calling conventions between functions, meaning what registers are used and what sizes the various C data types are. ISA (Instruction Set Architecture) refers to the instructions and registers a CPU has available.

Some 64-bit ISA CPUs have both a 64-bit ABI and a 32-bit ABI defined, the latter for compatibility with older CPUs in the family. GMP supports some CPUs like this in both ABIs. In fact within GMP 'ABI' means a combination of chip ABI, plus how GMP chooses to use it. For example in some 32-bit ABIs, GMP may support a limb as either a 32-bit `long` or a 64-bit `long long`.

By default GMP chooses the best ABI available for a given system, and this generally gives significantly greater speed. But an ABI can be chosen explicitly to make GMP compatible with other libraries, or particular application requirements. For example,

```
./configure ABI=32
```

In all cases it's vital that all object code used in a given program is compiled for the same ABI.

Usually a limb is implemented as a `long`. When a `long long` limb is used this is encoded in the generated `gmp.h`. This is convenient for applications, but it does mean that `gmp.h` will vary, and can't be just copied around. `gmp.h` remains compiler independent though, since all compilers for a particular ABI will be expected to use the same limb type.

Currently no attempt is made to follow whatever conventions a system has for installing library or header files built for a particular ABI. This will probably only matter when installing multiple builds of GMP, and it might be as simple as configuring with a special 'libdir', or it might require more than that. Note that builds for different ABIs need to done separately, with a fresh `./configure` and `make` each.

AMD64 ('x86_64')

>On AMD64 systems supporting both 32-bit and 64-bit modes for applications, the following ABI choices are available.

>>'ABI=64'   The 64-bit ABI uses 64-bit limbs and pointers and makes full use of the chip architecture. This is the default. Applications will usually not need special compiler flags, but for reference the option is

>>```
gcc -m64
```

>>'ABI=32'   The 32-bit ABI is the usual i386 conventions. This will be slower, and is not recommended except for inter-operating with other code not yet 64-bit capable. Applications must be compiled with

>>```
gcc -m32
```

>>(In GCC 2.95 and earlier there's no '-m32' option, it's the only mode.)

>>'ABI=x32' The x32 ABI uses 64-bit limbs but 32-bit pointers. Like the 64-bit ABI, it makes full use of the chip's arithmetic capabilities. This ABI is not supported by all operating systems.

>>```
gcc -mx32
```
```

HPPA 2.0 ('hppa2.0*', 'hppa64')

> 'ABI=2.0w'
>
>> The 2.0w ABI uses 64-bit limbs and pointers and is available on HP-UX 11 or up. Applications must be compiled with
>>
>> ```
>> gcc [built for 2.0w]
>> cc  +DD64
>> ```
>
> 'ABI=2.0n'
>
>> The 2.0n ABI means the 32-bit HPPA 1.0 ABI and all its normal calling conventions, but with 64-bit instructions permitted within functions. GMP uses a 64-bit long long for a limb. This ABI is available on hppa64 GNU/Linux and on HP-UX 10 or higher. Applications must be compiled with
>>
>> ```
>> gcc [built for 2.0n]
>> cc  +DA2.0 +e
>> ```
>>
>> Note that current versions of GCC (eg. 3.2) don't generate 64-bit instructions for long long operations and so may be slower than for 2.0w. (The GMP assembly code is the same though.)
>
> 'ABI=1.0' HPPA 2.0 CPUs can run all HPPA 1.0 and 1.1 code in the 32-bit HPPA 1.0 ABI. No special compiler options are needed for applications.

All three ABIs are available for CPU types 'hppa2.0w', 'hppa2.0' and 'hppa64', but for CPU type 'hppa2.0n' only 2.0n or 1.0 are considered.

Note that GCC on HP-UX has no options to choose between 2.0n and 2.0w modes, unlike HP cc. Instead it must be built for one or the other ABI. GMP will detect how it was built, and skip to the corresponding 'ABI'.

IA-64 under HP-UX ('ia64*-*-hpux*', 'itanium*-*-hpux*')

> HP-UX supports two ABIs for IA-64. GMP performance is the same in both.
>
> 'ABI=32' In the 32-bit ABI, pointers, ints and longs are 32 bits and GMP uses a 64 bit long long for a limb. Applications can be compiled without any special flags since this ABI is the default in both HP C and GCC, but for reference the flags are
>
>> ```
>> gcc  -milp32
>> cc   +DD32
>> ```
>
> 'ABI=64' In the 64-bit ABI, longs and pointers are 64 bits and GMP uses a long for a limb. Applications must be compiled with
>
>> ```
>> gcc  -mlp64
>> cc   +DD64
>> ```

On other IA-64 systems, GNU/Linux for instance, 'ABI=64' is the only choice.

MIPS under IRIX 6 ('mips*-*-irix[6789]')

> IRIX 6 always has a 64-bit MIPS 3 or better CPU, and supports ABIs o32, n32, and 64. n32 or 64 are recommended, and GMP performance will be the same in each. The default is n32.
>
> 'ABI=o32' The o32 ABI is 32-bit pointers and integers, and no 64-bit operations. GMP will be slower than in n32 or 64, this option only exists to support old compilers, eg. GCC 2.7.2. Applications can be compiled with no special flags on an old compiler, or on a newer compiler with

```
gcc  -mabi=32
cc   -32
```

'ABI=n32'   The n32 ABI is 32-bit pointers and integers, but with a 64-bit limb
            using a `long long`. Applications must be compiled with

```
gcc  -mabi=n32
cc   -n32
```

'ABI=64'   The 64-bit ABI is 64-bit pointers and integers. Applications must be
            compiled with

```
gcc  -mabi=64
cc   -64
```

Note that MIPS GNU/Linux, as of kernel version 2.2, doesn't have the necessary
support for n32 or 64 and so only gets a 32-bit limb and the MIPS 2 code.

PowerPC 64 ('powerpc64', 'powerpc620', 'powerpc630', 'powerpc970', 'power4', 'power5')

'ABI=mode64'

            The AIX 64 ABI uses 64-bit limbs and pointers and is the default on
            PowerPC 64 '*-*-aix*' systems. Applications must be compiled with

```
gcc  -maix64
xlc  -q64
```

            On 64-bit GNU/Linux, BSD, and Mac OS X/Darwin systems, the ap-
            plications must be compiled with

```
gcc  -m64
```

'ABI=mode32'

            The 'mode32' ABI uses a 64-bit `long long` limb but with the chip still in
            32-bit mode and using 32-bit calling conventions. This is the default for
            systems where the true 64-bit ABI is unavailable. No special compiler
            options are typically needed for applications. This ABI is not available
            under AIX.

'ABI=32'   This is the basic 32-bit PowerPC ABI, with a 32-bit limb. No special
            compiler options are needed for applications.

GMP's speed is greatest for the 'mode64' ABI, the 'mode32' ABI is 2nd best. In
'ABI=32' only the 32-bit ISA is used and this doesn't make full use of a 64-bit chip.

Sparc V9 ('sparc64', 'sparcv9', 'ultrasparc*')

'ABI=64'   The 64-bit V9 ABI is available on the various BSD sparc64 ports, recent
            versions of Sparc64 GNU/Linux, and Solaris 2.7 and up (when the kernel
            is in 64-bit mode). GCC 3.2 or higher, or Sun cc is required. On
            GNU/Linux, depending on the default gcc mode, applications must be
            compiled with

```
gcc  -m64
```

            On Solaris applications must be compiled with

```
gcc  -m64 -mptr64 -Wa,-xarch=v9 -mcpu=v9
cc   -xarch=v9
```

            On the BSD sparc64 systems no special options are required, since 64-
            bits is the only ABI available.

'ABI=32'   For the basic 32-bit ABI, GMP still uses as much of the V9 ISA as it
            can. In the Sun documentation this combination is known as "v8plus".

On GNU/Linux, depending on the default `gcc` mode, applications may need to be compiled with

```
gcc  -m32
```

On Solaris, no special compiler options are required for applications, though using something like the following is recommended. (`gcc` 2.8 and earlier only support '`-mv8`' though.)

```
gcc  -mv8plus
cc   -xarch=v8plus
```

GMP speed is greatest in '`ABI=64`', so it's the default where available. The speed is partly because there are extra registers available and partly because 64-bits is considered the more important case and has therefore had better code written for it.

Don't be confused by the names of the '`-m`' and '`-x`' compiler options, they're called '`arch`' but effectively control both ABI and ISA.

On Solaris 2.6 and earlier, only '`ABI=32`' is available since the kernel doesn't save all registers.

On Solaris 2.7 with the kernel in 32-bit mode, a normal native build will reject '`ABI=64`' because the resulting executables won't run. '`ABI=64`' can still be built if desired by making it look like a cross-compile, for example

```
./configure --build=none --host=sparcv9-sun-solaris2.7 ABI=64
```

2.3 Notes for Package Builds

GMP should present no great difficulties for packaging in a binary distribution.

Libtool is used to build the library and '`-version-info`' is set appropriately, having started from '`3:0:0`' in GMP 3.0 (see Section "Library interface versions" in *GNU Libtool*).

The GMP 4 series will be upwardly binary compatible in each release and will be upwardly binary compatible with all of the GMP 3 series. Additional function interfaces may be added in each release, so on systems where libtool versioning is not fully checked by the loader an auxiliary mechanism may be needed to express that a dynamic linked application depends on a new enough GMP.

An auxiliary mechanism may also be needed to express that `libgmpxx.la` (from `--enable-cxx`, see Section 2.1 [Build Options], page 3) requires `libgmp.la` from the same GMP version, since this is not done by the libtool versioning, nor otherwise. A mismatch will result in unresolved symbols from the linker, or perhaps the loader.

When building a package for a CPU family, care should be taken to use '`--host`' (or '`--build`') to choose the least common denominator among the CPUs which might use the package. For example this might mean plain '`sparc`' (meaning V7) for SPARCs.

For x86s, `--enable-fat` sets things up for a fat binary build, making a runtime selection of optimized low level routines. This is a good choice for packaging to run on a range of x86 chips.

Users who care about speed will want GMP built for their exact CPU type, to make best use of the available optimizations. Providing a way to suitably rebuild a package may be useful. This could be as simple as making it possible for a user to omit '`--build`' (and '`--host`') so '`./config.guess`' will detect the CPU. But a way to manually specify a '`--build`' will be wanted for systems where '`./config.guess`' is inexact.

On systems with multiple ABIs, a packaged build will need to decide which among the choices is to be provided, see Section 2.2 [ABI and ISA], page 8. A given run of '`./configure`' etc will only build one ABI. If a second ABI is also required then a second run of '`./configure`' etc must be made, starting from a clean directory tree ('`make distclean`').

As noted under "ABI and ISA", currently no attempt is made to follow system conventions for install locations that vary with ABI, such as `/usr/lib/sparcv9` for '`ABI=64`' as opposed to `/usr/lib` for '`ABI=32`'. A package build can override '`libdir`' and other standard variables as necessary.

Note that `gmp.h` is a generated file, and will be architecture and ABI dependent. When attempting to install two ABIs simultaneously it will be important that an application compile gets the correct `gmp.h` for its desired ABI. If compiler include paths don't vary with ABI options then it might be necessary to create a `/usr/include/gmp.h` which tests preprocessor symbols and chooses the correct actual `gmp.h`.

2.4 Notes for Particular Systems

AIX 3 and 4

> On systems '`*-*-aix[34]*`' shared libraries are disabled by default, since some versions of the native `ar` fail on the convenience libraries used. A shared build can be attempted with
>
>> `./configure --enable-shared --disable-static`
>
> Note that the '`--disable-static`' is necessary because in a shared build libtool makes `libgmp.a` a symlink to `libgmp.so`, apparently for the benefit of old versions of `ld` which only recognise `.a`, but unfortunately this is done even if a fully functional `ld` is available.

ARM

> On systems '`arm*-*-*`', versions of GCC up to and including 2.95.3 have a bug in unsigned division, giving wrong results for some operands. GMP '`./configure`' will demand GCC 2.95.4 or later.

Compaq C++

> Compaq C++ on OSF 5.1 has two flavours of `iostream`, a standard one and an old pre-standard one (see '`man iostream_intro`'). GMP can only use the standard one, which unfortunately is not the default but must be selected by defining `__USE_STD_IOSTREAM`. Configure with for instance
>
>> `./configure --enable-cxx CPPFLAGS=-D__USE_STD_IOSTREAM`

Floating Point Mode

> On some systems, the hardware floating point has a control mode which can set all operations to be done in a particular precision, for instance single, double or extended on x86 systems (x87 floating point). The GMP functions involving a `double` cannot be expected to operate to their full precision when the hardware is in single precision mode. Of course this affects all code, including application code, not just GMP.

FreeBSD 7.x, 8.x, 9.0, 9.1, 9.2

> `m4` in these releases of FreeBSD has an eval function which ignores its 2nd and 3rd arguments, which makes it unsuitable for `.asm` file processing. '`./configure`' will detect the problem and either abort or choose another m4 in the `PATH`. The bug is fixed in FreeBSD 9.3 and 10.0, so either upgrade or use GNU m4. Note that the FreeBSD package system installs GNU m4 under the name '`gm4`', which GMP cannot guess.

FreeBSD 7.x, 8.x, 9.x

> GMP releases starting with 6.0 do not support '`ABI=32`' on FreeBSD/amd64 prior to release 10.0 of the system. The cause is a broken `limits.h`, which GMP no longer works around.

MS-DOS and MS Windows

On an MS-DOS system DJGPP can be used to build GMP, and on an MS Windows system Cygwin, DJGPP and MINGW can be used. All three are excellent ports of GCC and the various GNU tools.

```
http://www.cygwin.com/
http://www.delorie.com/djgpp/
http://www.mingw.org/
```

Microsoft also publishes an Interix "Services for Unix" which can be used to build GMP on Windows (with a normal './configure'), but it's not free software.

MS Windows DLLs

On systems '*-*-cygwin*', '*-*-mingw*' and '*-*-pw32*' by default GMP builds only a static library, but a DLL can be built instead using

```
./configure --disable-static --enable-shared
```

Static and DLL libraries can't both be built, since certain export directives in gmp.h must be different.

A MINGW DLL build of GMP can be used with Microsoft C. Libtool doesn't install a .lib format import library, but it can be created with MS lib as follows, and copied to the install directory. Similarly for libmp and libgmpxx.

```
cd .libs
lib /def:libgmp-3.dll.def /out:libgmp-3.lib
```

MINGW uses the C runtime library 'msvcrt.dll' for I/O, so applications wanting to use the GMP I/O routines must be compiled with 'cl /MD' to do the same. If one of the other C runtime library choices provided by MS C is desired then the suggestion is to use the GMP string functions and confine I/O to the application.

Motorola 68k CPU Types

'm68k' is taken to mean 68000. 'm68020' or higher will give a performance boost on applicable CPUs. 'm68360' can be used for CPU32 series chips. 'm68302' can be used for "Dragonball" series chips, though this is merely a synonym for 'm68000'.

NetBSD 5.x

m4 in these releases of NetBSD has an eval function which ignores its 2nd and 3rd arguments, which makes it unsuitable for .asm file processing. './configure' will detect the problem and either abort or choose another m4 in the PATH. The bug is fixed in NetBSD 6, so either upgrade or use GNU m4. Note that the NetBSD package system installs GNU m4 under the name 'gm4', which GMP cannot guess.

OpenBSD 2.6

m4 in this release of OpenBSD has a bug in eval that makes it unsuitable for .asm file processing. './configure' will detect the problem and either abort or choose another m4 in the PATH. The bug is fixed in OpenBSD 2.7, so either upgrade or use GNU m4.

Power CPU Types

In GMP, CPU types 'power*' and 'powerpc*' will each use instructions not available on the other, so it's important to choose the right one for the CPU that will be used. Currently GMP has no assembly code support for using just the common instruction subset. To get executables that run on both, the current suggestion is to use the generic C code (--disable-assembly), possibly with appropriate compiler options (like '-mcpu=common' for gcc). CPU 'rs6000' (which is not a CPU but a family of workstations) is accepted by config.sub, but is currently equivalent to --disable-assembly.

Sparc CPU Types
'sparcv8' or 'supersparc' on relevant systems will give a significant performance increase over the V7 code selected by plain 'sparc'.

Sparc App Regs
The GMP assembly code for both 32-bit and 64-bit Sparc clobbers the "application registers" g2, g3 and g4, the same way that the GCC default '-mapp-regs' does (see Section "SPARC Options" in Using the GNU Compiler Collection (GCC)).

This makes that code unsuitable for use with the special V9 '-mcmodel=embmedany' (which uses g4 as a data segment pointer), and for applications wanting to use those registers for special purposes. In these cases the only suggestion currently is to build GMP with --disable-assembly to avoid the assembly code.

SunOS 4   /usr/bin/m4 lacks various features needed to process .asm files, and instead './configure' will automatically use /usr/5bin/m4, which we believe is always available (if not then use GNU m4).

x86 CPU Types
'i586', 'pentium' or 'pentiummmx' code is good for its intended P5 Pentium chips, but quite slow when run on Intel P6 class chips (PPro, P-II, P-III). 'i386' is a better choice when making binaries that must run on both.

x86 MMX and SSE2 Code
If the CPU selected has MMX code but the assembler doesn't support it, a warning is given and non-MMX code is used instead. This will be an inferior build, since the MMX code that's present is there because it's faster than the corresponding plain integer code. The same applies to SSE2.

Old versions of 'gas' don't support MMX instructions, in particular version 1.92.3 that comes with FreeBSD 2.2.8 or the more recent OpenBSD 3.1 doesn't.

Solaris 2.6 and 2.7 as generate incorrect object code for register to register movq instructions, and so can't be used for MMX code. Install a recent gas if MMX code is wanted on these systems.

2.5 Known Build Problems

You might find more up-to-date information at https://gmplib.org/.

Compiler link options
The version of libtool currently in use rather aggressively strips compiler options when linking a shared library. This will hopefully be relaxed in the future, but for now if this is a problem the suggestion is to create a little script to hide them, and for instance configure with

```
./configure CC=gcc-with-my-options
```

DJGPP ('*-*-msdosdjgpp*')
The DJGPP port of bash 2.03 is unable to run the 'configure' script, it exits silently, having died writing a preamble to config.log. Use bash 2.04 or higher.

'make all' was found to run out of memory during the final libgmp.la link on one system tested, despite having 64Mb available. Running 'make libgmp.la' directly helped, perhaps recursing into the various subdirectories uses up memory.

GNU binutils strip prior to 2.12
strip from GNU binutils 2.11 and earlier should not be used on the static libraries libgmp.a and libmp.a since it will discard all but the last of multiple archive members with the same name, like the three versions of init.o in libgmp.a. Binutils 2.12 or higher can be used successfully.

The shared libraries `libgmp.so` and `libmp.so` are not affected by this and any version of `strip` can be used on them.

`make` syntax error

On certain versions of SCO OpenServer 5 and IRIX 6.5 the native `make` is unable to handle the long dependencies list for `libgmp.la`. The symptom is a "syntax error" on the following line of the top-level `Makefile`.

```
libgmp.la: $(libgmp_la_OBJECTS) $(libgmp_la_DEPENDENCIES)
```

Either use GNU Make, or as a workaround remove `$(libgmp_la_DEPENDENCIES)` from that line (which will make the initial build work, but if any recompiling is done `libgmp.la` might not be rebuilt).

MacOS X ('`*-*-darwin*`')

Libtool currently only knows how to create shared libraries on MacOS X using the native `cc` (which is a modified GCC), not a plain GCC. A static-only build should work though ('`--disable-shared`').

NeXT prior to 3.3

The system compiler on old versions of NeXT was a massacred and old GCC, even if it called itself `cc`. This compiler cannot be used to build GMP, you need to get a real GCC, and install that. (NeXT may have fixed this in release 3.3 of their system.)

POWER and PowerPC

Bugs in GCC 2.7.2 (and 2.6.3) mean it can't be used to compile GMP on POWER or PowerPC. If you want to use GCC for these machines, get GCC 2.7.2.1 (or later).

Sequent Symmetry

Use the GNU assembler instead of the system assembler, since the latter has serious bugs.

Solaris 2.6 The system `sed` prints an error "Output line too long" when libtool builds `libgmp.la`. This doesn't seem to cause any obvious ill effects, but GNU `sed` is recommended, to avoid any doubt.

Sparc Solaris 2.7 with gcc 2.95.2 in '`ABI=32`'

A shared library build of GMP seems to fail in this combination, it builds but then fails the tests, apparently due to some incorrect data relocations within `gmp_randinit_lc_2exp_size`. The exact cause is unknown, '`--disable-shared`' is recommended.

2.6 Performance optimization

For optimal performance, build GMP for the exact CPU type of the target computer, see Section 2.1 [Build Options], page 3.

Unlike what is the case for most other programs, the compiler typically doesn't matter much, since GMP uses assembly language for the most critical operation.

In particular for long-running GMP applications, and applications demanding extremely large numbers, building and running the `tuneup` program in the `tune` subdirectory, can be important. For example,

```
cd tune
make tuneup
./tuneup
```

will generate better contents for the `gmp-mparam.h` parameter file.

To use the results, put the output in the file indicated in the 'Parameters for ...' header. Then recompile from scratch.

The `tuneup` program takes one useful parameter, '`-f NNN`', which instructs the program how long to check FFT multiply parameters. If you're going to use GMP for extremely large numbers, you may want to run `tuneup` with a large NNN value.

3 GMP Basics

Using functions, macros, data types, etc. not documented in this manual is strongly discouraged. If you do so your application is guaranteed to be incompatible with future versions of GMP.

3.1 Headers and Libraries

All declarations needed to use GMP are collected in the include file `gmp.h`. It is designed to work with both C and C++ compilers.

```
#include <gmp.h>
```

Note however that prototypes for GMP functions with `FILE *` parameters are only provided if `<stdio.h>` is included too.

```
#include <stdio.h>
#include <gmp.h>
```

Likewise `<stdarg.h>` is required for prototypes with `va_list` parameters, such as `gmp_vprintf`. And `<obstack.h>` for prototypes with `struct obstack` parameters, such as `gmp_obstack_printf`, when available.

All programs using GMP must link against the `libgmp` library. On a typical Unix-like system this can be done with '`-lgmp`', for example

```
gcc myprogram.c -lgmp
```

GMP C++ functions are in a separate `libgmpxx` library. This is built and installed if C++ support has been enabled (see Section 2.1 [Build Options], page 3). For example,

```
g++ mycxxprog.cc -lgmpxx -lgmp
```

GMP is built using Libtool and an application can use that to link if desired, see *GNU Libtool*.

If GMP has been installed to a non-standard location then it may be necessary to use '`-I`' and '`-L`' compiler options to point to the right directories, and some sort of run-time path for a shared library.

3.2 Nomenclature and Types

In this manual, *integer* usually means a multiple precision integer, as defined by the GMP library. The C data type for such integers is `mpz_t`. Here are some examples of how to declare such integers:

```
mpz_t sum;

struct foo { mpz_t x, y; };

mpz_t vec[20];
```

Rational number means a multiple precision fraction. The C data type for these fractions is `mpq_t`. For example:

```
mpq_t quotient;
```

Floating point number or *Float* for short, is an arbitrary precision mantissa with a limited precision exponent. The C data type for such objects is `mpf_t`. For example:

```
mpf_t fp;
```

The floating point functions accept and return exponents in the C type `mp_exp_t`. Currently this is usually a `long`, but on some systems it's an `int` for efficiency.

A *limb* means the part of a multi-precision number that fits in a single machine word. (We chose this word because a limb of the human body is analogous to a digit, only larger, and containing several digits.) Normally a limb is 32 or 64 bits. The C data type for a limb is `mp_limb_t`.

Counts of limbs of a multi-precision number represented in the C type `mp_size_t`. Currently this is normally a `long`, but on some systems it's an `int` for efficiency, and on some systems it will be `long long` in the future.

Counts of bits of a multi-precision number are represented in the C type `mp_bitcnt_t`. Currently this is always an `unsigned long`, but on some systems it will be an `unsigned long long` in the future.

Random state means an algorithm selection and current state data. The C data type for such objects is `gmp_randstate_t`. For example:

```
gmp_randstate_t rstate;
```

Also, in general `mp_bitcnt_t` is used for bit counts and ranges, and `size_t` is used for byte or character counts.

3.3 Function Classes

There are six classes of functions in the GMP library:

1. Functions for signed integer arithmetic, with names beginning with `mpz_`. The associated type is `mpz_t`. There are about 150 functions in this class. (see Chapter 5 [Integer Functions], page 30)

2. Functions for rational number arithmetic, with names beginning with `mpq_`. The associated type is `mpq_t`. There are about 35 functions in this class, but the integer functions can be used for arithmetic on the numerator and denominator separately. (see Chapter 6 [Rational Number Functions], page 46)

3. Functions for floating-point arithmetic, with names beginning with `mpf_`. The associated type is `mpf_t`. There are about 70 functions is this class. (see Chapter 7 [Floating-point Functions], page 50)

4. Fast low-level functions that operate on natural numbers. These are used by the functions in the preceding groups, and you can also call them directly from very time-critical user programs. These functions' names begin with `mpn_`. The associated type is array of `mp_limb_t`. There are about 60 (hard-to-use) functions in this class. (see Chapter 8 [Low-level Functions], page 58)

5. Miscellaneous functions. Functions for setting up custom allocation and functions for generating random numbers. (see Chapter 13 [Custom Allocation], page 89, and see Chapter 9 [Random Number Functions], page 69)

3.4 Variable Conventions

GMP functions generally have output arguments before input arguments. This notation is by analogy with the assignment operator. The BSD MP compatibility functions are exceptions, having the output arguments last.

GMP lets you use the same variable for both input and output in one call. For example, the main function for integer multiplication, `mpz_mul`, can be used to square x and put the result back in x with

```
mpz_mul (x, x, x);
```

Before you can assign to a GMP variable, you need to initialize it by calling one of the special initialization functions. When you're done with a variable, you need to clear it out, using one of the functions for that purpose. Which function to use depends on the type of variable. See the chapters on integer functions, rational number functions, and floating-point functions for details.

A variable should only be initialized once, or at least cleared between each initialization. After a variable has been initialized, it may be assigned to any number of times.

For efficiency reasons, avoid excessive initializing and clearing. In general, initialize near the start of a function and clear near the end. For example,

```
void
foo (void)
{
  mpz_t  n;
  int    i;
  mpz_init (n);
  for (i = 1; i < 100; i++)
    {
      mpz_mul (n, ...);
      mpz_fdiv_q (n, ...);
      ...
    }
  mpz_clear (n);
}
```

3.5 Parameter Conventions

When a GMP variable is used as a function parameter, it's effectively a call-by-reference, meaning if the function stores a value there it will change the original in the caller. Parameters which are input-only can be designated const to provoke a compiler error or warning on attempting to modify them.

When a function is going to return a GMP result, it should designate a parameter that it sets, like the library functions do. More than one value can be returned by having more than one output parameter, again like the library functions. A return of an mpz_t etc doesn't return the object, only a pointer, and this is almost certainly not what's wanted.

Here's an example accepting an mpz_t parameter, doing a calculation, and storing the result to the indicated parameter.

```
void
foo (mpz_t result, const mpz_t param, unsigned long n)
{
  unsigned long  i;
  mpz_mul_ui (result, param, n);
  for (i = 1; i < n; i++)
    mpz_add_ui (result, result, i*7);
}

int
main (void)
{
```

```
mpz_t   r, n;
mpz_init (r);
mpz_init_set_str (n, "123456", 0);
foo (r, n, 20L);
gmp_printf ("%Zd\n", r);
return 0;
}
```

`foo` works even if the mainline passes the same variable for `param` and `result`, just like the library functions. But sometimes it's tricky to make that work, and an application might not want to bother supporting that sort of thing.

For interest, the GMP types `mpz_t` etc are implemented as one-element arrays of certain structures. This is why declaring a variable creates an object with the fields GMP needs, but then using it as a parameter passes a pointer to the object. Note that the actual fields in each `mpz_t` etc are for internal use only and should not be accessed directly by code that expects to be compatible with future GMP releases.

3.6 Memory Management

The GMP types like `mpz_t` are small, containing only a couple of sizes, and pointers to allocated data. Once a variable is initialized, GMP takes care of all space allocation. Additional space is allocated whenever a variable doesn't have enough.

`mpz_t` and `mpq_t` variables never reduce their allocated space. Normally this is the best policy, since it avoids frequent reallocation. Applications that need to return memory to the heap at some particular point can use `mpz_realloc2`, or clear variables no longer needed.

`mpf_t` variables, in the current implementation, use a fixed amount of space, determined by the chosen precision and allocated at initialization, so their size doesn't change.

All memory is allocated using `malloc` and friends by default, but this can be changed, see Chapter 13 [Custom Allocation], page 89. Temporary memory on the stack is also used (via `alloca`), but this can be changed at build-time if desired, see Section 2.1 [Build Options], page 3.

3.7 Reentrancy

GMP is reentrant and thread-safe, with some exceptions:

- If configured with `--enable-alloca=malloc-notreentrant` (or with `--enable-alloca=notreentrant` when `alloca` is not available), then naturally GMP is not reentrant.

- `mpf_set_default_prec` and `mpf_init` use a global variable for the selected precision. `mpf_init2` can be used instead, and in the C++ interface an explicit precision to the `mpf_class` constructor.

- `mpz_random` and the other old random number functions use a global random state and are hence not reentrant. The newer random number functions that accept a `gmp_randstate_t` parameter can be used instead.

- `gmp_randinit` (obsolete) returns an error indication through a global variable, which is not thread safe. Applications are advised to use `gmp_randinit_default` or `gmp_randinit_lc_2exp` instead.

- `mp_set_memory_functions` uses global variables to store the selected memory allocation functions.

- If the memory allocation functions set by a call to `mp_set_memory_functions` (or `malloc` and friends by default) are not reentrant, then GMP will not be reentrant either.

- If the standard I/O functions such as `fwrite` are not reentrant then the GMP I/O functions using them will not be reentrant either.

- It's safe for two threads to read from the same GMP variable simultaneously, but it's not safe for one to read while another might be writing, nor for two threads to write simultaneously. It's not safe for two threads to generate a random number from the same `gmp_randstate_t` simultaneously, since this involves an update of that variable.

3.8 Useful Macros and Constants

`const int mp_bits_per_limb`   [Global Constant]
    The number of bits per limb.

`__GNU_MP_VERSION`   [Macro]
`__GNU_MP_VERSION_MINOR`   [Macro]
`__GNU_MP_VERSION_PATCHLEVEL`   [Macro]
    The major and minor GMP version, and patch level, respectively, as integers. For GMP i.j, these numbers will be i, j, and 0, respectively. For GMP i.j.k, these numbers will be i, j, and k, respectively.

`const char * const gmp_version`   [Global Constant]
    The GMP version number, as a null-terminated string, in the form "i.j.k". This release is "6.0.0". Note that the format "i.j" was used, before version 4.3.0, when k was zero.

`__GMP_CC`   [Macro]
`__GMP_CFLAGS`   [Macro]
    The compiler and compiler flags, respectively, used when compiling GMP, as strings.

3.9 Compatibility with older versions

This version of GMP is upwardly binary compatible with all 5.x, 4.x, and 3.x versions, and upwardly compatible at the source level with all 2.x versions, with the following exceptions.

- `mpn_gcd` had its source arguments swapped as of GMP 3.0, for consistency with other `mpn` functions.

- `mpf_get_prec` counted precision slightly differently in GMP 3.0 and 3.0.1, but in 3.1 reverted to the 2.x style.

- `mpn_bdivmod`, documented as preliminary in GMP 4, has been removed.

There are a number of compatibility issues between GMP 1 and GMP 2 that of course also apply when porting applications from GMP 1 to GMP 5. Please see the GMP 2 manual for details.

3.10 Demonstration programs

The `demos` subdirectory has some sample programs using GMP. These aren't built or installed, but there's a `Makefile` with rules for them. For instance,

```
make pexpr
./pexpr 68^975+10
```

The following programs are provided

- 'pexpr' is an expression evaluator, the program used on the GMP web page.

- The 'calc' subdirectory has a similar but simpler evaluator using `lex` and `yacc`.

- The 'expr' subdirectory is yet another expression evaluator, a library designed for ease of use within a C program. See `demos/expr/README` for more information.
- 'factorize' is a Pollard-Rho factorization program.
- 'isprime' is a command-line interface to the `mpz_probab_prime_p` function.
- 'primes' counts or lists primes in an interval, using a sieve.
- 'qcn' is an example use of `mpz_kronecker_ui` to estimate quadratic class numbers.
- The 'perl' subdirectory is a comprehensive perl interface to GMP. See `demos/perl/INSTALL` for more information. Documentation is in POD format in `demos/perl/GMP.pm`.

As an aside, consideration has been given at various times to some sort of expression evaluation within the main GMP library. Going beyond something minimal quickly leads to matters like user-defined functions, looping, fixnums for control variables, etc, which are considered outside the scope of GMP (much closer to language interpreters or compilers, See Chapter 14 [Language Bindings], page 91.) Something simple for program input convenience may yet be a possibility, a combination of the `expr` demo and the `pexpr` tree back-end perhaps. But for now the above evaluators are offered as illustrations.

3.11 Efficiency

Small Operands

On small operands, the time for function call overheads and memory allocation can be significant in comparison to actual calculation. This is unavoidable in a general purpose variable precision library, although GMP attempts to be as efficient as it can on both large and small operands.

Static Linking

On some CPUs, in particular the x86s, the static `libgmp.a` should be used for maximum speed, since the PIC code in the shared `libgmp.so` will have a small overhead on each function call and global data address. For many programs this will be insignificant, but for long calculations there's a gain to be had.

Initializing and Clearing

Avoid excessive initializing and clearing of variables, since this can be quite time consuming, especially in comparison to otherwise fast operations like addition.

A language interpreter might want to keep a free list or stack of initialized variables ready for use. It should be possible to integrate something like that with a garbage collector too.

Reallocations

An `mpz_t` or `mpq_t` variable used to hold successively increasing values will have its memory repeatedly `realloced`, which could be quite slow or could fragment memory, depending on the C library. If an application can estimate the final size then `mpz_init2` or `mpz_realloc2` can be called to allocate the necessary space from the beginning (see Section 5.1 [Initializing Integers], page 30).

It doesn't matter if a size set with `mpz_init2` or `mpz_realloc2` is too small, since all functions will do a further reallocation if necessary. Badly overestimating memory required will waste space though.

2exp Functions

It's up to an application to call functions like `mpz_mul_2exp` when appropriate. General purpose functions like `mpz_mul` make no attempt to identify powers of two or other special forms, because such inputs will usually be very rare and testing every time would be wasteful.

ui and si Functions

> The ui functions and the small number of si functions exist for convenience and should be used where applicable. But if for example an mpz_t contains a value that fits in an unsigned long there's no need extract it and call a ui function, just use the regular mpz function.

In-Place Operations

> mpz_abs, mpq_abs, mpf_abs, mpz_neg, mpq_neg and mpf_neg are fast when used for in-place operations like mpz_abs(x,x), since in the current implementation only a single field of x needs changing. On suitable compilers (GCC for instance) this is inlined too.
>
> mpz_add_ui, mpz_sub_ui, mpf_add_ui and mpf_sub_ui benefit from an in-place operation like mpz_add_ui(x,x,y), since usually only one or two limbs of x will need to be changed. The same applies to the full precision mpz_add etc if y is small. If y is big then cache locality may be helped, but that's all.
>
> mpz_mul is currently the opposite, a separate destination is slightly better. A call like mpz_mul(x,x,y) will, unless y is only one limb, make a temporary copy of x before forming the result. Normally that copying will only be a tiny fraction of the time for the multiply, so this is not a particularly important consideration.
>
> mpz_set, mpq_set, mpq_set_num, mpf_set, etc, make no attempt to recognise a copy of something to itself, so a call like mpz_set(x,x) will be wasteful. Naturally that would never be written deliberately, but if it might arise from two pointers to the same object then a test to avoid it might be desirable.

```
if (x != y)
    mpz_set (x, y);
```

> Note that it's never worth introducing extra mpz_set calls just to get in-place operations. If a result should go to a particular variable then just direct it there and let GMP take care of data movement.

Divisibility Testing (Small Integers)

> mpz_divisible_ui_p and mpz_congruent_ui_p are the best functions for testing whether an mpz_t is divisible by an individual small integer. They use an algorithm which is faster than mpz_tdiv_ui, but which gives no useful information about the actual remainder, only whether it's zero (or a particular value).
>
> However when testing divisibility by several small integers, it's best to take a remainder modulo their product, to save multi-precision operations. For instance to test whether a number is divisible by any of 23, 29 or 31 take a remainder modulo $23 \times 29 \times 31 = 20677$ and then test that.
>
> The division functions like mpz_tdiv_q_ui which give a quotient as well as a remainder are generally a little slower than the remainder-only functions like mpz_tdiv_ui. If the quotient is only rarely wanted then it's probably best to just take a remainder and then go back and calculate the quotient if and when it's wanted (mpz_divexact_ui can be used if the remainder is zero).

Rational Arithmetic

> The mpq functions operate on mpq_t values with no common factors in the numerator and denominator. Common factors are checked-for and cast out as necessary. In general, cancelling factors every time is the best approach since it minimizes the sizes for subsequent operations.
>
> However, applications that know something about the factorization of the values they're working with might be able to avoid some of the GCDs used for canonicalization, or swap them for divisions. For example when multiplying by a prime it's enough to check for factors of it in the denominator instead of doing a full GCD.

Or when forming a big product it might be known that very little cancellation will be possible, and so canonicalization can be left to the end.

The `mpq_numref` and `mpq_denref` macros give access to the numerator and denominator to do things outside the scope of the supplied `mpq` functions. See Section 6.5 [Applying Integer Functions], page 48.

The canonical form for rationals allows mixed-type `mpq_t` and integer additions or subtractions to be done directly with multiples of the denominator. This will be somewhat faster than `mpq_add`. For example,

```
/* mpq increment */
mpz_add (mpq_numref(q), mpq_numref(q), mpq_denref(q));

/* mpq += unsigned long */
mpz_addmul_ui (mpq_numref(q), mpq_denref(q), 123UL);

/* mpq -= mpz */
mpz_submul (mpq_numref(q), mpq_denref(q), z);
```

Number Sequences

Functions like `mpz_fac_ui`, `mpz_fib_ui` and `mpz_bin_uiui` are designed for calculating isolated values. If a range of values is wanted it's probably best to call to get a starting point and iterate from there.

Text Input/Output

Hexadecimal or octal are suggested for input or output in text form. Power-of-2 bases like these can be converted much more efficiently than other bases, like decimal. For big numbers there's usually nothing of particular interest to be seen in the digits, so the base doesn't matter much.

Maybe we can hope octal will one day become the normal base for everyday use, as proposed by King Charles XII of Sweden and later reformers.

3.12 Debugging

Stack Overflow

Depending on the system, a segmentation violation or bus error might be the only indication of stack overflow. See '`--enable-alloca`' choices in Section 2.1 [Build Options], page 3, for how to address this.

In new enough versions of GCC, '`-fstack-check`' may be able to ensure an overflow is recognised by the system before too much damage is done, or '`-fstack-limit-symbol`' or '`-fstack-limit-register`' may be able to add checking if the system itself doesn't do any (see Section "Options for Code Generation" in *Using the GNU Compiler Collection (GCC)*). These options must be added to the '`CFLAGS`' used in the GMP build (see Section 2.1 [Build Options], page 3), adding them just to an application will have no effect. Note also they're a slowdown, adding overhead to each function call and each stack allocation.

Heap Problems

The most likely cause of application problems with GMP is heap corruption. Failing to `init` GMP variables will have unpredictable effects, and corruption arising elsewhere in a program may well affect GMP. Initializing GMP variables more than once or failing to clear them will cause memory leaks.

In all such cases a `malloc` debugger is recommended. On a GNU or BSD system the standard C library `malloc` has some diagnostic facilities, see Section "Allocation Debugging" in *The GNU C Library Reference Manual*, or '`man 3 malloc`'. Other possibilities, in no particular order, include

```
http://www.inf.ethz.ch/personal/biere/projects/ccmalloc/
http://dmalloc.com/
http://www.perens.com/FreeSoftware/  (electric fence)
http://packages.debian.org/stable/devel/fda
http://www.gnupdate.org/components/leakbug/
http://people.redhat.com/~otaylor/memprof/
http://www.cbmamiga.demon.co.uk/mpatrol/
```

The GMP default allocation routines in `memory.c` also have a simple sentinel scheme which can be enabled with `#define DEBUG` in that file. This is mainly designed for detecting buffer overruns during GMP development, but might find other uses.

Stack Backtraces

On some systems the compiler options GMP uses by default can interfere with debugging. In particular on x86 and 68k systems '`-fomit-frame-pointer`' is used and this generally inhibits stack backtracing. Recompiling without such options may help while debugging, though the usual caveats about it potentially moving a memory problem or hiding a compiler bug will apply.

GDB, the GNU Debugger

A sample `.gdbinit` is included in the distribution, showing how to call some undocumented dump functions to print GMP variables from within GDB. Note that these functions shouldn't be used in final application code since they're undocumented and may be subject to incompatible changes in future versions of GMP.

Source File Paths

GMP has multiple source files with the same name, in different directories. For example `mpz`, `mpq` and `mpf` each have an `init.c`. If the debugger can't already determine the right one it may help to build with absolute paths on each C file. One way to do that is to use a separate object directory with an absolute path to the source directory.

```
cd /my/build/dir
/my/source/dir/gmp-6.0.0/configure
```

This works via `VPATH`, and might require GNU `make`. Alternately it might be possible to change the `.c.lo` rules appropriately.

Assertion Checking

The build option `--enable-assert` is available to add some consistency checks to the library (see Section 2.1 [Build Options], page 3). These are likely to be of limited value to most applications. Assertion failures are just as likely to indicate memory corruption as a library or compiler bug.

Applications using the low-level `mpn` functions, however, will benefit from `--enable-assert` since it adds checks on the parameters of most such functions, many of which have subtle restrictions on their usage. Note however that only the generic C code has checks, not the assembly code, so `--disable-assembly` should be used for maximum checking.

Temporary Memory Checking

The build option `--enable-alloca=debug` arranges that each block of temporary memory in GMP is allocated with a separate call to `malloc` (or the allocation function set with `mp_set_memory_functions`).

This can help a malloc debugger detect accesses outside the intended bounds, or detect memory not released. In a normal build, on the other hand, temporary memory is allocated in blocks which GMP divides up for its own use, or may be allocated with a compiler builtin `alloca` which will go nowhere near any malloc debugger hooks.

Maximum Debuggability

To summarize the above, a GMP build for maximum debuggability would be

```
./configure --disable-shared --enable-assert \
   --enable-alloca=debug --disable-assembly CFLAGS=-g
```

For C++, add '--enable-cxx CXXFLAGS=-g'.

Checker

The GCC checker (`https://savannah.nongnu.org/projects/checker/`) can be used with GMP. It contains a stub library which means GMP applications compiled with checker can use a normal GMP build.

A build of GMP with checking within GMP itself can be made. This will run very very slowly. On GNU/Linux for example,

```
./configure --disable-assembly CC=checkergcc
```

`--disable-assembly` must be used, since the GMP assembly code doesn't support the checking scheme. The GMP C++ features cannot be used, since current versions of checker (0.9.9.1) don't yet support the standard C++ library.

Valgrind

Valgrind (`http://valgrind.org/`) is a memory checker for x86, ARM, MIPS, PowerPC, and S/390. It translates and emulates machine instructions to do strong checks for uninitialized data (at the level of individual bits), memory accesses through bad pointers, and memory leaks.

Valgrind does not always support every possible instruction, in particular ones recently added to an ISA. Valgrind might therefore be incompatible with a recent GMP or even a less recent GMP which is compiled using a recent GCC.

GMP's assembly code sometimes promotes a read of the limbs to some larger size, for efficiency. GMP will do this even at the start and end of a multilimb operand, using naturally aligned operations on the larger type. This may lead to benign reads outside of allocated areas, triggering complaints from Valgrind. Valgrind's option '--partial-loads-ok=yes' should help.

Other Problems

Any suspected bug in GMP itself should be isolated to make sure it's not an application problem, see Chapter 4 [Reporting Bugs], page 29.

3.13 Profiling

Running a program under a profiler is a good way to find where it's spending most time and where improvements can be best sought. The profiling choices for a GMP build are as follows.

'--disable-profiling'

The default is to add nothing special for profiling.

It should be possible to just compile the mainline of a program with -p and use prof to get a profile consisting of timer-based sampling of the program counter. Most of the GMP assembly code has the necessary symbol information.

This approach has the advantage of minimizing interference with normal program operation, but on most systems the resolution of the sampling is quite low (10 milliseconds for instance), requiring long runs to get accurate information.

'--enable-profiling=prof'

Build with support for the system prof, which means '-p' added to the 'CFLAGS'.

This provides call counting in addition to program counter sampling, which allows the most frequently called routines to be identified, and an average time spent in each routine to be determined.

The x86 assembly code has support for this option, but on other processors the assembly routines will be as if compiled without '-p' and therefore won't appear in the call counts.

On some systems, such as GNU/Linux, '-p' in fact means '-pg' and in this case '--enable-profiling=gprof' described below should be used instead.

'--enable-profiling=gprof'

Build with support for gprof, which means '-pg' added to the 'CFLAGS'.

This provides call graph construction in addition to call counting and program counter sampling, which makes it possible to count calls coming from different locations. For example the number of calls to mpn_mul from mpz_mul versus the number from mpf_mul. The program counter sampling is still flat though, so only a total time in mpn_mul would be accumulated, not a separate amount for each call site.

The x86 assembly code has support for this option, but on other processors the assembly routines will be as if compiled without '-pg' and therefore not be included in the call counts.

On x86 and m68k systems '-pg' and '-fomit-frame-pointer' are incompatible, so the latter is omitted from the default flags in that case, which might result in poorer code generation.

Incidentally, it should be possible to use the gprof program with a plain '--enable-profiling=prof' build. But in that case only the 'gprof -p' flat profile and call counts can be expected to be valid, not the 'gprof -q' call graph.

'--enable-profiling=instrument'

Build with the GCC option '-finstrument-functions' added to the 'CFLAGS' (see Section "Options for Code Generation" in *Using the GNU Compiler Collection (GCC)*).

This inserts special instrumenting calls at the start and end of each function, allowing exact timing and full call graph construction.

This instrumenting is not normally a standard system feature and will require support from an external library, such as

    http://sourceforge.net/projects/fnccheck/

This should be included in 'LIBS' during the GMP configure so that test programs will link. For example,

    ./configure --enable-profiling=instrument LIBS=-lfc

On a GNU system the C library provides dummy instrumenting functions, so programs compiled with this option will link. In this case it's only necessary to ensure the correct library is added when linking an application.

The x86 assembly code supports this option, but on other processors the assembly routines will be as if compiled without '-finstrument-functions' meaning time spent in them will effectively be attributed to their caller.

3.14 Autoconf

Autoconf based applications can easily check whether GMP is installed. The only thing to be noted is that GMP library symbols from version 3 onwards have prefixes like __gmpz. The following therefore would be a simple test,

    AC_CHECK_LIB(gmp, __gmpz_init)

This just uses the default AC_CHECK_LIB actions for found or not found, but an application that must have GMP would want to generate an error if not found. For example,

```
AC_CHECK_LIB(gmp, __gmpz_init, ,
  [AC_MSG_ERROR([GNU MP not found, see https://gmplib.org/])])
```

If functions added in some particular version of GMP are required, then one of those can be used when checking. For example `mpz_mul_si` was added in GMP 3.1,

```
AC_CHECK_LIB(gmp, __gmpz_mul_si, ,
  [AC_MSG_ERROR(
  [GNU MP not found, or not 3.1 or up, see https://gmplib.org/])])
```

An alternative would be to test the version number in `gmp.h` using say `AC_EGREP_CPP`. That would make it possible to test the exact version, if some particular sub-minor release is known to be necessary.

In general it's recommended that applications should simply demand a new enough GMP rather than trying to provide supplements for features not available in past versions.

Occasionally an application will need or want to know the size of a type at configuration or preprocessing time, not just with `sizeof` in the code. This can be done in the normal way with `mp_limb_t` etc, but GMP 4.0 or up is best for this, since prior versions needed certain '-D' defines on systems using a `long long` limb. The following would suit Autoconf 2.50 or up,

```
AC_CHECK_SIZEOF(mp_limb_t, , [#include <gmp.h>])
```

3.15 Emacs

`C-h C-i` (`info-lookup-symbol`) is a good way to find documentation on C functions while editing (see Section "Info Documentation Lookup" in *The Emacs Editor*).

The GMP manual can be included in such lookups by putting the following in your `.emacs`,

```
(eval-after-load "info-look"
  '(let ((mode-value (assoc 'c-mode (assoc 'symbol info-lookup-alist))))
     (setcar (nthcdr 3 mode-value)
             (cons '("(gmp)Function Index" nil "^ -.* " "\\>")
                   (nth 3 mode-value)))))
```

4 Reporting Bugs

If you think you have found a bug in the GMP library, please investigate it and report it. We have made this library available to you, and it is not too much to ask you to report the bugs you find.

Before you report a bug, check it's not already addressed in Section 2.5 [Known Build Problems], page 14, or perhaps Section 2.4 [Notes for Particular Systems], page 12. You may also want to check `https://gmplib.org/` for patches for this release.

Please include the following in any report,

- The GMP version number, and if pre-packaged or patched then say so.
- A test program that makes it possible for us to reproduce the bug. Include instructions on how to run the program.
- A description of what is wrong. If the results are incorrect, in what way. If you get a crash, say so.
- If you get a crash, include a stack backtrace from the debugger if it's informative ('`where`' in `gdb`, or '`$C`' in `adb`).
- Please do not send core dumps, executables or `strace`s.
- The '`configure`' options you used when building GMP, if any.
- The output from '`configure`', as printed to stdout, with any options used.
- The name of the compiler and its version. For `gcc`, get the version with '`gcc -v`', otherwise perhaps '`what `which cc``', or similar.
- The output from running '`uname -a`'.
- The output from running '`./config.guess`', and from running '`./configfsf.guess`' (might be the same).
- If the bug is related to '`configure`', then the compressed contents of `config.log`.
- If the bug is related to an `asm` file not assembling, then the contents of `config.m4` and the offending line or lines from the temporary `mpn/tmp-<file>.s`.

Please make an effort to produce a self-contained report, with something definite that can be tested or debugged. Vague queries or piecemeal messages are difficult to act on and don't help the development effort.

It is not uncommon that an observed problem is actually due to a bug in the compiler; the GMP code tends to explore interesting corners in compilers.

If your bug report is good, we will do our best to help you get a corrected version of the library; if the bug report is poor, we won't do anything about it (except maybe ask you to send a better report).

Send your report to: `gmp-bugs@gmplib.org`.

If you think something in this manual is unclear, or downright incorrect, or if the language needs to be improved, please send a note to the same address.

5 Integer Functions

This chapter describes the GMP functions for performing integer arithmetic. These functions start with the prefix `mpz_`.

GMP integers are stored in objects of type `mpz_t`.

5.1 Initialization Functions

The functions for integer arithmetic assume that all integer objects are initialized. You do that by calling the function `mpz_init`. For example,

```
{
  mpz_t integ;
  mpz_init (integ);
  ...
  mpz_add (integ, ...);
  ...
  mpz_sub (integ, ...);

  /* Unless the program is about to exit, do ... */
  mpz_clear (integ);
}
```

As you can see, you can store new values any number of times, once an object is initialized.

void **mpz_init** (*mpz_t x*)   [Function]
    Initialize x, and set its value to 0.

void **mpz_inits** (*mpz_t x, ...*)   [Function]
    Initialize a NULL-terminated list of `mpz_t` variables, and set their values to 0.

void **mpz_init2** (*mpz_t x, mp_bitcnt_t n*)   [Function]
    Initialize x, with space for n-bit numbers, and set its value to 0. Calling this function instead of `mpz_init` or `mpz_inits` is never necessary; reallocation is handled automatically by GMP when needed.

    While n defines the initial space, x will grow automatically in the normal way, if necessary, for subsequent values stored. `mpz_init2` makes it possible to avoid such reallocations if a maximum size is known in advance.

    In preparation for an operation, GMP often allocates one limb more than ultimately needed. To make sure GMP will not perform reallocation for x, you need to add the number of bits in `mp_limb_t` to n.

void **mpz_clear** (*mpz_t x*)   [Function]
    Free the space occupied by x. Call this function for all `mpz_t` variables when you are done with them.

void **mpz_clears** (*mpz_t x, ...*)   [Function]
    Free the space occupied by a NULL-terminated list of `mpz_t` variables.

void **mpz_realloc2** (*mpz_t x, mp_bitcnt_t n*)   [Function]
    Change the space allocated for x to n bits. The value in x is preserved if it fits, or is set to 0 if not.

Calling this function is never necessary; reallocation is handled automatically by GMP when needed. But this function can be used to increase the space for a variable in order to avoid repeated automatic reallocations, or to decrease it to give memory back to the heap.

5.2 Assignment Functions

These functions assign new values to already initialized integers (see Section 5.1 [Initializing Integers], page 30).

void mpz_set (*mpz_t* **rop**, *const mpz_t* **op**)	[Function]
void mpz_set_ui (*mpz_t* **rop**, *unsigned long int* **op**)	[Function]
void mpz_set_si (*mpz_t* **rop**, *signed long int* **op**)	[Function]
void mpz_set_d (*mpz_t* **rop**, *double* **op**)	[Function]
void mpz_set_q (*mpz_t* **rop**, *const mpq_t* **op**)	[Function]
void mpz_set_f (*mpz_t* **rop**, *const mpf_t* **op**)	[Function]

Set the value of *rop* from *op*.

`mpz_set_d`, `mpz_set_q` and `mpz_set_f` truncate *op* to make it an integer.

int mpz_set_str (*mpz_t* **rop**, *const char* ***str**, *int* **base**)   [Function]
Set the value of *rop* from *str*, a null-terminated C string in base *base*. White space is allowed in the string, and is simply ignored.

The *base* may vary from 2 to 62, or if *base* is 0, then the leading characters are used: 0x and 0X for hexadecimal, 0b and 0B for binary, 0 for octal, or decimal otherwise.

For bases up to 36, case is ignored; upper-case and lower-case letters have the same value. For bases 37 to 62, upper-case letter represent the usual 10..35 while lower-case letter represent 36..61.

This function returns 0 if the entire string is a valid number in base *base*. Otherwise it returns -1.

void mpz_swap (*mpz_t* **rop1**, *mpz_t* **rop2**)   [Function]
Swap the values *rop1* and *rop2* efficiently.

5.3 Combined Initialization and Assignment Functions

For convenience, GMP provides a parallel series of initialize-and-set functions which initialize the output and then store the value there. These functions' names have the form `mpz_init_set...`

Here is an example of using one:

```
{
  mpz_t pie;
  mpz_init_set_str (pie, "3141592653589793238462643383279502884", 10);
  ...
  mpz_sub (pie, ...);
  ...
  mpz_clear (pie);
}
```

Once the integer has been initialized by any of the `mpz_init_set...` functions, it can be used as the source or destination operand for the ordinary integer functions. Don't use an initialize-and-set function on a variable already initialized!

void **mpz_init_set** (*mpz_t **rop**, const mpz_t **op***)   [Function]
void **mpz_init_set_ui** (*mpz_t **rop**, unsigned long int **op***)   [Function]
void **mpz_init_set_si** (*mpz_t **rop**, signed long int **op***)   [Function]
void **mpz_init_set_d** (*mpz_t **rop**, double **op***)   [Function]
 Initialize *rop* with limb space and set the initial numeric value from *op*.

int **mpz_init_set_str** (*mpz_t **rop**, const char ****str**, int **base***)   [Function]
 Initialize *rop* and set its value like **mpz_set_str** (see its documentation above for details).

 If the string is a correct base *base* number, the function returns 0; if an error occurs it returns
 −1. *rop* is initialized even if an error occurs. (I.e., you have to call **mpz_clear** for it.)

5.4 Conversion Functions

This section describes functions for converting GMP integers to standard C types. Functions
for converting *to* GMP integers are described in Section 5.2 [Assigning Integers], page 31 and
Section 5.12 [I/O of Integers], page 40.

unsigned long int **mpz_get_ui** (*const mpz_t **op***)   [Function]
 Return the value of *op* as an **unsigned long**.

 If *op* is too big to fit an **unsigned long** then just the least significant bits that do fit are
 returned. The sign of *op* is ignored, only the absolute value is used.

signed long int **mpz_get_si** (*const mpz_t **op***)   [Function]
 If *op* fits into a **signed long int** return the value of *op*. Otherwise return the least significant
 part of *op*, with the same sign as *op*.

 If *op* is too big to fit in a **signed long int**, the returned result is probably not very useful.
 To find out if the value will fit, use the function **mpz_fits_slong_p**.

double **mpz_get_d** (*const mpz_t **op***)   [Function]
 Convert *op* to a **double**, truncating if necessary (i.e. rounding towards zero).

 If the exponent from the conversion is too big, the result is system dependent. An infinity is
 returned where available. A hardware overflow trap may or may not occur.

double **mpz_get_d_2exp** (*signed long int ****exp**, const mpz_t **op***)   [Function]
 Convert *op* to a **double**, truncating if necessary (i.e. rounding towards zero), and returning
 the exponent separately.

 The return value is in the range $0.5 \le |d| < 1$ and the exponent is stored to ***exp**. $d * 2^{exp}$ is
 the (truncated) *op* value. If *op* is zero, the return is 0.0 and 0 is stored to ***exp**.

 This is similar to the standard C **frexp** function (see Section "Normalization Functions" in
 The GNU C Library Reference Manual).

char * **mpz_get_str** (*char ****str**, int **base**, const mpz_t **op***)   [Function]
 Convert *op* to a string of digits in base *base*. The base argument may vary from 2 to 62 or
 from −2 to −36.

 For *base* in the range 2..36, digits and lower-case letters are used; for −2..−36, digits and
 upper-case letters are used; for 37..62, digits, upper-case letters, and lower-case letters (in
 that significance order) are used.

If *str* is NULL, the result string is allocated using the current allocation function (see Chapter 13 [Custom Allocation], page 89). The block will be `strlen(str)+1` bytes, that being exactly enough for the string and null-terminator.

If *str* is not NULL, it should point to a block of storage large enough for the result, that being `mpz_sizeinbase (op, base) + 2`. The two extra bytes are for a possible minus sign, and the null-terminator.

A pointer to the result string is returned, being either the allocated block, or the given *str*.

5.5 Arithmetic Functions

void mpz_add (*mpz_t* **rop**, *const mpz_t* **op1**, *const mpz_t* **op2**)   [Function]
void mpz_add_ui (*mpz_t* **rop**, *const mpz_t* **op1**, *unsigned long int* **op2**)   [Function]
    Set *rop* to *op1* + *op2*.

void mpz_sub (*mpz_t* **rop**, *const mpz_t* **op1**, *const mpz_t* **op2**)   [Function]
void mpz_sub_ui (*mpz_t* **rop**, *const mpz_t* **op1**, *unsigned long int* **op2**)   [Function]
void mpz_ui_sub (*mpz_t* **rop**, *unsigned long int* **op1**, *const mpz_t* **op2**)   [Function]
    Set *rop* to *op1* − *op2*.

void mpz_mul (*mpz_t* **rop**, *const mpz_t* **op1**, *const mpz_t* **op2**)   [Function]
void mpz_mul_si (*mpz_t* **rop**, *const mpz_t* **op1**, *long int* **op2**)   [Function]
void mpz_mul_ui (*mpz_t* **rop**, *const mpz_t* **op1**, *unsigned long int* **op2**)   [Function]
    Set *rop* to *op1* × *op2*.

void mpz_addmul (*mpz_t* **rop**, *const mpz_t* **op1**, *const mpz_t* **op2**)   [Function]
void mpz_addmul_ui (*mpz_t* **rop**, *const mpz_t* **op1**, *unsigned long int* **op2**)   [Function]
    Set *rop* to *rop* + *op1* × *op2*.

void mpz_submul (*mpz_t* **rop**, *const mpz_t* **op1**, *const mpz_t* **op2**)   [Function]
void mpz_submul_ui (*mpz_t* **rop**, *const mpz_t* **op1**, *unsigned long int* **op2**)   [Function]
    Set *rop* to *rop* − *op1* × *op2*.

void mpz_mul_2exp (*mpz_t* **rop**, *const mpz_t* **op1**, *mp_bitcnt_t* **op2**)   [Function]
    Set *rop* to $op1 \times 2^{op2}$. This operation can also be defined as a left shift by *op2* bits.

void mpz_neg (*mpz_t* **rop**, *const mpz_t* **op**)   [Function]
    Set *rop* to −*op*.

void mpz_abs (*mpz_t* **rop**, *const mpz_t* **op**)   [Function]
    Set *rop* to the absolute value of *op*.

5.6 Division Functions

Division is undefined if the divisor is zero. Passing a zero divisor to the division or modulo functions (including the modular powering functions `mpz_powm` and `mpz_powm_ui`), will cause an intentional division by zero. This lets a program handle arithmetic exceptions in these functions the same way as for normal C `int` arithmetic.

void mpz_cdiv_q (*mpz_t* **q**, *const mpz_t* **n**, *const mpz_t* **d**)   [Function]
void mpz_cdiv_r (*mpz_t* **r**, *const mpz_t* **n**, *const mpz_t* **d**)   [Function]
void mpz_cdiv_qr (*mpz_t* **q**, *mpz_t* **r**, *const mpz_t* **n**, *const mpz_t* **d**)   [Function]

unsigned long int mpz_cdiv_q_ui (*mpz_t* **q**, *const mpz_t* **n**,   [Function]
     unsigned long int **d**)

unsigned long int mpz_cdiv_r_ui (*mpz_t* **r**, *const mpz_t* **n**,   [Function]
     unsigned long int **d**)

unsigned long int mpz_cdiv_qr_ui (*mpz_t* **q**, *mpz_t* **r**, *const mpz_t* **n**,   [Function]
     unsigned long int **d**)

unsigned long int mpz_cdiv_ui (*const mpz_t* **n**, *unsigned long int* **d**)   [Function]

void mpz_cdiv_q_2exp (*mpz_t* **q**, *const mpz_t* **n**, *mp_bitcnt_t* **b**)   [Function]

void mpz_cdiv_r_2exp (*mpz_t* **r**, *const mpz_t* **n**, *mp_bitcnt_t* **b**)   [Function]

void mpz_fdiv_q (*mpz_t* **q**, *const mpz_t* **n**, *const mpz_t* **d**)   [Function]

void mpz_fdiv_r (*mpz_t* **r**, *const mpz_t* **n**, *const mpz_t* **d**)   [Function]

void mpz_fdiv_qr (*mpz_t* **q**, *mpz_t* **r**, *const mpz_t* **n**, *const mpz_t* **d**)   [Function]

unsigned long int mpz_fdiv_q_ui (*mpz_t* **q**, *const mpz_t* **n**,   [Function]
     unsigned long int **d**)

unsigned long int mpz_fdiv_r_ui (*mpz_t* **r**, *const mpz_t* **n**,   [Function]
     unsigned long int **d**)

unsigned long int mpz_fdiv_qr_ui (*mpz_t* **q**, *mpz_t* **r**, *const mpz_t* **n**,   [Function]
     unsigned long int **d**)

unsigned long int mpz_fdiv_ui (*const mpz_t* **n**, *unsigned long int* **d**)   [Function]

void mpz_fdiv_q_2exp (*mpz_t* **q**, *const mpz_t* **n**, *mp_bitcnt_t* **b**)   [Function]

void mpz_fdiv_r_2exp (*mpz_t* **r**, *const mpz_t* **n**, *mp_bitcnt_t* **b**)   [Function]

void mpz_tdiv_q (*mpz_t* **q**, *const mpz_t* **n**, *const mpz_t* **d**)   [Function]

void mpz_tdiv_r (*mpz_t* **r**, *const mpz_t* **n**, *const mpz_t* **d**)   [Function]

void mpz_tdiv_qr (*mpz_t* **q**, *mpz_t* **r**, *const mpz_t* **n**, *const mpz_t* **d**)   [Function]

unsigned long int mpz_tdiv_q_ui (*mpz_t* **q**, *const mpz_t* **n**,   [Function]
     unsigned long int **d**)

unsigned long int mpz_tdiv_r_ui (*mpz_t* **r**, *const mpz_t* **n**,   [Function]
     unsigned long int **d**)

unsigned long int mpz_tdiv_qr_ui (*mpz_t* **q**, *mpz_t* **r**, *const mpz_t* **n**,   [Function]
     unsigned long int **d**)

unsigned long int mpz_tdiv_ui (*const mpz_t* **n**, *unsigned long int* **d**)   [Function]

void mpz_tdiv_q_2exp (*mpz_t* **q**, *const mpz_t* **n**, *mp_bitcnt_t* **b**)   [Function]

void mpz_tdiv_r_2exp (*mpz_t* **r**, *const mpz_t* **n**, *mp_bitcnt_t* **b**)   [Function]

Divide n by d, forming a quotient q and/or remainder r. For the 2exp functions, $d = 2^b$. The rounding is in three styles, each suiting different applications.

- cdiv rounds q up towards $+\infty$, and r will have the opposite sign to d. The c stands for "ceil".

- fdiv rounds q down towards $-\infty$, and r will have the same sign as d. The f stands for "floor".

- tdiv rounds q towards zero, and r will have the same sign as n. The t stands for "truncate".

In all cases q and r will satisfy $n = qd + r$, and r will satisfy $0 \le |r| < |d|$.

The q functions calculate only the quotient, the r functions only the remainder, and the qr functions calculate both. Note that for qr the same variable cannot be passed for both q and r, or results will be unpredictable.

For the ui variants the return value is the remainder, and in fact returning the remainder is all the div_ui functions do. For tdiv and cdiv the remainder can be negative, so for those the return value is the absolute value of the remainder.

For the `2exp` variants the divisor is 2^b. These functions are implemented as right shifts and bit masks, but of course they round the same as the other functions.

For positive n both `mpz_fdiv_q_2exp` and `mpz_tdiv_q_2exp` are simple bitwise right shifts. For negative n, `mpz_fdiv_q_2exp` is effectively an arithmetic right shift treating n as twos complement the same as the bitwise logical functions do, whereas `mpz_tdiv_q_2exp` effectively treats n as sign and magnitude.

void mpz_mod (*mpz_t* **r**, *const mpz_t* **n**, *const mpz_t* **d**)   [Function]
unsigned long int mpz_mod_ui (*mpz_t* **r**, *const mpz_t* **n**,   [Function]
      unsigned long int **d**)
    Set r to $n \bmod d$. The sign of the divisor is ignored; the result is always non-negative.

    `mpz_mod_ui` is identical to `mpz_fdiv_r_ui` above, returning the remainder as well as setting r. See `mpz_fdiv_ui` above if only the return value is wanted.

void mpz_divexact (*mpz_t* **q**, *const mpz_t* **n**, *const mpz_t* **d**)   [Function]
void mpz_divexact_ui (*mpz_t* **q**, *const mpz_t* **n**, *unsigned long* **d**)   [Function]
    Set q to n/d. These functions produce correct results only when it is known in advance that d divides n.

    These routines are much faster than the other division functions, and are the best choice when exact division is known to occur, for example reducing a rational to lowest terms.

int mpz_divisible_p (*const mpz_t* **n**, *const mpz_t* **d**)   [Function]
int mpz_divisible_ui_p (*const mpz_t* **n**, *unsigned long int* **d**)   [Function]
int mpz_divisible_2exp_p (*const mpz_t* **n**, *mp_bitcnt_t* **b**)   [Function]
    Return non-zero if n is exactly divisible by d, or in the case of `mpz_divisible_2exp_p` by 2^b.

    n is divisible by d if there exists an integer q satisfying $n = qd$. Unlike the other division functions, $d = 0$ is accepted and following the rule it can be seen that only 0 is considered divisible by 0.

int mpz_congruent_p (*const mpz_t* **n**, *const mpz_t* **c**, *const mpz_t* **d**)   [Function]
int mpz_congruent_ui_p (*const mpz_t* **n**, *unsigned long int* **c**, *unsigned long*   [Function]
    int **d**)
int mpz_congruent_2exp_p (*const mpz_t* **n**, *const mpz_t* **c**, *mp_bitcnt_t* **b**)   [Function]
    Return non-zero if n is congruent to c modulo d, or in the case of `mpz_congruent_2exp_p` modulo 2^b.

    n is congruent to c mod d if there exists an integer q satisfying $n = c + qd$. Unlike the other division functions, $d = 0$ is accepted and following the rule it can be seen that n and c are considered congruent mod 0 only when exactly equal.

5.7 Exponentiation Functions

void mpz_powm (*mpz_t* **rop**, *const mpz_t* **base**, *const mpz_t* **exp**, *const mpz_t*   [Function]
    mod)
void mpz_powm_ui (*mpz_t* **rop**, *const mpz_t* **base**, *unsigned long int* **exp**,   [Function]
    const mpz_t **mod**)
    Set rop to $base^{exp} \bmod mod$.

    Negative exp is supported if an inverse $base^{-1} \bmod mod$ exists (see `mpz_invert` in Section 5.9 [Number Theoretic Functions], page 37). If an inverse doesn't exist then a divide by zero is raised.

void **mpz_powm_sec** (*mpz_t* **rop**, *const mpz_t* **base**, *const mpz_t* **exp**, *const*   [Function]
      mpz_t **mod**)
    Set *rop* to $base^{exp}$ mod *mod*.

    It is required that $exp > 0$ and that *mod* is odd.

    This function is designed to take the same time and have the same cache access patterns
    for any two same-size arguments, assuming that function arguments are placed at the same
    position and that the machine state is identical upon function entry. This function is intended
    for cryptographic purposes, where resilience to side-channel attacks is desired.

void **mpz_pow_ui** (*mpz_t* **rop**, *const mpz_t* **base**, *unsigned long int* **exp**)   [Function]
void **mpz_ui_pow_ui** (*mpz_t* **rop**, *unsigned long int* **base**, *unsigned long int*   [Function]
      exp)
    Set *rop* to $base^{exp}$. The case 0^0 yields 1.

5.8 Root Extraction Functions

int **mpz_root** (*mpz_t* **rop**, *const mpz_t* **op**, *unsigned long int* **n**)   [Function]
    Set *rop* to $\lfloor \sqrt[n]{op} \rfloor$, the truncated integer part of the *n*th root of *op*. Return non-zero if the
    computation was exact, i.e., if *op* is *rop* to the *n*th power.

void **mpz_rootrem** (*mpz_t* **root**, *mpz_t* **rem**, *const mpz_t* **u**, *unsigned long int*   [Function]
      n)
    Set *root* to $\lfloor \sqrt[n]{u} \rfloor$, the truncated integer part of the *n*th root of *u*. Set *rem* to the remainder,
    $(u - root^n)$.

void **mpz_sqrt** (*mpz_t* **rop**, *const mpz_t* **op**)   [Function]
    Set *rop* to $\lfloor \sqrt{op} \rfloor$, the truncated integer part of the square root of *op*.

void **mpz_sqrtrem** (*mpz_t* **rop1**, *mpz_t* **rop2**, *const mpz_t* **op**)   [Function]
    Set *rop1* to $\lfloor \sqrt{op} \rfloor$, like **mpz_sqrt**. Set *rop2* to the remainder $(op - rop1^2)$, which will be
    zero if *op* is a perfect square.

    If *rop1* and *rop2* are the same variable, the results are undefined.

int **mpz_perfect_power_p** (*const mpz_t* **op**)   [Function]
    Return non-zero if *op* is a perfect power, i.e., if there exist integers *a* and *b*, with $b > 1$, such
    that $op = a^b$.

    Under this definition both 0 and 1 are considered to be perfect powers. Negative values of
    op are accepted, but of course can only be odd perfect powers.

int **mpz_perfect_square_p** (*const mpz_t* **op**)   [Function]
    Return non-zero if *op* is a perfect square, i.e., if the square root of *op* is an integer. Under
    this definition both 0 and 1 are considered to be perfect squares.

5.9 Number Theoretic Functions

int **mpz_probab_prime_p** (*const mpz_t* **n**, *int* **reps**)   [Function]
    Determine whether n is prime. Return 2 if n is definitely prime, return 1 if n is probably
    prime (without being certain), or return 0 if n is definitely composite.

    This function does some trial divisions, then some Miller-Rabin probabilistic primality tests.
    The argument *reps* controls how many such tests are done; a higher value will reduce the
    chances of a composite being returned as "probably prime". 25 is a reasonable number; a
    composite number will then be identified as a prime with a probability of less than 2^{-50}.

    Miller-Rabin and similar tests can be more properly called compositeness tests. Numbers
    which fail are known to be composite but those which pass might be prime or might be
    composite. Only a few composites pass, hence those which pass are considered probably
    prime.

void **mpz_nextprime** (*mpz_t* **rop**, *const mpz_t* **op**)   [Function]
    Set *rop* to the next prime greater than *op*.

    This function uses a probabilistic algorithm to identify primes. For practical purposes it's
    adequate, the chance of a composite passing will be extremely small.

void **mpz_gcd** (*mpz_t* **rop**, *const mpz_t* **op1**, *const mpz_t* **op2**)   [Function]
    Set *rop* to the greatest common divisor of *op1* and *op2*. The result is always positive even if
    one or both input operands are negative. Except if both inputs are zero; then this function
    defines $gcd(0, 0) = 0$.

unsigned long int **mpz_gcd_ui** (*mpz_t* **rop**, *const mpz_t* **op1**, *unsigned*   [Function]
        long int **op2**)
    Compute the greatest common divisor of *op1* and *op2*. If *rop* is not NULL, store the result
    there.

    If the result is small enough to fit in an **unsigned long int**, it is returned. If the result does
    not fit, 0 is returned, and the result is equal to the argument *op1*. Note that the result will
    always fit if *op2* is non-zero.

void **mpz_gcdext** (*mpz_t* **g**, *mpz_t* **s**, *mpz_t* **t**, *const mpz_t* **a**, *const mpz_t* **b**)   [Function]
    Set g to the greatest common divisor of a and b, and in addition set s and t to coefficients
    satisfying $as + bt = g$. The value in g is always positive, even if one or both of a and b
    are negative (or zero if both inputs are zero). The values in s and t are chosen such that
    normally, $|s| < |b|/(2g)$ and $|t| < |a|/(2g)$, and these relations define s and t uniquely. There
    are a few exceptional cases:

    If $|a| = |b|$, then $s = 0$, $t = sgn(b)$.

    Otherwise, $s = sgn(a)$ if $b = 0$ or $|b| = 2g$, and $t = sgn(b)$ if $a = 0$ or $|a| = 2g$.

    In all cases, $s = 0$ if and only if $g = |b|$, i.e., if b divides a or $a = b = 0$.

    If t is NULL then that value is not computed.

void **mpz_lcm** (*mpz_t* **rop**, *const mpz_t* **op1**, *const mpz_t* **op2**)   [Function]
void **mpz_lcm_ui** (*mpz_t* **rop**, *const mpz_t* **op1**, *unsigned long* **op2**)   [Function]
    Set *rop* to the least common multiple of *op1* and *op2*. *rop* is always positive, irrespective of
    the signs of *op1* and *op2*. *rop* will be zero if either *op1* or *op2* is zero.

`int mpz_invert` (*mpz_t* **rop**, *const mpz_t* **op1**, *const mpz_t* **op2**)   [Function]
Compute the inverse of *op1* modulo *op2* and put the result in *rop*. If the inverse exists, the return value is non-zero and *rop* will satisfy $0 < rop < |op2|$. If an inverse doesn't exist the return value is zero and *rop* is undefined. The behaviour of this function is undefined when *op2* is zero.

`int mpz_jacobi` (*const mpz_t* **a**, *const mpz_t* **b**)   [Function]
Calculate the Jacobi symbol $\left(\frac{a}{b}\right)$. This is defined only for *b* odd.

`int mpz_legendre` (*const mpz_t* **a**, *const mpz_t* **p**)   [Function]
Calculate the Legendre symbol $\left(\frac{a}{p}\right)$. This is defined only for *p* an odd positive prime, and for such *p* it's identical to the Jacobi symbol.

`int mpz_kronecker` (*const mpz_t* **a**, *const mpz_t* **b**)   [Function]
`int mpz_kronecker_si` (*const mpz_t* **a**, *long* **b**)   [Function]
`int mpz_kronecker_ui` (*const mpz_t* **a**, *unsigned long* **b**)   [Function]
`int mpz_si_kronecker` (*long* **a**, *const mpz_t* **b**)   [Function]
`int mpz_ui_kronecker` (*unsigned long* **a**, *const mpz_t* **b**)   [Function]
Calculate the Jacobi symbol $\left(\frac{a}{b}\right)$ with the Kronecker extension $\left(\frac{a}{2}\right) = \left(\frac{2}{a}\right)$ when *a* odd, or $\left(\frac{a}{2}\right) = 0$ when *a* even.

When *b* is odd the Jacobi symbol and Kronecker symbol are identical, so `mpz_kronecker_ui` etc can be used for mixed precision Jacobi symbols too.

For more information see Henri Cohen section 1.4.2 (see Appendix B [References], page 125), or any number theory textbook. See also the example program `demos/qcn.c` which uses `mpz_kronecker_ui`.

`mp_bitcnt_t mpz_remove` (*mpz_t* **rop**, *const mpz_t* **op**, *const mpz_t* **f**)   [Function]
Remove all occurrences of the factor *f* from *op* and store the result in *rop*. The return value is how many such occurrences were removed.

`void mpz_fac_ui` (*mpz_t* **rop**, *unsigned long int* **n**)   [Function]
`void mpz_2fac_ui` (*mpz_t* **rop**, *unsigned long int* **n**)   [Function]
`void mpz_mfac_uiui` (*mpz_t* **rop**, *unsigned long int* **n**, *unsigned long int* **m**)   [Function]
Set *rop* to the factorial of *n*: `mpz_fac_ui` computes the plain factorial $n!$, `mpz_2fac_ui` computes the double-factorial $n!!$, and `mpz_mfac_uiui` the *m*-multi-factorial $n!^{(m)}$.

`void mpz_primorial_ui` (*mpz_t* **rop**, *unsigned long int* **n**)   [Function]
Set *rop* to the primorial of *n*, i.e. the product of all positive prime numbers $\leq n$.

`void mpz_bin_ui` (*mpz_t* **rop**, *const mpz_t* **n**, *unsigned long int* **k**)   [Function]
`void mpz_bin_uiui` (*mpz_t* **rop**, *unsigned long int* **n**, *unsigned long int* **k**)   [Function]
Compute the binomial coefficient $\binom{n}{k}$ and store the result in *rop*. Negative values of *n* are supported by `mpz_bin_ui`, using the identity $\binom{-n}{k} = (-1)^k \binom{n+k-1}{k}$, see Knuth volume 1 section 1.2.6 part G.

`void mpz_fib_ui` (*mpz_t* **fn**, *unsigned long int* **n**)   [Function]
`void mpz_fib2_ui` (*mpz_t* **fn**, *mpz_t* **fnsub1**, *unsigned long int* **n**)   [Function]
`mpz_fib_ui` sets *fn* to to F_n, the *n*'th Fibonacci number. `mpz_fib2_ui` sets *fn* to F_n, and *fnsub1* to F_{n-1}.

These functions are designed for calculating isolated Fibonacci numbers. When a sequence of values is wanted it's best to start with `mpz_fib2_ui` and iterate the defining $F_{n+1} = F_n + F_{n-1}$ or similar.

void **mpz_lucnum_ui** (*mpz_t* **ln**, *unsigned long int* **n**)   [Function]

void **mpz_lucnum2_ui** (*mpz_t* **ln**, *mpz_t* **lnsub1**, *unsigned long int* **n**)   [Function]

> `mpz_lucnum_ui` sets *ln* to to L_n, the *n*'th Lucas number. `mpz_lucnum2_ui` sets *ln* to L_n, and *lnsub1* to L_{n-1}.

> These functions are designed for calculating isolated Lucas numbers. When a sequence of values is wanted it's best to start with `mpz_lucnum2_ui` and iterate the defining $L_{n+1} = L_n + L_{n-1}$ or similar.

> The Fibonacci numbers and Lucas numbers are related sequences, so it's never necessary to call both `mpz_fib2_ui` and `mpz_lucnum2_ui`. The formulas for going from Fibonacci to Lucas can be found in Section 15.7.5 [Lucas Numbers Algorithm], page 112, the reverse is straightforward too.

5.10 Comparison Functions

int **mpz_cmp** (*const mpz_t* **op1**, *const mpz_t* **op2**)   [Function]

int **mpz_cmp_d** (*const mpz_t* **op1**, *double* **op2**)   [Function]

int **mpz_cmp_si** (*const mpz_t* **op1**, *signed long int* **op2**)   [Macro]

int **mpz_cmp_ui** (*const mpz_t* **op1**, *unsigned long int* **op2**)   [Macro]

> Compare *op1* and *op2*. Return a positive value if $op1 > op2$, zero if $op1 = op2$, or a negative value if $op1 < op2$.

> `mpz_cmp_ui` and `mpz_cmp_si` are macros and will evaluate their arguments more than once. `mpz_cmp_d` can be called with an infinity, but results are undefined for a NaN.

int **mpz_cmpabs** (*const mpz_t* **op1**, *const mpz_t* **op2**)   [Function]

int **mpz_cmpabs_d** (*const mpz_t* **op1**, *double* **op2**)   [Function]

int **mpz_cmpabs_ui** (*const mpz_t* **op1**, *unsigned long int* **op2**)   [Function]

> Compare the absolute values of *op1* and *op2*. Return a positive value if $|op1| > |op2|$, zero if $|op1| = |op2|$, or a negative value if $|op1| < |op2|$.

> `mpz_cmpabs_d` can be called with an infinity, but results are undefined for a NaN.

int **mpz_sgn** (*const mpz_t* **op**)   [Macro]

> Return $+1$ if $op > 0$, 0 if $op = 0$, and -1 if $op < 0$.

> This function is actually implemented as a macro. It evaluates its argument multiple times.

5.11 Logical and Bit Manipulation Functions

These functions behave as if twos complement arithmetic were used (although sign-magnitude is the actual implementation). The least significant bit is number 0.

void **mpz_and** (*mpz_t* **rop**, *const mpz_t* **op1**, *const mpz_t* **op2**)   [Function]

> Set *rop* to *op1* bitwise-and *op2*.

void **mpz_ior** (*mpz_t* **rop**, *const mpz_t* **op1**, *const mpz_t* **op2**)   [Function]

> Set *rop* to *op1* bitwise inclusive-or *op2*.

void **mpz_xor** (*mpz_t* **rop**, *const mpz_t* **op1**, *const mpz_t* **op2**)   [Function]
    Set *rop* to *op1* bitwise exclusive-or *op2*.

void **mpz_com** (*mpz_t* **rop**, *const mpz_t* **op**)   [Function]
    Set *rop* to the one's complement of *op*.

mp_bitcnt_t **mpz_popcount** (*const mpz_t* **op**)   [Function]
    If $op \geq 0$, return the population count of *op*, which is the number of 1 bits in the binary
    representation. If $op < 0$, the number of 1s is infinite, and the return value is the largest
    possible `mp_bitcnt_t`.

mp_bitcnt_t **mpz_hamdist** (*const mpz_t* **op1**, *const mpz_t* **op2**)   [Function]
    If *op1* and *op2* are both ≥ 0 or both < 0, return the hamming distance between the two
    operands, which is the number of bit positions where *op1* and *op2* have different bit values.
    If one operand is ≥ 0 and the other < 0 then the number of bits different is infinite, and the
    return value is the largest possible `mp_bitcnt_t`.

mp_bitcnt_t **mpz_scan0** (*const mpz_t* **op**, *mp_bitcnt_t* **starting_bit**)   [Function]
mp_bitcnt_t **mpz_scan1** (*const mpz_t* **op**, *mp_bitcnt_t* **starting_bit**)   [Function]
    Scan *op*, starting from bit *starting_bit*, towards more significant bits, until the first 0 or 1 bit
    (respectively) is found. Return the index of the found bit.

    If the bit at *starting_bit* is already what's sought, then *starting_bit* is returned.

    If there's no bit found, then the largest possible `mp_bitcnt_t` is returned. This will happen
    in `mpz_scan0` past the end of a negative number, or `mpz_scan1` past the end of a nonnegative
    number.

void **mpz_setbit** (*mpz_t* **rop**, *mp_bitcnt_t* **bit_index**)   [Function]
    Set bit *bit_index* in *rop*.

void **mpz_clrbit** (*mpz_t* **rop**, *mp_bitcnt_t* **bit_index**)   [Function]
    Clear bit *bit_index* in *rop*.

void **mpz_combit** (*mpz_t* **rop**, *mp_bitcnt_t* **bit_index**)   [Function]
    Complement bit *bit_index* in *rop*.

int **mpz_tstbit** (*const mpz_t* **op**, *mp_bitcnt_t* **bit_index**)   [Function]
    Test bit *bit_index* in *op* and return 0 or 1 accordingly.

5.12 Input and Output Functions

Functions that perform input from a stdio stream, and functions that output to a stdio stream,
of mpz numbers. Passing a `NULL` pointer for a *stream* argument to any of these functions will
make them read from `stdin` and write to `stdout`, respectively.

When using any of these functions, it is a good idea to include `stdio.h` before `gmp.h`, since that
will allow `gmp.h` to define prototypes for these functions.

See also Chapter 10 [Formatted Output], page 71 and Chapter 11 [Formatted Input], page 76.

size_t **mpz_out_str** (*FILE* ***stream**, *int* **base**, *const mpz_t* **op**)   [Function]
    Output *op* on stdio stream *stream*, as a string of digits in base *base*. The base argument may
    vary from 2 to 62 or from -2 to -36.

For *base* in the range 2..36, digits and lower-case letters are used; for −2..−36, digits and upper-case letters are used; for 37..62, digits, upper-case letters, and lower-case letters (in that significance order) are used.

Return the number of bytes written, or if an error occurred, return 0.

size_t mpz_inp_str (*mpz_t* `rop`, *FILE **`stream`, *int* `base`)   [Function]
    Input a possibly white-space preceded string in base *base* from stdio stream *stream*, and put the read integer in *rop*.

    The *base* may vary from 2 to 62, or if *base* is 0, then the leading characters are used: `0x` and `0X` for hexadecimal, `0b` and `0B` for binary, `0` for octal, or decimal otherwise.

    For bases up to 36, case is ignored; upper-case and lower-case letters have the same value. For bases 37 to 62, upper-case letter represent the usual 10..35 while lower-case letter represent 36..61.

    Return the number of bytes read, or if an error occurred, return 0.

size_t mpz_out_raw (*FILE **`stream`, *const mpz_t* `op`)   [Function]
    Output *op* on stdio stream *stream*, in raw binary format. The integer is written in a portable format, with 4 bytes of size information, and that many bytes of limbs. Both the size and the limbs are written in decreasing significance order (i.e., in big-endian).

    The output can be read with `mpz_inp_raw`.

    Return the number of bytes written, or if an error occurred, return 0.

    The output of this can not be read by `mpz_inp_raw` from GMP 1, because of changes necessary for compatibility between 32-bit and 64-bit machines.

size_t mpz_inp_raw (*mpz_t* `rop`, *FILE **`stream`)   [Function]
    Input from stdio stream *stream* in the format written by `mpz_out_raw`, and put the result in *rop*. Return the number of bytes read, or if an error occurred, return 0.

    This routine can read the output from `mpz_out_raw` also from GMP 1, in spite of changes necessary for compatibility between 32-bit and 64-bit machines.

5.13 Random Number Functions

The random number functions of GMP come in two groups; older function that rely on a global state, and newer functions that accept a state parameter that is read and modified. Please see the Chapter 9 [Random Number Functions], page 69 for more information on how to use and not to use random number functions.

void mpz_urandomb (*mpz_t* `rop`, *gmp_randstate_t* `state`, *mp_bitcnt_t* `n`)   [Function]
    Generate a uniformly distributed random integer in the range 0 to $2^n - 1$, inclusive.

    The variable *state* must be initialized by calling one of the `gmp_randinit` functions (Section 9.1 [Random State Initialization], page 69) before invoking this function.

void mpz_urandomm (*mpz_t* `rop`, *gmp_randstate_t* `state`, *const mpz_t* `n`)   [Function]
    Generate a uniform random integer in the range 0 to $n - 1$, inclusive.

    The variable *state* must be initialized by calling one of the `gmp_randinit` functions (Section 9.1 [Random State Initialization], page 69) before invoking this function.

void **mpz_rrandomb** (*mpz_t* **rop**, *gmp_randstate_t* **state**, *mp_bitcnt_t* **n**)   [Function]
    Generate a random integer with long strings of zeros and ones in the binary representation. Useful for testing functions and algorithms, since this kind of random numbers have proven to be more likely to trigger corner-case bugs. The random number will be in the range 0 to $2^n - 1$, inclusive.

    The variable *state* must be initialized by calling one of the **gmp_randinit** functions (Section 9.1 [Random State Initialization], page 69) before invoking this function.

void **mpz_random** (*mpz_t* **rop**, *mp_size_t* **max_size**)   [Function]
    Generate a random integer of at most *max_size* limbs. The generated random number doesn't satisfy any particular requirements of randomness. Negative random numbers are generated when *max_size* is negative.

    This function is obsolete. Use **mpz_urandomb** or **mpz_urandomm** instead.

void **mpz_random2** (*mpz_t* **rop**, *mp_size_t* **max_size**)   [Function]
    Generate a random integer of at most *max_size* limbs, with long strings of zeros and ones in the binary representation. Useful for testing functions and algorithms, since this kind of random numbers have proven to be more likely to trigger corner-case bugs. Negative random numbers are generated when *max_size* is negative.

    This function is obsolete. Use **mpz_rrandomb** instead.

5.14 Integer Import and Export

mpz_t variables can be converted to and from arbitrary words of binary data with the following functions.

void **mpz_import** (*mpz_t* **rop**, *size_t* **count**, *int* **order**, *size_t* **size**, *int*   [Function]
        endian, *size_t* **nails**, *const void ***op**)
    Set *rop* from an array of word data at *op*.

    The parameters specify the format of the data. *count* many words are read, each *size* bytes. *order* can be 1 for most significant word first or -1 for least significant first. Within each word *endian* can be 1 for most significant byte first, -1 for least significant first, or 0 for the native endianness of the host CPU. The most significant *nails* bits of each word are skipped, this can be 0 to use the full words.

    There is no sign taken from the data, *rop* will simply be a positive integer. An application can handle any sign itself, and apply it for instance with **mpz_neg**.

    There are no data alignment restrictions on *op*, any address is allowed.

    Here's an example converting an array of **unsigned long** data, most significant element first, and host byte order within each value.

```
unsigned long  a[20];
/* Initialize z and a */
mpz_import (z, 20, 1, sizeof(a[0]), 0, 0, a);
```

    This example assumes the full **sizeof** bytes are used for data in the given type, which is usually true, and certainly true for **unsigned long** everywhere we know of. However on Cray vector systems it may be noted that **short** and **int** are always stored in 8 bytes (and with **sizeof** indicating that) but use only 32 or 46 bits. The *nails* feature can account for this, by passing for instance 8*sizeof(int)-INT_BIT.

void * mpz_export (*void *rop*, *size_t *countp*, *int* order, *size_t* **size**, *int*   [Function]
         endian, *size_t* **nails**, *const mpz_t* **op**)
  Fill *rop* with word data from *op*.

  The parameters specify the format of the data produced. Each word will be *size* bytes and
  order can be 1 for most significant word first or -1 for least significant first. Within each
  word *endian* can be 1 for most significant byte first, -1 for least significant first, or 0 for the
  native endianness of the host CPU. The most significant *nails* bits of each word are unused
  and set to zero, this can be 0 to produce full words.

  The number of words produced is written to *countp*, or *countp* can be NULL to discard the
  count. *rop* must have enough space for the data, or if *rop* is NULL then a result array of
  the necessary size is allocated using the current GMP allocation function (see Chapter 13
  [Custom Allocation], page 89). In either case the return value is the destination used, either
  rop or the allocated block.

  If *op* is non-zero then the most significant word produced will be non-zero. If *op* is zero then
  the count returned will be zero and nothing written to *rop*. If *rop* is NULL in this case, no
  block is allocated, just NULL is returned.

  The sign of *op* is ignored, just the absolute value is exported. An application can use mpz_sgn
  to get the sign and handle it as desired. (see Section 5.10 [Integer Comparisons], page 39)

  There are no data alignment restrictions on *rop*, any address is allowed.

  When an application is allocating space itself the required size can be determined with a
  calculation like the following. Since mpz_sizeinbase always returns at least 1, count here
  will be at least one, which avoids any portability problems with malloc(0), though if z is
  zero no space at all is actually needed (or written).

```
numb = 8*size - nail;
count = (mpz_sizeinbase (z, 2) + numb-1) / numb;
p = malloc (count * size);
```

5.15 Miscellaneous Functions

int mpz_fits_ulong_p (*const mpz_t* op)   [Function]
int mpz_fits_slong_p (*const mpz_t* op)   [Function]
int mpz_fits_uint_p (*const mpz_t* op)   [Function]
int mpz_fits_sint_p (*const mpz_t* op)   [Function]
int mpz_fits_ushort_p (*const mpz_t* op)   [Function]
int mpz_fits_sshort_p (*const mpz_t* op)   [Function]
  Return non-zero iff the value of *op* fits in an unsigned long int, signed long int, unsigned
  int, signed int, unsigned short int, or signed short int, respectively. Otherwise, return zero.

int mpz_odd_p (*const mpz_t* op)   [Macro]
int mpz_even_p (*const mpz_t* op)   [Macro]
  Determine whether *op* is odd or even, respectively. Return non-zero if yes, zero if no. These
  macros evaluate their argument more than once.

size_t mpz_sizeinbase (*const mpz_t* op, *int* base)   [Function]
  Return the size of *op* measured in number of digits in the given *base*. *base* can vary from 2
  to 62. The sign of *op* is ignored, just the absolute value is used. The result will be either

exact or 1 too big. If *base* is a power of 2, the result is always exact. If *op* is zero the return value is always 1.

This function can be used to determine the space required when converting *op* to a string. The right amount of allocation is normally two more than the value returned by `mpz_sizeinbase`, one extra for a minus sign and one for the null-terminator.

It will be noted that `mpz_sizeinbase(op,2)` can be used to locate the most significant 1 bit in *op*, counting from 1. (Unlike the bitwise functions which start from 0, See Section 5.11 [Logical and Bit Manipulation Functions], page 39.)

5.16 Special Functions

The functions in this section are for various special purposes. Most applications will not need them.

void mpz_array_init (*mpz_t* **integer_array**, *mp_size_t* **array_size**,   [Function]
      mp_size_t **fixed_num_bits**)
This is an obsolete function. Do not use it.

void * _mpz_realloc (*mpz_t* **integer**, *mp_size_t* **new_alloc**)   [Function]
Change the space for *integer* to *new_alloc* limbs. The value in *integer* is preserved if it fits, or is set to 0 if not. The return value is not useful to applications and should be ignored.

`mpz_realloc2` is the preferred way to accomplish allocation changes like this. `mpz_realloc2` and `_mpz_realloc` are the same except that `_mpz_realloc` takes its size in limbs.

mp_limb_t mpz_getlimbn (*const mpz_t* **op**, *mp_size_t* **n**)   [Function]
Return limb number *n* from *op*. The sign of *op* is ignored, just the absolute value is used. The least significant limb is number 0.

`mpz_size` can be used to find how many limbs make up *op*. `mpz_getlimbn` returns zero if *n* is outside the range 0 to `mpz_size(op)-1`.

size_t mpz_size (*const mpz_t* **op**)   [Function]
Return the size of *op* measured in number of limbs. If *op* is zero, the returned value will be zero.

const mp_limb_t * mpz_limbs_read (*const mpz_t* **x**)   [Function]
Return a pointer to the limb array representing the absolute value of *x*. The size of the array is `mpz_size(x)`. Intended for read access only.

mp_limb_t * mpz_limbs_write (*mpz_t* **x**, *mp_size_t* **n**)   [Function]
mp_limb_t * mpz_limbs_modify (*mpz_t* **x**, *mp_size_t* **n**)   [Function]
Return a pointer to the limb array, intended for write access. The array is reallocated as needed, to make room for *n* limbs. Requires $n > 0$. The `mpz_limbs_modify` function returns an array that holds the old absolute value of *x*, while `mpz_limbs_write` may destroy the old value and return an array with unspecified contents.

void mpz_limbs_finish (*mpz_t* **x**, *mp_size_t* **s**)   [Function]
Updates the internal size field of *x*. Used after writing to the limb array pointer returned by `mpz_limbs_write` or `mpz_limbs_modify` is completed. The array should contain |*s*| valid limbs, representing the new absolute value for *x*, and the sign of *x* is taken from the sign of *s*. This function never reallocates *x*, so the limb pointer remains valid.

```
void foo (mpz_t x)
{
  mp_size_t n, i;
  mp_limb_t *xp;

  n = mpz_size (x);
  xp = mpz_limbs_modify(x, 2*n);
  for (i = 0; i < n; i++)
    xp[n+i] = xp[n-1-i];
  mpz_limbs_finish (x, mpz_sgn (x) < 0 ? - 2*n : 2*n);
}
```

mpz_srcptr mpz_roinit_n (*mpz_t x, const mp_limb_t *xp, mp_size_t xs*) [Function]
  Special initialization of x, using the given limb array and size. x should be treated as read-only: it can be passed safely as input to any mpz function, but not as an output. The array xp must point to at least a readable limb, its size is |xs|, and the sign of x is the sign of xs. For convenience, the function returns x, but cast to a const pointer type.

```
void foo (mpz_t x)
{
  static const mp_limb_t y[3] = { 0x1, 0x2, 0x3 };
  mpz_t tmp;
  mpz_add (x, x, mpz_roinit_n (tmp, y, 3));
}
```

mpz_t MPZ_ROINIT_N (*mp_limb_t *xp, mp_size_t xs*) [Macro]
  This macro expands to an initializer which can be assigned to an mpz_t variable. The limb array xp must point to at least a readable limb, moreover, unlike the mpz_roinit_n function, the array must be normalized: if xs is non-zero, then xp[|xs| − 1] must be non-zero. Intended primarily for constant values. Using it for non-constant values requires a C compiler supporting C99.

```
void foo (mpz_t x)
{
  static const mp_limb_t ya[3] = { 0x1, 0x2, 0x3 };
  static const mpz_t y = MPZ_ROINIT_N ((mp_limb_t *) ya, 3);

  mpz_add (x, x, y);
}
```

6 Rational Number Functions

This chapter describes the GMP functions for performing arithmetic on rational numbers. These functions start with the prefix `mpq_`.

Rational numbers are stored in objects of type `mpq_t`.

All rational arithmetic functions assume operands have a canonical form, and canonicalize their result. The canonical from means that the denominator and the numerator have no common factors, and that the denominator is positive. Zero has the unique representation 0/1.

Pure assignment functions do not canonicalize the assigned variable. It is the responsibility of the user to canonicalize the assigned variable before any arithmetic operations are performed on that variable.

void **mpq_canonicalize** (*mpq_t op*)   [Function]
> Remove any factors that are common to the numerator and denominator of *op*, and make the denominator positive.

6.1 Initialization and Assignment Functions

void **mpq_init** (*mpq_t x*)   [Function]
> Initialize *x* and set it to 0/1. Each variable should normally only be initialized once, or at least cleared out (using the function `mpq_clear`) between each initialization.

void **mpq_inits** (*mpq_t x, ...*)   [Function]
> Initialize a NULL-terminated list of `mpq_t` variables, and set their values to 0/1.

void **mpq_clear** (*mpq_t x*)   [Function]
> Free the space occupied by *x*. Make sure to call this function for all `mpq_t` variables when you are done with them.

void **mpq_clears** (*mpq_t x, ...*)   [Function]
> Free the space occupied by a NULL-terminated list of `mpq_t` variables.

void **mpq_set** (*mpq_t rop, const mpq_t op*)   [Function]
void **mpq_set_z** (*mpq_t rop, const mpz_t op*)   [Function]
> Assign *rop* from *op*.

void **mpq_set_ui** (*mpq_t rop, unsigned long int op1, unsigned long int op2*)   [Function]
void **mpq_set_si** (*mpq_t rop, signed long int op1, unsigned long int op2*)   [Function]
> Set the value of *rop* to *op1/op2*. Note that if *op1* and *op2* have common factors, *rop* has to be passed to `mpq_canonicalize` before any operations are performed on *rop*.

int **mpq_set_str** (*mpq_t rop, const char *str, int base*)   [Function]
> Set *rop* from a null-terminated string *str* in the given *base*.
>
> The string can be an integer like "41" or a fraction like "41/152". The fraction must be in canonical form (see Chapter 6 [Rational Number Functions], page 46), or if not then `mpq_canonicalize` must be called.
>
> The numerator and optional denominator are parsed the same as in `mpz_set_str` (see Section 5.2 [Assigning Integers], page 31). White space is allowed in the string, and is simply ignored. The *base* can vary from 2 to 62, or if *base* is 0 then the leading characters are used:

`0x` or `0X` for hex, `0b` or `0B` for binary, `0` for octal, or decimal otherwise. Note that this is done separately for the numerator and denominator, so for instance `0xEF/100` is $239/100$, whereas `0xEF/0x100` is $239/256$.

The return value is 0 if the entire string is a valid number, or -1 if not.

void **mpq_swap** (*mpq_t* **rop1**, *mpq_t* **rop2**)   [Function]
> Swap the values *rop1* and *rop2* efficiently.

6.2 Conversion Functions

double **mpq_get_d** (*const mpq_t* **op**)   [Function]
> Convert *op* to a `double`, truncating if necessary (i.e. rounding towards zero).

> If the exponent from the conversion is too big or too small to fit a `double` then the result is system dependent. For too big an infinity is returned when available. For too small 0.0 is normally returned. Hardware overflow, underflow and denorm traps may or may not occur.

void **mpq_set_d** (*mpq_t* **rop**, *double* **op**)   [Function]
void **mpq_set_f** (*mpq_t* **rop**, *const mpf_t* **op**)   [Function]
> Set *rop* to the value of *op*. There is no rounding, this conversion is exact.

char * **mpq_get_str** (*char *str*, *int* **base**, *const mpq_t* **op**)   [Function]
> Convert *op* to a string of digits in base *base*. The base may vary from 2 to 36. The string will be of the form 'num/den', or if the denominator is 1 then just 'num'.

> If *str* is `NULL`, the result string is allocated using the current allocation function (see Chapter 13 [Custom Allocation], page 89). The block will be `strlen(str)+1` bytes, that being exactly enough for the string and null-terminator.

> If *str* is not `NULL`, it should point to a block of storage large enough for the result, that being

> ```
> mpz_sizeinbase (mpq_numref(op), base)
>   + mpz_sizeinbase (mpq_denref(op), base) + 3
> ```

The three extra bytes are for a possible minus sign, possible slash, and the null-terminator.

A pointer to the result string is returned, being either the allocated block, or the given *str*.

6.3 Arithmetic Functions

void **mpq_add** (*mpq_t* **sum**, *const mpq_t* **addend1**, *const mpq_t* **addend2**)   [Function]
> Set *sum* to *addend1* + *addend2*.

void **mpq_sub** (*mpq_t* **difference**, *const mpq_t* **minuend**, *const mpq_t*   [Function]
> **subtrahend**)
> Set *difference* to *minuend* − *subtrahend*.

void **mpq_mul** (*mpq_t* **product**, *const mpq_t* **multiplier**, *const mpq_t*   [Function]
> **multiplicand**)
> Set *product* to *multiplier* × *multiplicand*.

void **mpq_mul_2exp** (*mpq_t* **rop**, *const mpq_t* **op1**, *mp_bitcnt_t* **op2**)   [Function]
> Set *rop* to $op1 \times 2^{op2}$.

void **mpq_div** (*mpq_t* `quotient`, *const mpq_t* `dividend`, *const mpq_t*   [Function]
      `divisor`)
     Set *quotient* to *dividend/divisor*.

void **mpq_div_2exp** (*mpq_t* `rop`, *const mpq_t* `op1`, *mp_bitcnt_t* `op2`)   [Function]
     Set *rop* to $op1/2^{op2}$.

void **mpq_neg** (*mpq_t* `negated_operand`, *const mpq_t* `operand`)   [Function]
     Set *negated_operand* to $-operand$.

void **mpq_abs** (*mpq_t* `rop`, *const mpq_t* `op`)   [Function]
     Set *rop* to the absolute value of *op*.

void **mpq_inv** (*mpq_t* `inverted_number`, *const mpq_t* `number`)   [Function]
     Set *inverted_number* to 1/*number*. If the new denominator is zero, this routine will divide
     by zero.

6.4 Comparison Functions

int **mpq_cmp** (*const mpq_t* `op1`, *const mpq_t* `op2`)   [Function]
     Compare *op1* and *op2*. Return a positive value if $op1 > op2$, zero if $op1 = op2$, and a
     negative value if $op1 < op2$.

     To determine if two rationals are equal, **mpq_equal** is faster than `mpq_cmp`.

int **mpq_cmp_ui** (*const mpq_t* `op1`, *unsigned long int* `num2`, *unsigned long int*   [Macro]
      `den2`)
int **mpq_cmp_si** (*const mpq_t* `op1`, *long int* `num2`, *unsigned long int* `den2`)   [Macro]
     Compare *op1* and *num2/den2*. Return a positive value if $op1 > num2/den2$, zero if $op1 =
     num2/den2$, and a negative value if $op1 < num2/den2$.

     num2 and *den2* are allowed to have common factors.

     These functions are implemented as a macros and evaluate their arguments multiple times.

int **mpq_sgn** (*const mpq_t* `op`)   [Macro]
     Return $+1$ if $op > 0$, 0 if $op = 0$, and -1 if $op < 0$.

     This function is actually implemented as a macro. It evaluates its argument multiple times.

int **mpq_equal** (*const mpq_t* `op1`, *const mpq_t* `op2`)   [Function]
     Return non-zero if *op1* and *op2* are equal, zero if they are non-equal. Although `mpq_cmp` can
     be used for the same purpose, this function is much faster.

6.5 Applying Integer Functions to Rationals

The set of `mpq` functions is quite small. In particular, there are few functions for either input
or output. The following functions give direct access to the numerator and denominator of an
`mpq_t`.

Note that if an assignment to the numerator and/or denominator could take an `mpq_t` out
of the canonical form described at the start of this chapter (see Chapter 6 [Rational Number
Functions], page 46) then `mpq_canonicalize` must be called before any other `mpq` functions are
applied to that `mpq_t`.

mpz_t mpq_numref (*const mpq_t* op)   [Macro]
mpz_t mpq_denref (*const mpq_t* op)   [Macro]
> Return a reference to the numerator and denominator of *op*, respectively. The mpz functions can be used on the result of these macros.

void mpq_get_num (*mpz_t* numerator, *const mpq_t* rational)   [Function]
void mpq_get_den (*mpz_t* denominator, *const mpq_t* rational)   [Function]
void mpq_set_num (*mpq_t* rational, *const mpz_t* numerator)   [Function]
void mpq_set_den (*mpq_t* rational, *const mpz_t* denominator)   [Function]
> Get or set the numerator or denominator of a rational. These functions are equivalent to calling mpz_set with an appropriate mpq_numref or mpq_denref. Direct use of mpq_numref or mpq_denref is recommended instead of these functions.

6.6 Input and Output Functions

Functions that perform input from a stdio stream, and functions that output to a stdio stream, of mpq numbers. Passing a NULL pointer for a *stream* argument to any of these functions will make them read from stdin and write to stdout, respectively.

When using any of these functions, it is a good idea to include stdio.h before gmp.h, since that will allow gmp.h to define prototypes for these functions.

See also Chapter 10 [Formatted Output], page 71 and Chapter 11 [Formatted Input], page 76.

size_t mpq_out_str (*FILE *stream*, *int* base, *const mpq_t* op)   [Function]
> Output *op* on stdio stream *stream*, as a string of digits in base *base*. The base may vary from 2 to 36. Output is in the form 'num/den' or if the denominator is 1 then just 'num'.
>
> Return the number of bytes written, or if an error occurred, return 0.

size_t mpq_inp_str (*mpq_t* rop, *FILE *stream*, *int* base)   [Function]
> Read a string of digits from *stream* and convert them to a rational in *rop*. Any initial whitespace characters are read and discarded. Return the number of characters read (including white space), or 0 if a rational could not be read.
>
> The input can be a fraction like '17/63' or just an integer like '123'. Reading stops at the first character not in this form, and white space is not permitted within the string. If the input might not be in canonical form, then mpq_canonicalize must be called (see Chapter 6 [Rational Number Functions], page 46).
>
> The *base* can be between 2 and 36, or can be 0 in which case the leading characters of the string determine the base, '0x' or '0X' for hexadecimal, '0' for octal, or decimal otherwise. The leading characters are examined separately for the numerator and denominator of a fraction, so for instance '0x10/11' is 16/11, whereas '0x10/0x11' is 16/17.

7 Floating-point Functions

GMP floating point numbers are stored in objects of type `mpf_t` and functions operating on them have an `mpf_` prefix.

The mantissa of each float has a user-selectable precision, limited only by available memory. Each variable has its own precision, and that can be increased or decreased at any time.

The exponent of each float is a fixed precision, one machine word on most systems. In the current implementation the exponent is a count of limbs, so for example on a 32-bit system this means a range of roughly $2^{-68719476768}$ to $2^{68719476736}$, or on a 64-bit system this will be greater. Note however that `mpf_get_str` can only return an exponent which fits an `mp_exp_t` and currently `mpf_set_str` doesn't accept exponents bigger than a `long`.

Each variable keeps a size for the mantissa data actually in use. This means that if a float is exactly represented in only a few bits then only those bits will be used in a calculation, even if the selected precision is high.

All calculations are performed to the precision of the destination variable. Each function is defined to calculate with "infinite precision" followed by a truncation to the destination precision, but of course the work done is only what's needed to determine a result under that definition.

The precision selected by the user for a variable is a minimum value, GMP may increase it to facilitate efficient calculation. Currently this means rounding up to a whole limb, and then sometimes having a further partial limb, depending on the high limb of the mantissa.

The mantissa is stored in binary. One consequence of this is that decimal fractions like 0.1 cannot be represented exactly. The same is true of plain IEEE `double` floats. This makes both highly unsuitable for calculations involving money or other values that should be exact decimal fractions. (Suitably scaled integers, or perhaps rationals, are better choices.)

The `mpf` functions and variables have no special notion of infinity or not-a-number, and applications must take care not to overflow the exponent or results will be unpredictable. This might change in a future release.

Note that the `mpf` functions are *not* intended as a smooth extension to IEEE P754 arithmetic. In particular results obtained on one computer often differ from the results on a computer with a different word size.

The GMP extension library MPFR (http://mpfr.org) is an alternative to GMP's `mpf` functions. MPFR provides well-defined precision and accurate rounding, and thereby naturally extends IEEE P754.

7.1 Initialization Functions

void mpf_set_default_prec (*mp_bitcnt_t prec*)   [Function]
  Set the default precision to be **at least** *prec* bits. All subsequent calls to `mpf_init` will use this precision, but previously initialized variables are unaffected.

mp_bitcnt_t mpf_get_default_prec (*void*)   [Function]
  Return the default precision actually used.

An `mpf_t` object must be initialized before storing the first value in it. The functions `mpf_init` and `mpf_init2` are used for that purpose.

void **mpf_init** (*mpf_t* **x**)   [Function]
:   Initialize *x* to 0. Normally, a variable should be initialized once only or at least be cleared, using `mpf_clear`, between initializations. The precision of *x* is undefined unless a default precision has already been established by a call to `mpf_set_default_prec`.

void **mpf_init2** (*mpf_t* **x**, *mp_bitcnt_t* **prec**)   [Function]
:   Initialize *x* to 0 and set its precision to be **at least** *prec* bits. Normally, a variable should be initialized once only or at least be cleared, using `mpf_clear`, between initializations.

void **mpf_inits** (*mpf_t* **x**, *...*)   [Function]
:   Initialize a NULL-terminated list of `mpf_t` variables, and set their values to 0. The precision of the initialized variables is undefined unless a default precision has already been established by a call to `mpf_set_default_prec`.

void **mpf_clear** (*mpf_t* **x**)   [Function]
:   Free the space occupied by *x*. Make sure to call this function for all `mpf_t` variables when you are done with them.

void **mpf_clears** (*mpf_t* **x**, *...*)   [Function]
:   Free the space occupied by a NULL-terminated list of `mpf_t` variables.

Here is an example on how to initialize floating-point variables:

```
{
  mpf_t x, y;
  mpf_init (x);          /* use default precision */
  mpf_init2 (y, 256);    /* precision at least 256 bits */
  ...
  /* Unless the program is about to exit, do ... */
  mpf_clear (x);
  mpf_clear (y);
}
```

The following three functions are useful for changing the precision during a calculation. A typical use would be for adjusting the precision gradually in iterative algorithms like Newton-Raphson, making the computation precision closely match the actual accurate part of the numbers.

mp_bitcnt_t **mpf_get_prec** (*const mpf_t* **op**)   [Function]
:   Return the current precision of *op*, in bits.

void **mpf_set_prec** (*mpf_t* **rop**, *mp_bitcnt_t* **prec**)   [Function]
:   Set the precision of *rop* to be **at least** *prec* bits. The value in *rop* will be truncated to the new precision.

    This function requires a call to `realloc`, and so should not be used in a tight loop.

void **mpf_set_prec_raw** (*mpf_t* **rop**, *mp_bitcnt_t* **prec**)   [Function]
:   Set the precision of *rop* to be **at least** *prec* bits, without changing the memory allocated.

    prec must be no more than the allocated precision for *rop*, that being the precision when *rop* was initialized, or in the most recent `mpf_set_prec`.

    The value in *rop* is unchanged, and in particular if it had a higher precision than *prec* it will retain that higher precision. New values written to *rop* will use the new *prec*.

Before calling `mpf_clear` or the full `mpf_set_prec`, another `mpf_set_prec_raw` call must be made to restore *rop* to its original allocated precision. Failing to do so will have unpredictable results.

`mpf_get_prec` can be used before `mpf_set_prec_raw` to get the original allocated precision. After `mpf_set_prec_raw` it reflects the *prec* value set.

`mpf_set_prec_raw` is an efficient way to use an `mpf_t` variable at different precisions during a calculation, perhaps to gradually increase precision in an iteration, or just to use various different precisions for different purposes during a calculation.

7.2 Assignment Functions

These functions assign new values to already initialized floats (see Section 7.1 [Initializing Floats], page 50).

void mpf_set (*mpf_t* **rop**, *const mpf_t* **op**)   [Function]
void mpf_set_ui (*mpf_t* **rop**, *unsigned long int* **op**)   [Function]
void mpf_set_si (*mpf_t* **rop**, *signed long int* **op**)   [Function]
void mpf_set_d (*mpf_t* **rop**, *double* **op**)   [Function]
void mpf_set_z (*mpf_t* **rop**, *const mpz_t* **op**)   [Function]
void mpf_set_q (*mpf_t* **rop**, *const mpq_t* **op**)   [Function]
  Set the value of *rop* from *op*.

int mpf_set_str (*mpf_t* **rop**, *const char* ***str**, *int* **base**)   [Function]
  Set the value of *rop* from the string in *str*. The string is of the form 'M@N' or, if the base is 10 or less, alternatively 'MeN'. 'M' is the mantissa and 'N' is the exponent. The mantissa is always in the specified base. The exponent is either in the specified base or, if *base* is negative, in decimal. The decimal point expected is taken from the current locale, on systems providing `localeconv`.

  The argument *base* may be in the ranges 2 to 62, or −62 to −2. Negative values are used to specify that the exponent is in decimal.

  For bases up to 36, case is ignored; upper-case and lower-case letters have the same value; for bases 37 to 62, upper-case letter represent the usual 10..35 while lower-case letter represent 36..61.

  Unlike the corresponding `mpz` function, the base will not be determined from the leading characters of the string if *base* is 0. This is so that numbers like '0.23' are not interpreted as octal.

  White space is allowed in the string, and is simply ignored. [This is not really true; white-space is ignored in the beginning of the string and within the mantissa, but not in other places, such as after a minus sign or in the exponent. We are considering changing the definition of this function, making it fail when there is any white-space in the input, since that makes a lot of sense. Please tell us your opinion about this change. Do you really want it to accept "3 14" as meaning 314 as it does now?]

  This function returns 0 if the entire string is a valid number in base *base*. Otherwise it returns −1.

void mpf_swap (*mpf_t* **rop1**, *mpf_t* **rop2**)   [Function]
  Swap *rop1* and *rop2* efficiently. Both the values and the precisions of the two variables are swapped.

7.3 Combined Initialization and Assignment Functions

For convenience, GMP provides a parallel series of initialize-and-set functions which initialize the output and then store the value there. These functions' names have the form `mpf_init_set...`

Once the float has been initialized by any of the `mpf_init_set...` functions, it can be used as the source or destination operand for the ordinary float functions. Don't use an initialize-and-set function on a variable already initialized!

void `mpf_init_set` (*mpf_t **rop**, const mpf_t **op*)	[Function]
void `mpf_init_set_ui` (*mpf_t **rop**, unsigned long int **op*)	[Function]
void `mpf_init_set_si` (*mpf_t **rop**, signed long int **op*)	[Function]
void `mpf_init_set_d` (*mpf_t **rop**, double **op*)	[Function]

Initialize *rop* and set its value from *op*.

The precision of *rop* will be taken from the active default precision, as set by `mpf_set_default_prec`.

int `mpf_init_set_str` (*mpf_t **rop**, const char ****str**, int **base*)   [Function]
Initialize *rop* and set its value from the string in *str*. See `mpf_set_str` above for details on the assignment operation.

Note that *rop* is initialized even if an error occurs. (I.e., you have to call `mpf_clear` for it.)

The precision of *rop* will be taken from the active default precision, as set by `mpf_set_default_prec`.

7.4 Conversion Functions

double `mpf_get_d` (*const mpf_t **op*)   [Function]
Convert *op* to a `double`, truncating if necessary (i.e. rounding towards zero).

If the exponent in *op* is too big or too small to fit a `double` then the result is system dependent. For too big an infinity is returned when available. For too small 0.0 is normally returned. Hardware overflow, underflow and denorm traps may or may not occur.

double `mpf_get_d_2exp` (*signed long int ****exp**, const mpf_t **op*)   [Function]
Convert *op* to a `double`, truncating if necessary (i.e. rounding towards zero), and with an exponent returned separately.

The return value is in the range $0.5 \le |d| < 1$ and the exponent is stored to **exp*. $d \times 2^{exp}$ is the (truncated) *op* value. If *op* is zero, the return is 0.0 and 0 is stored to **exp*.

This is similar to the standard C `frexp` function (see Section "Normalization Functions" in *The GNU C Library Reference Manual*).

long `mpf_get_si` (*const mpf_t **op*)	[Function]
unsigned long `mpf_get_ui` (*const mpf_t **op*)	[Function]

Convert *op* to a `long` or `unsigned long`, truncating any fraction part. If *op* is too big for the return type, the result is undefined.

See also `mpf_fits_slong_p` and `mpf_fits_ulong_p` (see Section 7.8 [Miscellaneous Float Functions], page 56).

`char * mpf_get_str` (*char *str*, *mp_exp_t *expptr*, *int base*, *size_t*   [Function]
    n_digits, *const mpf_t op*)
> Convert *op* to a string of digits in base *base*. The base argument may vary from 2 to 62 or from −2 to −36. Up to *n_digits* digits will be generated. Trailing zeros are not returned. No more digits than can be accurately represented by *op* are ever generated. If *n_digits* is 0 then that accurate maximum number of digits are generated.
>
> For *base* in the range 2..36, digits and lower-case letters are used; for −2..−36, digits and upper-case letters are used; for 37..62, digits, upper-case letters, and lower-case letters (in that significance order) are used.
>
> If *str* is NULL, the result string is allocated using the current allocation function (see Chapter 13 [Custom Allocation], page 89). The block will be `strlen(str)+1` bytes, that being exactly enough for the string and null-terminator.
>
> If *str* is not NULL, it should point to a block of *n_digits* + 2 bytes, that being enough for the mantissa, a possible minus sign, and a null-terminator. When *n_digits* is 0 to get all significant digits, an application won't be able to know the space required, and *str* should be NULL in that case.
>
> The generated string is a fraction, with an implicit radix point immediately to the left of the first digit. The applicable exponent is written through the *expptr* pointer. For example, the number 3.1416 would be returned as string `"31416"` and exponent 1.
>
> When *op* is zero, an empty string is produced and the exponent returned is 0.
>
> A pointer to the result string is returned, being either the allocated block or the given *str*.

7.5 Arithmetic Functions

`void mpf_add` (*mpf_t rop*, *const mpf_t op1*, *const mpf_t op2*)   [Function]
`void mpf_add_ui` (*mpf_t rop*, *const mpf_t op1*, *unsigned long int op2*)   [Function]
> Set *rop* to *op1* + *op2*.

`void mpf_sub` (*mpf_t rop*, *const mpf_t op1*, *const mpf_t op2*)   [Function]
`void mpf_ui_sub` (*mpf_t rop*, *unsigned long int op1*, *const mpf_t op2*)   [Function]
`void mpf_sub_ui` (*mpf_t rop*, *const mpf_t op1*, *unsigned long int op2*)   [Function]
> Set *rop* to *op1* − *op2*.

`void mpf_mul` (*mpf_t rop*, *const mpf_t op1*, *const mpf_t op2*)   [Function]
`void mpf_mul_ui` (*mpf_t rop*, *const mpf_t op1*, *unsigned long int op2*)   [Function]
> Set *rop* to *op1* × *op2*.

Division is undefined if the divisor is zero, and passing a zero divisor to the divide functions will make these functions intentionally divide by zero. This lets the user handle arithmetic exceptions in these functions in the same manner as other arithmetic exceptions.

`void mpf_div` (*mpf_t rop*, *const mpf_t op1*, *const mpf_t op2*)   [Function]
`void mpf_ui_div` (*mpf_t rop*, *unsigned long int op1*, *const mpf_t op2*)   [Function]
`void mpf_div_ui` (*mpf_t rop*, *const mpf_t op1*, *unsigned long int op2*)   [Function]
> Set *rop* to *op1*/*op2*.

`void mpf_sqrt` (*mpf_t rop*, *const mpf_t op*)   [Function]
`void mpf_sqrt_ui` (*mpf_t rop*, *unsigned long int op*)   [Function]
> Set *rop* to $\sqrt{op}$.

void **mpf_pow_ui** (*mpf_t **rop**, const mpf_t **op1**, unsigned long int **op2**)   [Function]
    Set *rop* to *op1^{op2}*.

void **mpf_neg** (*mpf_t **rop**, const mpf_t **op**)   [Function]
    Set *rop* to $-op$.

void **mpf_abs** (*mpf_t **rop**, const mpf_t **op**)   [Function]
    Set *rop* to the absolute value of *op*.

void **mpf_mul_2exp** (*mpf_t **rop**, const mpf_t **op1**, mp_bitcnt_t **op2**)   [Function]
    Set *rop* to $op1 \times 2^{op2}$.

void **mpf_div_2exp** (*mpf_t **rop**, const mpf_t **op1**, mp_bitcnt_t **op2**)   [Function]
    Set *rop* to $op1/2^{op2}$.

7.6 Comparison Functions

int **mpf_cmp** (*const mpf_t **op1**, const mpf_t **op2**)   [Function]
int **mpf_cmp_d** (*const mpf_t **op1**, double **op2**)   [Function]
int **mpf_cmp_ui** (*const mpf_t **op1**, unsigned long int **op2**)   [Function]
int **mpf_cmp_si** (*const mpf_t **op1**, signed long int **op2**)   [Function]
    Compare *op1* and *op2*. Return a positive value if *op1* > *op2*, zero if *op1* = *op2*, and a
    negative value if *op1* < *op2*.

    mpf_cmp_d can be called with an infinity, but results are undefined for a NaN.

int **mpf_eq** (*const mpf_t **op1**, const mpf_t **op2**, mp_bitcnt_t **op3**)   [Function]
    Return non-zero if the first *op3* bits of *op1* and *op2* are equal, zero otherwise. I.e., test if
    op1 and *op2* are approximately equal.

    Caution 1: All version of GMP up to version 4.2.4 compared just whole limbs, meaning
    sometimes more than *op3* bits, sometimes fewer.

    Caution 2: This function will consider XXX11...111 and XX100...000 different, even if ... is
    replaced by a semi-infinite number of bits. Such numbers are really just one ulp off, and
    should be considered equal.

void **mpf_reldiff** (*mpf_t **rop**, const mpf_t **op1**, const mpf_t **op2**)   [Function]
    Compute the relative difference between *op1* and *op2* and store the result in *rop*. This is
    $|op1 - op2|/op1$.

int **mpf_sgn** (*const mpf_t **op**)   [Macro]
    Return +1 if *op* > 0, 0 if *op* = 0, and −1 if *op* < 0.

    This function is actually implemented as a macro. It evaluates its argument multiple times.

7.7 Input and Output Functions

Functions that perform input from a stdio stream, and functions that output to a stdio stream,
of mpf numbers. Passing a NULL pointer for a *stream* argument to any of these functions will
make them read from stdin and write to stdout, respectively.

When using any of these functions, it is a good idea to include stdio.h before gmp.h, since that
will allow gmp.h to define prototypes for these functions.

See also Chapter 10 [Formatted Output], page 71 and Chapter 11 [Formatted Input], page 76.

size_t mpf_out_str (*FILE *stream, int base, size_t n_digits, const*   [Function]
       mpf_t op)

    Print *op* to *stream*, as a string of digits. Return the number of bytes written, or if an error
    occurred, return 0.

    The mantissa is prefixed with an '0.' and is in the given *base*, which may vary from 2 to 62
    or from −2 to −36. An exponent is then printed, separated by an 'e', or if the base is greater
    than 10 then by an '@'. The exponent is always in decimal. The decimal point follows the
    current locale, on systems providing `localeconv`.

    For *base* in the range 2..36, digits and lower-case letters are used; for −2..−36, digits and
    upper-case letters are used; for 37..62, digits, upper-case letters, and lower-case letters (in
    that significance order) are used.

    Up to *n_digits* will be printed from the mantissa, except that no more digits than are accu-
    rately representable by *op* will be printed. *n_digits* can be 0 to select that accurate maximum.

size_t mpf_inp_str (*mpf_t rop, FILE *stream, int base*)   [Function]

    Read a string in base *base* from *stream*, and put the read float in *rop*. The string is of
    the form 'M@N' or, if the base is 10 or less, alternatively 'MeN'. 'M' is the mantissa and 'N' is
    the exponent. The mantissa is always in the specified base. The exponent is either in the
    specified base or, if *base* is negative, in decimal. The decimal point expected is taken from
    the current locale, on systems providing `localeconv`.

    The argument *base* may be in the ranges 2 to 36, or −36 to −2. Negative values are used to
    specify that the exponent is in decimal.

    Unlike the corresponding `mpz` function, the base will not be determined from the leading
    characters of the string if *base* is 0. This is so that numbers like '0.23' are not interpreted
    as octal.

    Return the number of bytes read, or if an error occurred, return 0.

7.8 Miscellaneous Functions

void mpf_ceil (*mpf_t rop, const mpf_t op*)   [Function]
void mpf_floor (*mpf_t rop, const mpf_t op*)   [Function]
void mpf_trunc (*mpf_t rop, const mpf_t op*)   [Function]

    Set *rop* to *op* rounded to an integer. `mpf_ceil` rounds to the next higher integer, `mpf_floor`
    to the next lower, and `mpf_trunc` to the integer towards zero.

int mpf_integer_p (*const mpf_t op*)   [Function]

    Return non-zero if *op* is an integer.

int mpf_fits_ulong_p (*const mpf_t op*)   [Function]
int mpf_fits_slong_p (*const mpf_t op*)   [Function]
int mpf_fits_uint_p (*const mpf_t op*)   [Function]
int mpf_fits_sint_p (*const mpf_t op*)   [Function]
int mpf_fits_ushort_p (*const mpf_t op*)   [Function]
int mpf_fits_sshort_p (*const mpf_t op*)   [Function]

    Return non-zero if *op* would fit in the respective C data type, when truncated to an integer.

void **mpf_urandomb** (*mpf_t* **rop**, *gmp_randstate_t* **state**, *mp_bitcnt_t*   [Function]
   nbits)

Generate a uniformly distributed random float in *rop*, such that $0 \leq rop < 1$, with *nbits* significant bits in the mantissa or less if the precision of *rop* is smaller.

The variable *state* must be initialized by calling one of the **gmp_randinit** functions (Section 9.1 [Random State Initialization], page 69) before invoking this function.

void **mpf_random2** (*mpf_t* **rop**, *mp_size_t* **max_size**, *mp_exp_t* **exp**)   [Function]

Generate a random float of at most *max_size* limbs, with long strings of zeros and ones in the binary representation. The exponent of the number is in the interval $-exp$ to *exp* (in limbs). This function is useful for testing functions and algorithms, since these kind of random numbers have proven to be more likely to trigger corner-case bugs. Negative random numbers are generated when *max_size* is negative.

8 Low-level Functions

This chapter describes low-level GMP functions, used to implement the high-level GMP functions, but also intended for time-critical user code.

These functions start with the prefix `mpn_`.

The `mpn` functions are designed to be as fast as possible, **not** to provide a coherent calling interface. The different functions have somewhat similar interfaces, but there are variations that make them hard to use. These functions do as little as possible apart from the real multiple precision computation, so that no time is spent on things that not all callers need.

A source operand is specified by a pointer to the least significant limb and a limb count. A destination operand is specified by just a pointer. It is the responsibility of the caller to ensure that the destination has enough space for storing the result.

With this way of specifying operands, it is possible to perform computations on subranges of an argument, and store the result into a subrange of a destination.

A common requirement for all functions is that each source area needs at least one limb. No size argument may be zero. Unless otherwise stated, in-place operations are allowed where source and destination are the same, but not where they only partly overlap.

The `mpn` functions are the base for the implementation of the `mpz_`, `mpf_`, and `mpq_` functions.

This example adds the number beginning at $s1p$ and the number beginning at $s2p$ and writes the sum at $destp$. All areas have n limbs.

```
cy = mpn_add_n (destp, s1p, s2p, n)
```

It should be noted that the `mpn` functions make no attempt to identify high or low zero limbs on their operands, or other special forms. On random data such cases will be unlikely and it'd be wasteful for every function to check every time. An application knowing something about its data can take steps to trim or perhaps split its calculations.

In the notation used below, a source operand is identified by the pointer to the least significant limb, and the limb count in braces. For example, $\{s1p, s1n\}$.

`mp_limb_t mpn_add_n` (*mp_limb_t* **rp**, *const mp_limb_t* **s1p**, *const*   [Function]
        mp_limb_t **s2p**, *mp_size_t* **n**)
>   Add $\{s1p, n\}$ and $\{s2p, n\}$, and write the n least significant limbs of the result to rp. Return carry, either 0 or 1.

>   This is the lowest-level function for addition. It is the preferred function for addition, since it is written in assembly for most CPUs. For addition of a variable to itself (i.e., $s1p$ equals $s2p$) use `mpn_lshift` with a count of 1 for optimal speed.

`mp_limb_t mpn_add_1` (*mp_limb_t* **rp**, *const mp_limb_t* **s1p**, *mp_size_t* **n**,   [Function]
        mp_limb_t **s2limb**)
>   Add $\{s1p, n\}$ and $s2limb$, and write the n least significant limbs of the result to rp. Return carry, either 0 or 1.

`mp_limb_t mpn_add` (*mp_limb_t* **rp**, *const mp_limb_t* **s1p**, *mp_size_t* **s1n**,   [Function]
        const mp_limb_t **s2p**, *mp_size_t* **s2n**)
>   Add $\{s1p, s1n\}$ and $\{s2p, s2n\}$, and write the $s1n$ least significant limbs of the result to rp. Return carry, either 0 or 1.

This function requires that *s1n* is greater than or equal to *s2n*.

mp_limb_t mpn_sub_n (*mp_limb_t* ***rp**, *const mp_limb_t* ***s1p**, *const*   [Function]
          mp_limb_t ***s2p**, *mp_size_t* **n**)
Subtract {*s2p*, *n*} from {*s1p*, *n*}, and write the *n* least significant limbs of the result to *rp*.
Return borrow, either 0 or 1.

This is the lowest-level function for subtraction. It is the preferred function for subtraction, since it is written in assembly for most CPUs.

mp_limb_t mpn_sub_1 (*mp_limb_t* ***rp**, *const mp_limb_t* ***s1p**, *mp_size_t* **n**,   [Function]
          mp_limb_t **s2limb**)
Subtract *s2limb* from {*s1p*, *n*}, and write the *n* least significant limbs of the result to *rp*.
Return borrow, either 0 or 1.

mp_limb_t mpn_sub (*mp_limb_t* ***rp**, *const mp_limb_t* ***s1p**, *mp_size_t* **s1n**,   [Function]
          const mp_limb_t ***s2p**, *mp_size_t* **s2n**)
Subtract {*s2p*, *s2n*} from {*s1p*, *s1n*}, and write the *s1n* least significant limbs of the result to
rp. Return borrow, either 0 or 1.

This function requires that *s1n* is greater than or equal to *s2n*.

mp_limb_t mpn_neg (*mp_limb_t* ***rp**, *const mp_limb_t* ***sp**, *mp_size_t* **n**)   [Function]
Perform the negation of {*sp*, *n*}, and write the result to {*rp*, *n*}. This is equivalent to calling
mpn_sub_n with a *n*-limb zero minuend and passing {*sp*, *n*} as subtrahend. Return borrow,
either 0 or 1.

void mpn_mul_n (*mp_limb_t* ***rp**, *const mp_limb_t* ***s1p**, *const mp_limb_t*   [Function]
          ***s2p**, *mp_size_t* **n**)
Multiply {*s1p*, *n*} and {*s2p*, *n*}, and write the 2*n-limb result to *rp*.

The destination has to have space for 2*n limbs, even if the product's most significant limb
is zero. No overlap is permitted between the destination and either source.

If the two input operands are the same, use **mpn_sqr**.

mp_limb_t mpn_mul (*mp_limb_t* ***rp**, *const mp_limb_t* ***s1p**, *mp_size_t* **s1n**,   [Function]
          const mp_limb_t ***s2p**, *mp_size_t* **s2n**)
Multiply {*s1p*, *s1n*} and {*s2p*, *s2n*}, and write the (*s1n*+*s2n*)-limb result to *rp*. Return the
most significant limb of the result.

The destination has to have space for *s1n* + *s2n* limbs, even if the product's most significant
limb is zero. No overlap is permitted between the destination and either source.

This function requires that *s1n* is greater than or equal to *s2n*.

void mpn_sqr (*mp_limb_t* ***rp**, *const mp_limb_t* ***s1p**, *mp_size_t* **n**)   [Function]
Compute the square of {*s1p*, *n*} and write the 2*n-limb result to *rp*.

The destination has to have space for 2*n* limbs, even if the result's most significant limb is
zero. No overlap is permitted between the destination and the source.

`mp_limb_t mpn_mul_1` (*mp_limb_t* ***rp**, *const mp_limb_t* ***s1p**, *mp_size_t* **n**,   [Function]
    mp_limb_t **s2limb**)

Multiply {*s1p*, *n*} by *s2limb*, and write the *n* least significant limbs of the product to *rp*. Return the most significant limb of the product. {*s1p*, *n*} and {*rp*, *n*} are allowed to overlap provided $rp \leq s1p$.

This is a low-level function that is a building block for general multiplication as well as other operations in GMP. It is written in assembly for most CPUs.

Don't call this function if *s2limb* is a power of 2; use `mpn_lshift` with a count equal to the logarithm of *s2limb* instead, for optimal speed.

`mp_limb_t mpn_addmul_1` (*mp_limb_t* ***rp**, *const mp_limb_t* ***s1p**, *mp_size_t*   [Function]
    n, *mp_limb_t* **s2limb**)

Multiply {*s1p*, *n*} and *s2limb*, and add the *n* least significant limbs of the product to {*rp*, *n*} and write the result to *rp*. Return the most significant limb of the product, plus carry-out from the addition.

This is a low-level function that is a building block for general multiplication as well as other operations in GMP. It is written in assembly for most CPUs.

`mp_limb_t mpn_submul_1` (*mp_limb_t* ***rp**, *const mp_limb_t* ***s1p**, *mp_size_t*   [Function]
    n, *mp_limb_t* **s2limb**)

Multiply {*s1p*, *n*} and *s2limb*, and subtract the *n* least significant limbs of the product from {*rp*, *n*} and write the result to *rp*. Return the most significant limb of the product, plus borrow-out from the subtraction.

This is a low-level function that is a building block for general multiplication and division as well as other operations in GMP. It is written in assembly for most CPUs.

`void mpn_tdiv_qr` (*mp_limb_t* ***qp**, *mp_limb_t* ***rp**, *mp_size_t* **qxn**, *const*   [Function]
    mp_limb_t ***np**, *mp_size_t* **nn**, *const mp_limb_t* ***dp**, *mp_size_t* **dn**)

Divide {*np*, *nn*} by {*dp*, *dn*} and put the quotient at {*qp*, *nn*−*dn*+1} and the remainder at {*rp*, *dn*}. The quotient is rounded towards 0.

No overlap is permitted between arguments, except that *np* might equal *rp*. The dividend size *nn* must be greater than or equal to divisor size *dn*. The most significant limb of the divisor must be non-zero. The *qxn* operand must be zero.

`mp_limb_t mpn_divrem` (*mp_limb_t* ***r1p**, *mp_size_t* **qxn**, *mp_limb_t* ***rs2p**,   [Function]
    mp_size_t **rs2n**, *const mp_limb_t* ***s3p**, *mp_size_t* **s3n**)

[This function is obsolete. Please call `mpn_tdiv_qr` instead for best performance.]

Divide {*rs2p*, *rs2n*} by {*s3p*, *s3n*}, and write the quotient at *r1p*, with the exception of the most significant limb, which is returned. The remainder replaces the dividend at *rs2p*; it will be *s3n* limbs long (i.e., as many limbs as the divisor).

In addition to an integer quotient, *qxn* fraction limbs are developed, and stored after the integral limbs. For most usages, *qxn* will be zero.

It is required that *rs2n* is greater than or equal to *s3n*. It is required that the most significant bit of the divisor is set.

If the quotient is not needed, pass *rs2p* + *s3n* as *r1p*. Aside from that special case, no overlap between arguments is permitted.

Return the most significant limb of the quotient, either 0 or 1.

The area at *r1p* needs to be *rs2n* − *s3n* + *qxn* limbs large.

mp_limb_t mpn_divrem_1 (*mp_limb_t *r1p*, *mp_size_t* **qxn**, *mp_limb_t *s2p*,   [Function]
     mp_size_t **s2n**, *mp_limb_t* **s3limb**)

mp_limb_t mpn_divmod_1 (*mp_limb_t *r1p*, *mp_limb_t *s2p*, *mp_size_t* **s2n**,   [Macro]
     mp_limb_t **s3limb**)

> Divide {*s2p*, *s2n*} by *s3limb*, and write the quotient at *r1p*. Return the remainder.

> The integer quotient is written to {*r1p+qxn*, *s2n*} and in addition *qxn* fraction limbs are developed and written to {*r1p*, *qxn*}. Either or both *s2n* and *qxn* can be zero. For most usages, *qxn* will be zero.

> mpn_divmod_1 exists for upward source compatibility and is simply a macro calling mpn_divrem_1 with a *qxn* of 0.

> The areas at *r1p* and *s2p* have to be identical or completely separate, not partially overlapping.

mp_limb_t mpn_divmod (*mp_limb_t *r1p*, *mp_limb_t *rs2p*, *mp_size_t* **rs2n**,   [Function]
     const mp_limb_t *s3p, *mp_size_t* **s3n**)

> [This function is obsolete. Please call mpn_tdiv_qr instead for best performance.]

mp_limb_t mpn_divexact_by3 (*mp_limb_t *rp*, *mp_limb_t *sp*, *mp_size_t* **n**)   [Macro]

mp_limb_t mpn_divexact_by3c (*mp_limb_t *rp*, *mp_limb_t *sp*,   [Function]
     mp_size_t **n**, *mp_limb_t* **carry**)

> Divide {*sp*, *n*} by 3, expecting it to divide exactly, and writing the result to {*rp*, *n*}. If 3 divides exactly, the return value is zero and the result is the quotient. If not, the return value is non-zero and the result won't be anything useful.

> mpn_divexact_by3c takes an initial carry parameter, which can be the return value from a previous call, so a large calculation can be done piece by piece from low to high. mpn_divexact_by3 is simply a macro calling mpn_divexact_by3c with a 0 carry parameter.

> These routines use a multiply-by-inverse and will be faster than mpn_divrem_1 on CPUs with fast multiplication but slow division.

> The source a, result q, size n, initial carry i, and return value c satisfy $cb^n + a - i = 3q$, where $b = 2^{\text{GMP\_NUMB\_BITS}}$. The return c is always 0, 1 or 2, and the initial carry i must also be 0, 1 or 2 (these are both borrows really). When $c = 0$ clearly $q = (a - i)/3$. When $c \neq 0$, the remainder $(a - i) \bmod 3$ is given by $3 - c$, because $b \equiv 1 \bmod 3$ (when mp_bits_per_limb is even, which is always so currently).

mp_limb_t mpn_mod_1 (*const mp_limb_t *s1p*, *mp_size_t* **s1n**, *mp_limb_t*   [Function]
     s2limb)

> Divide {*s1p*, *s1n*} by *s2limb*, and return the remainder. *s1n* can be zero.

mp_limb_t mpn_lshift (*mp_limb_t *rp*, *const mp_limb_t *sp*, *mp_size_t* **n**,   [Function]
     unsigned int **count**)

> Shift {*sp*, *n*} left by *count* bits, and write the result to {*rp*, *n*}. The bits shifted out at the left are returned in the least significant *count* bits of the return value (the rest of the return value is zero).

> *count* must be in the range 1 to mp_bits_per_limb−1. The regions {*sp*, *n*} and {*rp*, *n*} may overlap, provided $rp \geq sp$.

This function is written in assembly for most CPUs.

mp_limb_t mpn_rshift (*mp_limb_t* ***rp**, *const mp_limb_t* ***sp**, *mp_size_t* **n**,   [Function]
          unsigned int **count**)
Shift $\{sp, n\}$ right by *count* bits, and write the result to $\{rp, n\}$. The bits shifted out at the right are returned in the most significant *count* bits of the return value (the rest of the return value is zero).

count must be in the range 1 to **mp_bits_per_limb**-1. The regions $\{sp, n\}$ and $\{rp, n\}$ may overlap, provided $rp \leq sp$.

This function is written in assembly for most CPUs.

int mpn_cmp (*const mp_limb_t* ***s1p**, *const mp_limb_t* ***s2p**, *mp_size_t* **n**)   [Function]
Compare $\{s1p, n\}$ and $\{s2p, n\}$ and return a positive value if $s1 > s2$, 0 if they are equal, or a negative value if $s1 < s2$.

mp_size_t mpn_gcd (*mp_limb_t* ***rp**, *mp_limb_t* ***xp**, *mp_size_t* **xn**,   [Function]
          mp_limb_t ***yp**, *mp_size_t* **yn**)
Set $\{rp, retval\}$ to the greatest common divisor of $\{xp, xn\}$ and $\{yp, yn\}$. The result can be up to *yn* limbs, the return value is the actual number produced. Both source operands are destroyed.

It is required that $xn \geq yn > 0$, and the most significant limb of $\{yp, yn\}$ must be non-zero. No overlap is permitted between $\{xp, xn\}$ and $\{yp, yn\}$.

mp_limb_t mpn_gcd_1 (*const mp_limb_t* ***xp**, *mp_size_t* **xn**, *mp_limb_t*   [Function]
          ylimb)
Return the greatest common divisor of $\{xp, xn\}$ and *ylimb*. Both operands must be non-zero.

mp_size_t mpn_gcdext (*mp_limb_t* ***gp**, *mp_limb_t* ***sp**, *mp_size_t* ***sn**,   [Function]
          mp_limb_t ***up**, *mp_size_t* **un**, *mp_limb_t* ***vp**, *mp_size_t* **vn**)
Let U be defined by $\{up, un\}$ and let V be defined by $\{vp, vn\}$.

Compute the greatest common divisor G of U and V. Compute a cofactor S such that $G = US + VT$. The second cofactor T is not computed but can easily be obtained from $(G - US)/V$ (the division will be exact). It is required that $un \geq vn > 0$, and the most significant limb of $\{vp, vn\}$ must be non-zero.

S satisfies $S = 1$ or $|S| < V/(2G)$. $S = 0$ if and only if V divides U (i.e., $G = V$).

Store G at *gp* and let the return value define its limb count. Store S at *sp* and let $|*sn|$ define its limb count. S can be negative; when this happens *sn will be negative. The area at *gp* should have room for *vn* limbs and the area at *sp* should have room for $vn + 1$ limbs.

Both source operands are destroyed.

Compatibility notes: GMP 4.3.0 and 4.3.1 defined S less strictly. Earlier as well as later GMP releases define S as described here. GMP releases before GMP 4.3.0 required additional space for both input and output areas. More precisely, the areas $\{up, un+1\}$ and $\{vp, vn+1\}$ were destroyed (i.e. the operands plus an extra limb past the end of each), and the areas pointed to by *gp* and *sp* should each have room for $un + 1$ limbs.

mp_size_t mpn_sqrtrem (*mp_limb_t *r1p, mp_limb_t *r2p, const*   [Function]
      mp_limb_t *sp, mp_size_t n)

Compute the square root of $\{sp, n\}$ and put the result at $\{r1p, \lceil n/2 \rceil\}$ and the remainder at $\{r2p, retval\}$. *r2p* needs space for *n* limbs, but the return value indicates how many are produced.

The most significant limb of $\{sp, n\}$ must be non-zero. The areas $\{r1p, \lceil n/2 \rceil\}$ and $\{sp, n\}$ must be completely separate. The areas $\{r2p, n\}$ and $\{sp, n\}$ must be either identical or completely separate.

If the remainder is not wanted then *r2p* can be NULL, and in this case the return value is zero or non-zero according to whether the remainder would have been zero or non-zero.

A return value of zero indicates a perfect square. See also **mpn_perfect_square_p**.

size_t mpn_sizeinbase (*const mp_limb_t *xp, mp_size_t n, int base*)   [Function]

Return the size of $\{xp,n\}$ measured in number of digits in the given *base*. *base* can vary from 2 to 62. Requires $n > 0$ and $xp[n-1] > 0$. The result will be either exact or 1 too big. If *base* is a power of 2, the result is always exact.

mp_size_t mpn_get_str (*unsigned char *str, int base, mp_limb_t *s1p,*   [Function]
      mp_size_t s1n)

Convert $\{s1p, s1n\}$ to a raw unsigned char array at *str* in base *base*, and return the number of characters produced. There may be leading zeros in the string. The string is not in ASCII; to convert it to printable format, add the ASCII codes for '0' or 'A', depending on the base and range. *base* can vary from 2 to 256.

The most significant limb of the input $\{s1p, s1n\}$ must be non-zero. The input $\{s1p, s1n\}$ is clobbered, except when *base* is a power of 2, in which case it's unchanged.

The area at *str* has to have space for the largest possible number represented by a *s1n* long limb array, plus one extra character.

mp_size_t mpn_set_str (*mp_limb_t *rp, const unsigned char *str, size_t*   [Function]
      strsize, int base)

Convert bytes $\{str,strsize\}$ in the given *base* to limbs at *rp*.

$str[0]$ is the most significant input byte and $str[strsize-1]$ is the least significant input byte. Each byte should be a value in the range 0 to $base - 1$, not an ASCII character. *base* can vary from 2 to 256.

The converted value is $\{rp,rn\}$ where *rn* is the return value. If the most significant input byte $str[0]$ is non-zero, then $rp[rn-1]$ will be non-zero, else $rp[rn-1]$ and some number of subsequent limbs may be zero.

The area at *rp* has to have space for the largest possible number with *strsize* digits in the chosen base, plus one extra limb.

The input must have at least one byte, and no overlap is permitted between $\{str,strsize\}$ and the result at *rp*.

mp_bitcnt_t mpn_scan0 (*const mp_limb_t *s1p, mp_bitcnt_t bit*)   [Function]

Scan *s1p* from bit position *bit* for the next clear bit.

It is required that there be a clear bit within the area at *s1p* at or beyond bit position *bit*, so that the function has something to return.

mp_bitcnt_t mpn_scan1 (*const mp_limb_t *s1p, mp_bitcnt_t* **bit**)   [Function]
    Scan *s1p* from bit position *bit* for the next set bit.

    It is required that there be a set bit within the area at *s1p* at or beyond bit position *bit*, so that the function has something to return.

void mpn_random (*mp_limb_t *r1p, mp_size_t* **r1n**)   [Function]
void mpn_random2 (*mp_limb_t *r1p, mp_size_t* **r1n**)   [Function]
    Generate a random number of length *r1n* and store it at *r1p*. The most significant limb is always non-zero. mpn_random generates uniformly distributed limb data, mpn_random2 generates long strings of zeros and ones in the binary representation.

    mpn_random2 is intended for testing the correctness of the mpn routines.

mp_bitcnt_t mpn_popcount (*const mp_limb_t *s1p, mp_size_t* **n**)   [Function]
    Count the number of set bits in $\{s1p, n\}$.

mp_bitcnt_t mpn_hamdist (*const mp_limb_t *s1p, const mp_limb_t *s2p,*   [Function]
    mp_size_t **n**)
    Compute the hamming distance between $\{s1p, n\}$ and $\{s2p, n\}$, which is the number of bit positions where the two operands have different bit values.

int mpn_perfect_square_p (*const mp_limb_t *s1p, mp_size_t* **n**)   [Function]
    Return non-zero iff $\{s1p, n\}$ is a perfect square. The most significant limb of the input $\{s1p, n\}$ must be non-zero.

void mpn_and_n (*mp_limb_t *rp, const mp_limb_t *s1p, const mp_limb_t*   [Function]
    *s2p, mp_size_t **n**)
    Perform the bitwise logical and of $\{s1p, n\}$ and $\{s2p, n\}$, and write the result to $\{rp, n\}$.

void mpn_ior_n (*mp_limb_t *rp, const mp_limb_t *s1p, const mp_limb_t*   [Function]
    *s2p, mp_size_t **n**)
    Perform the bitwise logical inclusive or of $\{s1p, n\}$ and $\{s2p, n\}$, and write the result to $\{rp, n\}$.

void mpn_xor_n (*mp_limb_t *rp, const mp_limb_t *s1p, const mp_limb_t*   [Function]
    *s2p, mp_size_t **n**)
    Perform the bitwise logical exclusive or of $\{s1p, n\}$ and $\{s2p, n\}$, and write the result to $\{rp, n\}$.

void mpn_andn_n (*mp_limb_t *rp, const mp_limb_t *s1p, const mp_limb_t*   [Function]
    *s2p, mp_size_t **n**)
    Perform the bitwise logical and of $\{s1p, n\}$ and the bitwise complement of $\{s2p, n\}$, and write the result to $\{rp, n\}$.

void mpn_iorn_n (*mp_limb_t *rp, const mp_limb_t *s1p, const mp_limb_t*   [Function]
    *s2p, mp_size_t **n**)
    Perform the bitwise logical inclusive or of $\{s1p, n\}$ and the bitwise complement of $\{s2p, n\}$, and write the result to $\{rp, n\}$.

void mpn_nand_n (*mp_limb_t *rp, const mp_limb_t *s1p, const mp_limb_t*   [Function]
    *s2p, mp_size_t **n**)
    Perform the bitwise logical and of $\{s1p, n\}$ and $\{s2p, n\}$, and write the bitwise complement of the result to $\{rp, n\}$.

void **mpn_nior_n** (*mp_limb_t* ***rp**, *const mp_limb_t* ***s1p**, *const mp_limb_t*   [Function]
         ***s2p**, *mp_size_t* **n**)
   Perform the bitwise logical inclusive or of {*s1p*, *n*} and {*s2p*, *n*}, and write the bitwise
   complement of the result to {*rp*, *n*}.

void **mpn_xnor_n** (*mp_limb_t* ***rp**, *const mp_limb_t* ***s1p**, *const mp_limb_t*   [Function]
         ***s2p**, *mp_size_t* **n**)
   Perform the bitwise logical exclusive or of {*s1p*, *n*} and {*s2p*, *n*}, and write the bitwise
   complement of the result to {*rp*, *n*}.

void **mpn_com** (*mp_limb_t* ***rp**, *const mp_limb_t* ***sp**, *mp_size_t* **n**)   [Function]
   Perform the bitwise complement of {*sp*, *n*}, and write the result to {*rp*, *n*}.

void **mpn_copyi** (*mp_limb_t* ***rp**, *const mp_limb_t* ***s1p**, *mp_size_t* **n**)   [Function]
   Copy from {*s1p*, *n*} to {*rp*, *n*}, increasingly.

void **mpn_copyd** (*mp_limb_t* ***rp**, *const mp_limb_t* ***s1p**, *mp_size_t* **n**)   [Function]
   Copy from {*s1p*, *n*} to {*rp*, *n*}, decreasingly.

void **mpn_zero** (*mp_limb_t* ***rp**, *mp_size_t* **n**)   [Function]
   Zero {*rp*, *n*}.

8.1 Low-level functions for cryptography

The functions prefixed with **mpn_sec_** and **mpn_cnd_** are designed to perform the exact same
low-level operations and have the same cache access patterns for any two same-size arguments,
assuming that function arguments are placed at the same position and that the machine state is
identical upon function entry. These functions are intended for cryptographic purposes, where
resilience to side-channel attacks is desired.

These functions are less efficient than their "leaky" counterparts; their performance for operands
of the sizes typically used for cryptographic applications is between 15% and 100% worse. For
larger operands, these functions might be inadequate, since they rely on asymptotically elementary
algorithms.

These functions do not make any explicit allocations. Those of these functions that need scratch
space accept a scratch space operand. This convention allows callers to keep sensitive data in
designated memory areas. Note however that compilers may choose to spill scalar values used
within these functions to their stack frame and that such scalars may contain sensitive data.

In addition to these specially crafted functions, the following mpn functions are naturally side-
channel resistant: **mpn_add_n**, **mpn_sub_n**, **mpn_lshift**, **mpn_rshift**, **mpn_zero**, **mpn_copyi**,
mpn_copyd, **mpn_com**, and the logical function (**mpn_and_n**, etc).

There are some exceptions from the side-channel resilience: (1) Some assembly implementations
of **mpn_lshift** identify shift-by-one as a special case. This is a problem iff the shift count is a
function of sensitive data. (2) Alpha ev6 and Pentium4 using 64-bit limbs have leaky **mpn_add_n**
and **mpn_sub_n**. (3) Alpha ev6 has a leaky **mpn_mul_1** which also makes **mpn_sec_mul** on those
systems unsafe.

mp_limb_t mpn_cnd_add_n (*mp_limb_t* **cnd**, *mp_limb_t* ***rp***, *const*   [Function]
        mp_limb_t ***s1p***, *const mp_limb_t* ***s2p***, *mp_size_t* **n**)

mp_limb_t mpn_cnd_sub_n (*mp_limb_t* **cnd**, *mp_limb_t* ***rp***, *const*   [Function]
        mp_limb_t ***s1p***, *const mp_limb_t* ***s2p***, *mp_size_t* **n**)

These functions do conditional addition and subtraction. If *cnd* is non-zero, they produce the same result as a regular mpn_add_n or mpn_sub_n, and if *cnd* is zero, they copy {*s1p*,*n*} to the result area and return zero. The functions are designed to have timing and memory access patterns depending only on size and location of the data areas, but independent of the condition *cnd*. Like for mpn_add_n and mpn_sub_n, on most machines, the timing will also be independent of the actual limb values.

mp_limb_t mpn_sec_add_1 (*mp_limb_t* ***rp***, *const mp_limb_t* ***ap***, *mp_size_t*   [Function]
        n, *mp_limb_t* **b**, *mp_limb_t* ***tp***)

mp_limb_t mpn_sec_sub_1 (*mp_limb_t* ***rp***, *const mp_limb_t* ***ap***, *mp_size_t*   [Function]
        n, *mp_limb_t* **b**, *mp_limb_t* ***tp***)

Set R to $A + b$ or $A - b$, respectively, where $R = \{rp,n\}$, $A = \{ap,n\}$, and b is a single limb. Returns carry.

These functions take $O(N)$ time, unlike the leaky functions mpn_add_1 which are $O(1)$ on average. They require scratch space of mpn_sec_add_1_itch(**n**) and mpn_sec_sub_1_itch(**n**) limbs, respectively, to be passed in the *tp* parameter. The scratch space requirements are guaranteed to increase monotonously in the operand size.

void mpn_sec_mul (*mp_limb_t* ***rp***, *const mp_limb_t* ***ap***, *mp_size_t* **an**, *const*   [Function]
        mp_limb_t ***bp***, *mp_size_t* **bn**, *mp_limb_t* ***tp***)

mp_size_t mpn_sec_mul_itch (*mp_size_t* **an**, *mp_size_t* **bn**)   [Function]

Set R to $A \times B$, where $A = \{ap,an\}$, $B = \{bp,bn\}$, and $R = \{rp,an + bn\}$.

It is required that $an \geq bn > 0$.

No overlapping between R and the input operands is allowed. For $A = B$, use mpn_sec_sqr for optimal performance.

This function requires scratch space of mpn_sec_mul_itch(**an**, **bn**) limbs to be passed in the *tp* parameter. The scratch space requirements are guaranteed to increase monotonously in the operand sizes.

void mpn_sec_sqr (*mp_limb_t* ***rp***, *const mp_limb_t* ***ap***, *mp_size_t* **an**,   [Function]
        mp_limb_t ***tp***)

mp_size_t mpn_sec_sqr_itch (*mp_size_t* **an**)   [Function]

Set R to A^2, where $A = \{ap,an\}$, and $R = \{rp,2an\}$.

It is required that $an > 0$.

No overlapping between R and the input operands is allowed.

This function requires scratch space of mpn_sec_sqr_itch(**an**) limbs to be passed in the *tp* parameter. The scratch space requirements are guaranteed to increase monotonously in the operand size.

void mpn_sec_powm (*mp_limb_t* ***rp***, *const mp_limb_t* ***bp***, *mp_size_t* **bn**,   [Function]
        const mp_limb_t ***ep***, *mp_bitcnt_t* **enb**, *const mp_limb_t* ***mp***, *mp_size_t* **n**,
        mp_limb_t ***tp***)

mp_size_t mpn_sec_powm_itch (*mp_size_t* **bn**, *mp_bitcnt_t* **enb**, *size_t* **n**)   [Function]

Set R to $B^E \bmod M$, where $R = \{rp,n\}$, $M = \{mp,n\}$, and $E = \{ep, \lceil enb/\text{GMP\_NUMB\_BITS} \rceil\}$.

It is required that $B > 0$, that $M > 0$ is odd, and that $E < 2^{enb}$.

No overlapping between R and the input operands is allowed.

This function requires scratch space of `mpn_sec_powm_itch(bn, enb, n)` limbs to be passed in the *tp* parameter. The scratch space requirements are guaranteed to increase monotonously in the operand sizes.

`void mpn_sec_tabselect` (*mp_limb_t* ***rp**, *const mp_limb_t* ***tab**, *mp_size_t*   [Function]
     n, *mp_size_t* **nents**, *mp_size_t* **which**)
Select entry *which* from table *tab*, which has *nents* entries, each *n* limbs. Store the selected entry at *rp*.

This function reads the entire table to avoid side-channel information leaks.

`mp_limb_t mpn_sec_div_qr` (*mp_limb_t* ***qp**, *mp_limb_t* ***np**, *mp_size_t* **nn**,   [Function]
     const mp_limb_t ***dp**, *mp_size_t* **dn**, *mp_limb_t* ***tp**)
`mp_size_t mpn_sec_div_qr_itch` (*mp_size_t* **nn**, *mp_size_t* **dn**)   [Function]
Set Q to $\lfloor N/D \rfloor$ and R to $N \bmod D$, where $N = \{np,nn\}$, $D = \{dp,dn\}$, Q's most significant limb is the function return value and the remaining limbs are $\{qp,nn\text{-}dn\}$, and $R = \{np,dn\}$.

It is required that $nn \geq dn \geq 1$, and that $dp[dn - 1] \neq 0$. This does not imply that $N \geq D$ since N might be zero-padded.

Note the overlapping between N and R. No other operand overlapping is allowed. The entire space occupied by N is overwritten.

This function requires scratch space of `mpn_sec_div_qr_itch(nn, dn)` limbs to be passed in the *tp* parameter.

`void mpn_sec_div_r` (*mp_limb_t* ***np**, *mp_size_t* **nn**, *const mp_limb_t* ***dp**,   [Function]
     mp_size_t **dn**, *mp_limb_t* ***tp**)
`mp_size_t mpn_sec_div_r_itch` (*mp_size_t* **nn**, *mp_size_t* **dn**)   [Function]
Set R to $N \bmod D$, where $N = \{np,nn\}$, $D = \{dp,dn\}$, and $R = \{np,dn\}$.

It is required that $nn \geq dn \geq 1$, and that $dp[dn - 1] \neq 0$. This does not imply that $N \geq D$ since N might be zero-padded.

Note the overlapping between N and R. No other operand overlapping is allowed. The entire space occupied by N is overwritten.

This function requires scratch space of `mpn_sec_div_r_itch(nn, dn)` limbs to be passed in the *tp* parameter.

`int mpn_sec_invert` (*mp_limb_t* ***rp**, *mp_limb_t* ***ap**, *const mp_limb_t* ***mp**,   [Function]
     mp_size_t **n**, *mp_bitcnt_t* **nbcnt**, *mp_limb_t* ***tp**)
`mp_size_t mpn_sec_invert_itch` (*mp_size_t* **n**)   [Function]
Set R to $A^{-1} \bmod M$, where $R = \{rp,n\}$, $A = \{ap,n\}$, and $M = \{mp,n\}$. **This function's interface is preliminary.**

If an inverse exists, return 1, otherwise return 0 and leave R undefined. In either case, the input A is destroyed.

It is required that M is odd, and that $nbcnt \geq \lceil \log(A + 1) \rceil + \lceil \log(M + 1) \rceil$. A safe choice is $nbcnt = 2n \times$ `GMP_NUMB_BITS`, but a smaller value might improve performance if M or A are known to have leading zero bits.

This function requires scratch space of `mpn_sec_invert_itch(n)` limbs to be passed in the *tp* parameter.

8.2 Nails

Everything in this section is highly experimental and may disappear or be subject to incompatible changes in a future version of GMP.

Nails are an experimental feature whereby a few bits are left unused at the top of each `mp_limb_t`. This can significantly improve carry handling on some processors.

All the `mpn` functions accepting limb data will expect the nail bits to be zero on entry, and will return data with the nails similarly all zero. This applies both to limb vectors and to single limb arguments.

Nails can be enabled by configuring with '`--enable-nails`'. By default the number of bits will be chosen according to what suits the host processor, but a particular number can be selected with '`--enable-nails=N`'.

At the mpn level, a nail build is neither source nor binary compatible with a non-nail build, strictly speaking. But programs acting on limbs only through the mpn functions are likely to work equally well with either build, and judicious use of the definitions below should make any program compatible with either build, at the source level.

For the higher level routines, meaning `mpz` etc, a nail build should be fully source and binary compatible with a non-nail build.

`GMP_NAIL_BITS`   [Macro]
`GMP_NUMB_BITS`   [Macro]
`GMP_LIMB_BITS`   [Macro]
> `GMP_NAIL_BITS` is the number of nail bits, or 0 when nails are not in use. `GMP_NUMB_BITS` is the number of data bits in a limb. `GMP_LIMB_BITS` is the total number of bits in an `mp_limb_t`. In all cases
>
> ```
> GMP_LIMB_BITS == GMP_NAIL_BITS + GMP_NUMB_BITS
> ```

`GMP_NAIL_MASK`   [Macro]
`GMP_NUMB_MASK`   [Macro]
> Bit masks for the nail and number parts of a limb. `GMP_NAIL_MASK` is 0 when nails are not in use.
>
> `GMP_NAIL_MASK` is not often needed, since the nail part can be obtained with `x >> GMP_NUMB_BITS`, and that means one less large constant, which can help various RISC chips.

`GMP_NUMB_MAX`   [Macro]
> The maximum value that can be stored in the number part of a limb. This is the same as `GMP_NUMB_MASK`, but can be used for clarity when doing comparisons rather than bit-wise operations.

The term "nails" comes from finger or toe nails, which are at the ends of a limb (arm or leg). "numb" is short for number, but is also how the developers felt after trying for a long time to come up with sensible names for these things.

In the future (the distant future most likely) a non-zero nail might be permitted, giving non-unique representations for numbers in a limb vector. This would help vector processors since carries would only ever need to propagate one or two limbs.

9 Random Number Functions

Sequences of pseudo-random numbers in GMP are generated using a variable of type `gmp_randstate_t`, which holds an algorithm selection and a current state. Such a variable must be initialized by a call to one of the `gmp_randinit` functions, and can be seeded with one of the `gmp_randseed` functions.

The functions actually generating random numbers are described in Section 5.13 [Integer Random Numbers], page 41, and Section 7.8 [Miscellaneous Float Functions], page 56.

The older style random number functions don't accept a `gmp_randstate_t` parameter but instead share a global variable of that type. They use a default algorithm and are currently not seeded (though perhaps that will change in the future). The new functions accepting a `gmp_randstate_t` are recommended for applications that care about randomness.

9.1 Random State Initialization

void **gmp_randinit_default** (*gmp_randstate_t* **state**)   [Function]
> Initialize *state* with a default algorithm. This will be a compromise between speed and randomness, and is recommended for applications with no special requirements. Currently this is `gmp_randinit_mt`.

void **gmp_randinit_mt** (*gmp_randstate_t* **state**)   [Function]
> Initialize *state* for a Mersenne Twister algorithm. This algorithm is fast and has good randomness properties.

void **gmp_randinit_lc_2exp** (*gmp_randstate_t* **state**, *const mpz_t* **a**,   [Function]
>   *unsigned long* **c**, *mp_bitcnt_t* **m2exp**)
> Initialize *state* with a linear congruential algorithm $X = (aX + c) \bmod 2^{m2exp}$.

> The low bits of X in this algorithm are not very random. The least significant bit will have a period no more than 2, and the second bit no more than 4, etc. For this reason only the high half of each X is actually used.

> When a random number of more than $m2exp/2$ bits is to be generated, multiple iterations of the recurrence are used and the results concatenated.

int **gmp_randinit_lc_2exp_size** (*gmp_randstate_t* **state**, *mp_bitcnt_t*   [Function]
>   **size**)
> Initialize *state* for a linear congruential algorithm as per `gmp_randinit_lc_2exp`. *a*, *c* and *m2exp* are selected from a table, chosen so that *size* bits (or more) of each X will be used, i.e. $m2exp/2 \geq size$.

> If successful the return value is non-zero. If *size* is bigger than the table data provides then the return value is zero. The maximum *size* currently supported is 128.

void **gmp_randinit_set** (*gmp_randstate_t* **rop**, *gmp_randstate_t* **op**)   [Function]
> Initialize *rop* with a copy of the algorithm and state from *op*.

void **gmp_randinit** (*gmp_randstate_t* **state**, *gmp_randalg_t* **alg**, . . .)   [Function]
> **This function is obsolete.**

> Initialize *state* with an algorithm selected by *alg*. The only choice is `GMP_RAND_ALG_LC`, which is `gmp_randinit_lc_2exp_size` described above. A third parameter of type **unsigned long**

is required, this is the *size* for that function. `GMP_RAND_ALG_DEFAULT` or 0 are the same as `GMP_RAND_ALG_LC`.

`gmp_randinit` sets bits in the global variable `gmp_errno` to indicate an error. `GMP_ERROR_UNSUPPORTED_ARGUMENT` if *alg* is unsupported, or `GMP_ERROR_INVALID_ARGUMENT` if the *size* parameter is too big. It may be noted this error reporting is not thread safe (a good reason to use `gmp_randinit_lc_2exp_size` instead).

void gmp_randclear (*gmp_randstate_t* **state**)   [Function]
    Free all memory occupied by *state*.

9.2 Random State Seeding

void gmp_randseed (*gmp_randstate_t* **state**, *const mpz_t* **seed**)   [Function]
void gmp_randseed_ui (*gmp_randstate_t* **state**, *unsigned long int* **seed**)   [Function]
    Set an initial seed value into *state*.

The size of a seed determines how many different sequences of random numbers that it's possible to generate. The "quality" of the seed is the randomness of a given seed compared to the previous seed used, and this affects the randomness of separate number sequences. The method for choosing a seed is critical if the generated numbers are to be used for important applications, such as generating cryptographic keys.

Traditionally the system time has been used to seed, but care needs to be taken with this. If an application seeds often and the resolution of the system clock is low, then the same sequence of numbers might be repeated. Also, the system time is quite easy to guess, so if unpredictability is required then it should definitely not be the only source for the seed value. On some systems there's a special device `/dev/random` which provides random data better suited for use as a seed.

9.3 Random State Miscellaneous

unsigned long gmp_urandomb_ui (*gmp_randstate_t* **state**, *unsigned long*   [Function]
      n)
    Return a uniformly distributed random number of *n* bits, i.e. in the range 0 to $2^n - 1$ inclusive. *n* must be less than or equal to the number of bits in an `unsigned long`.

unsigned long gmp_urandomm_ui (*gmp_randstate_t* **state**, *unsigned long*   [Function]
      n)
    Return a uniformly distributed random number in the range 0 to $n - 1$, inclusive.

10 Formatted Output

10.1 Format Strings

`gmp_printf` and friends accept format strings similar to the standard C `printf` (see Section "Formatted Output" in *The GNU C Library Reference Manual*). A format specification is of the form

```
% [flags] [width] [.[precision]] [type] conv
```

GMP adds types 'Z', 'Q' and 'F' for `mpz_t`, `mpq_t` and `mpf_t` respectively, 'M' for `mp_limb_t`, and 'N' for an `mp_limb_t` array. 'Z', 'Q', 'M' and 'N' behave like integers. 'Q' will print a '/' and a denominator, if needed. 'F' behaves like a float. For example,

```
mpz_t z;
gmp_printf ("%s is an mpz %Zd\n", "here", z);

mpq_t q;
gmp_printf ("a hex rational: %#40Qx\n", q);

mpf_t f;
int   n;
gmp_printf ("fixed point mpf %.*Ff with %d digits\n", n, f, n);

mp_limb_t l;
gmp_printf ("limb %Mu\n", l);

const mp_limb_t *ptr;
mp_size_t       size;
gmp_printf ("limb array %Nx\n", ptr, size);
```

For 'N' the limbs are expected least significant first, as per the `mpn` functions (see Chapter 8 [Low-level Functions], page 58). A negative size can be given to print the value as a negative.

All the standard C `printf` types behave the same as the C library `printf`, and can be freely intermixed with the GMP extensions. In the current implementation the standard parts of the format string are simply handed to `printf` and only the GMP extensions handled directly.

The flags accepted are as follows. GLIBC style '’' is only for the standard C types (not the GMP types), and only if the C library supports it.

0	pad with zeros (rather than spaces)
#	show the base with '0x', '0X' or '0'
+	always show a sign
(space)	show a space or a '-' sign
’	group digits, GLIBC style (not GMP types)

The optional width and precision can be given as a number within the format string, or as a '*' to take an extra parameter of type `int`, the same as the standard `printf`.

The standard types accepted are as follows. 'h' and 'l' are portable, the rest will depend on the compiler (or include files) for the type and the C library for the output.

h	short
hh	char

j	intmax_t or uintmax_t
l	long or wchar_t
ll	long long
L	long double
q	quad_t or u_quad_t
t	ptrdiff_t
z	size_t

The GMP types are

F	mpf_t, float conversions
Q	mpq_t, integer conversions
M	mp_limb_t, integer conversions
N	mp_limb_t array, integer conversions
Z	mpz_t, integer conversions

The conversions accepted are as follows. 'a' and 'A' are always supported for mpf_t but depend on the C library for standard C float types. 'm' and 'p' depend on the C library.

a A	hex floats, C99 style
c	character
d	decimal integer
e E	scientific format float
f	fixed point float
i	same as d
g G	fixed or scientific float
m	strerror string, GLIBC style
n	store characters written so far
o	octal integer
p	pointer
s	string
u	unsigned integer
x X	hex integer

'o', 'x' and 'X' are unsigned for the standard C types, but for types 'Z', 'Q' and 'N' they are signed. 'u' is not meaningful for 'Z', 'Q' and 'N'.

'M' is a proxy for the C library 'l' or 'L', according to the size of mp_limb_t. Unsigned conversions will be usual, but a signed conversion can be used and will interpret the value as a twos complement negative.

'n' can be used with any type, even the GMP types.

Other types or conversions that might be accepted by the C library printf cannot be used through gmp_printf, this includes for instance extensions registered with GLIBC register_printf_function. Also currently there's no support for POSIX '$' style numbered arguments (perhaps this will be added in the future).

The precision field has its usual meaning for integer 'Z' and float 'F' types, but is currently undefined for 'Q' and should not be used with that.

mpf_t conversions only ever generate as many digits as can be accurately represented by the operand, the same as mpf_get_str does. Zeros will be used if necessary to pad to the requested precision. This happens even for an 'f' conversion of an mpf_t which is an integer, for instance

2^{1024} in an `mpf_t` of 128 bits precision will only produce about 40 digits, then pad with zeros to the decimal point. An empty precision field like '%.Fe' or '%.Ff' can be used to specifically request just the significant digits. Without any dot and thus no precision field, a precision value of 6 will be used. Note that these rules mean that '%Ff', '%.Ff', and '%.0Ff' will all be different.

The decimal point character (or string) is taken from the current locale settings on systems which provide `localeconv` (see Section "Locales and Internationalization" in *The GNU C Library Reference Manual*). The C library will normally do the same for standard float output.

The format string is only interpreted as plain `chars`, multibyte characters are not recognised. Perhaps this will change in the future.

10.2 Functions

Each of the following functions is similar to the corresponding C library function. The basic `printf` forms take a variable argument list. The `vprintf` forms take an argument pointer, see Section "Variadic Functions" in *The GNU C Library Reference Manual*, or 'man 3 `va_start`'.

It should be emphasised that if a format string is invalid, or the arguments don't match what the format specifies, then the behaviour of any of these functions will be unpredictable. GCC format string checking is not available, since it doesn't recognise the GMP extensions.

The file based functions `gmp_printf` and `gmp_fprintf` will return -1 to indicate a write error. Output is not "atomic", so partial output may be produced if a write error occurs. All the functions can return -1 if the C library `printf` variant in use returns -1, but this shouldn't normally occur.

int gmp_printf (*const char *fmt*, ...)   [Function]
int gmp_vprintf (*const char *fmt*, *va_list ap*)   [Function]
> Print to the standard output `stdout`. Return the number of characters written, or -1 if an error occurred.

int gmp_fprintf (*FILE *fp*, *const char *fmt*, ...)   [Function]
int gmp_vfprintf (*FILE *fp*, *const char *fmt*, *va_list ap*)   [Function]
> Print to the stream *fp*. Return the number of characters written, or -1 if an error occurred.

int gmp_sprintf (*char *buf*, *const char *fmt*, ...)   [Function]
int gmp_vsprintf (*char *buf*, *const char *fmt*, *va_list ap*)   [Function]
> Form a null-terminated string in *buf*. Return the number of characters written, excluding the terminating null.
>
> No overlap is permitted between the space at *buf* and the string *fmt*.
>
> These functions are not recommended, since there's no protection against exceeding the space available at *buf*.

int gmp_snprintf (*char *buf*, *size_t* `size`, *const char *fmt*, ...)   [Function]
int gmp_vsnprintf (*char *buf*, *size_t* `size`, *const char *fmt*, *va_list ap*) [Function]
> Form a null-terminated string in *buf*. No more than *size* bytes will be written. To get the full output, *size* must be enough for the string and null-terminator.
>
> The return value is the total number of characters which ought to have been produced, excluding the terminating null. If *retval* $\geq$ *size* then the actual output has been truncated to the first *size* -1 characters, and a null appended.
>
> No overlap is permitted between the region {*buf*,*size*} and the *fmt* string.

Notice the return value is in ISO C99 `snprintf` style. This is so even if the C library `vsnprintf` is the older GLIBC 2.0.x style.

int gmp_asprintf (*char **pp, const char *fmt, . . .*)   [Function]
int gmp_vasprintf (*char **pp, const char *fmt, va_list* **ap**)   [Function]
> Form a null-terminated string in a block of memory obtained from the current memory allocation function (see Chapter 13 [Custom Allocation], page 89). The block will be the size of the string and null-terminator. The address of the block in stored to **pp*. The return value is the number of characters produced, excluding the null-terminator.

> Unlike the C library `asprintf`, `gmp_asprintf` doesn't return −1 if there's no more memory available, it lets the current allocation function handle that.

int gmp_obstack_printf (*struct obstack *ob, const char *fmt, . . .*)   [Function]
int gmp_obstack_vprintf (*struct obstack *ob, const char *fmt, va_list* **ap**) [Function]
> Append to the current object in *ob*. The return value is the number of characters written. A null-terminator is not written.

> *fmt* cannot be within the current object in *ob*, since that object might move as it grows.

> These functions are available only when the C library provides the obstack feature, which probably means only on GNU systems, see Section "Obstacks" in *The GNU C Library Reference Manual*.

10.3 C++ Formatted Output

The following functions are provided in `libgmpxx` (see Section 3.1 [Headers and Libraries], page 17), which is built if C++ support is enabled (see Section 2.1 [Build Options], page 3). Prototypes are available from `<gmp.h>`.

ostream& operator<< (*ostream&* **stream**, *const mpz_t* **op**)   [Function]
> Print *op* to *stream*, using its `ios` formatting settings. `ios::width` is reset to 0 after output, the same as the standard `ostream` `operator<<` routines do.

> In hex or octal, *op* is printed as a signed number, the same as for decimal. This is unlike the standard `operator<<` routines on `int` etc, which instead give twos complement.

ostream& operator<< (*ostream&* **stream**, *const mpq_t* **op**)   [Function]
> Print *op* to *stream*, using its `ios` formatting settings. `ios::width` is reset to 0 after output, the same as the standard `ostream` `operator<<` routines do.

> Output will be a fraction like '5/9', or if the denominator is 1 then just a plain integer like '123'.

> In hex or octal, *op* is printed as a signed value, the same as for decimal. If `ios::showbase` is set then a base indicator is shown on both the numerator and denominator (if the denominator is required).

ostream& operator<< (*ostream&* **stream**, *const mpf_t* **op**)   [Function]
> Print *op* to *stream*, using its `ios` formatting settings. `ios::width` is reset to 0 after output, the same as the standard `ostream` `operator<<` routines do.

> The decimal point follows the standard library float `operator<<`, which on recent systems means the `std::locale` imbued on *stream*.

Hex and octal are supported, unlike the standard `operator<<` on `double`. The mantissa will be in hex or octal, the exponent will be in decimal. For hex the exponent delimiter is an '@'. This is as per `mpf_out_str`.

`ios::showbase` is supported, and will put a base on the mantissa, for example hex '0x1.8' or '0x0.8', or octal '01.4' or '00.4'. This last form is slightly strange, but at least differentiates itself from decimal.

These operators mean that GMP types can be printed in the usual C++ way, for example,

```
mpz_t   z;
int     n;
...
cout << "iteration " << n << " value " << z << "\n";
```

But note that `ostream` output (and `istream` input, see Section 11.3 [C++ Formatted Input], page 78) is the only overloading available for the GMP types and that for instance using + with an `mpz_t` will have unpredictable results. For classes with overloading, see Chapter 12 [C++ Class Interface], page 80.

11 Formatted Input

11.1 Formatted Input Strings

`gmp_scanf` and friends accept format strings similar to the standard C `scanf` (see Section "Formatted Input" in *The GNU C Library Reference Manual*). A format specification is of the form

```
% [flags] [width] [type] conv
```

GMP adds types 'Z', 'Q' and 'F' for `mpz_t`, `mpq_t` and `mpf_t` respectively. 'Z' and 'Q' behave like integers. 'Q' will read a '/' and a denominator, if present. 'F' behaves like a float.

GMP variables don't require an & when passed to `gmp_scanf`, since they're already "call-by-reference". For example,

```
/* to read say "a(5) = 1234" */
int    n;
mpz_t z;
gmp_scanf ("a(%d) = %Zd\n", &n, z);

mpq_t q1, q2;
gmp_sscanf ("0377 + 0x10/0x11", "%Qi + %Qi", q1, q2);

/* to read say "topleft (1.55,-2.66)" */
mpf_t x, y;
char  buf[32];
gmp_scanf ("%31s (%Ff,%Ff)", buf, x, y);
```

All the standard C `scanf` types behave the same as in the C library `scanf`, and can be freely intermixed with the GMP extensions. In the current implementation the standard parts of the format string are simply handed to `scanf` and only the GMP extensions handled directly.

The flags accepted are as follows. 'a' and ''' will depend on support from the C library, and ''' cannot be used with GMP types.

*	read but don't store
a	allocate a buffer (string conversions)
'	grouped digits, GLIBC style (not GMP types)

The standard types accepted are as follows. 'h' and 'l' are portable, the rest will depend on the compiler (or include files) for the type and the C library for the input.

h	short
hh	char
j	`intmax_t` or `uintmax_t`
l	long int, double or `wchar_t`
ll	long long
L	long double
q	`quad_t` or `u_quad_t`
t	`ptrdiff_t`
z	`size_t`

The GMP types are

F	`mpf_t`, float conversions
Q	`mpq_t`, integer conversions
Z	`mpz_t`, integer conversions

The conversions accepted are as follows. 'p' and '[' will depend on support from the C library, the rest are standard.

c	character or characters
d	decimal integer
e E f g	float
G	
i	integer with base indicator
n	characters read so far
o	octal integer
p	pointer
s	string of non-whitespace characters
u	decimal integer
x X	hex integer
[	string of characters in a set

'e', 'E', 'f', 'g' and 'G' are identical, they all read either fixed point or scientific format, and either upper or lower case 'e' for the exponent in scientific format.

C99 style hex float format (`printf %a`, see Section 10.1 [Formatted Output Strings], page 71) is always accepted for `mpf_t`, but for the standard float types it will depend on the C library.

'x' and 'X' are identical, both accept both upper and lower case hexadecimal.

'o', 'u', 'x' and 'X' all read positive or negative values. For the standard C types these are described as "unsigned" conversions, but that merely affects certain overflow handling, negatives are still allowed (per `strtoul`, see Section "Parsing of Integers" in The GNU C Library Reference Manual). For GMP types there are no overflows, so 'd' and 'u' are identical.

'Q' type reads the numerator and (optional) denominator as given. If the value might not be in canonical form then `mpq_canonicalize` must be called before using it in any calculations (see Chapter 6 [Rational Number Functions], page 46).

'Qi' will read a base specification separately for the numerator and denominator. For example '0x10/11' would be 16/11, whereas '0x10/0x11' would be 16/17.

'n' can be used with any of the types above, even the GMP types. '*' to suppress assignment is allowed, though in that case it would do nothing at all.

Other conversions or types that might be accepted by the C library `scanf` cannot be used through `gmp_scanf`.

Whitespace is read and discarded before a field, except for 'c' and '[' conversions.

For float conversions, the decimal point character (or string) expected is taken from the current locale settings on systems which provide `localeconv` (see Section "Locales and Internationalization" in The GNU C Library Reference Manual). The C library will normally do the same for standard float input.

The format string is only interpreted as plain `chars`, multibyte characters are not recognised. Perhaps this will change in the future.

11.2 Formatted Input Functions

Each of the following functions is similar to the corresponding C library function. The plain `scanf` forms take a variable argument list. The `vscanf` forms take an argument pointer, see Section "Variadic Functions" in *The GNU C Library Reference Manual*, or '`man 3 va_start`'.

It should be emphasised that if a format string is invalid, or the arguments don't match what the format specifies, then the behaviour of any of these functions will be unpredictable. GCC format string checking is not available, since it doesn't recognise the GMP extensions.

No overlap is permitted between the *fmt* string and any of the results produced.

int gmp_scanf (*const char *fmt, ...*)   [Function]
int gmp_vscanf (*const char *fmt, va_list* **ap**)   [Function]
    Read from the standard input `stdin`.

int gmp_fscanf (*FILE *fp, const char *fmt, ...*)   [Function]
int gmp_vfscanf (*FILE *fp, const char *fmt, va_list* **ap**)   [Function]
    Read from the stream *fp*.

int gmp_sscanf (*const char *s, const char *fmt, ...*)   [Function]
int gmp_vsscanf (*const char *s, const char *fmt, va_list* **ap**)   [Function]
    Read from a null-terminated string *s*.

The return value from each of these functions is the same as the standard C99 `scanf`, namely the number of fields successfully parsed and stored. '`%n`' fields and fields read but suppressed by '`*`' don't count towards the return value.

If end of input (or a file error) is reached before a character for a field or a literal, and if no previous non-suppressed fields have matched, then the return value is `EOF` instead of 0. A whitespace character in the format string is only an optional match and doesn't induce an `EOF` in this fashion. Leading whitespace read and discarded for a field don't count as characters for that field.

For the GMP types, input parsing follows C99 rules, namely one character of lookahead is used and characters are read while they continue to meet the format requirements. If this doesn't provide a complete number then the function terminates, with that field not stored nor counted towards the return value. For instance with `mpf_t` an input '`1.23e-XYZ`' would be read up to the '`X`' and that character pushed back since it's not a digit. The string '`1.23e-`' would then be considered invalid since an '`e`' must be followed by at least one digit.

For the standard C types, in the current implementation GMP calls the C library `scanf` functions, which might have looser rules about what constitutes a valid input.

Note that `gmp_sscanf` is the same as `gmp_fscanf` and only does one character of lookahead when parsing. Although clearly it could look at its entire input, it is deliberately made identical to `gmp_fscanf`, the same way C99 `sscanf` is the same as `fscanf`.

11.3 C++ Formatted Input

The following functions are provided in `libgmpxx` (see Section 3.1 [Headers and Libraries], page 17), which is built only if C++ support is enabled (see Section 2.1 [Build Options], page 3). Prototypes are available from `<gmp.h>`.

istream& operator>> (*istream&* **stream**, *mpz_t* **rop**)   [Function]
    Read *rop* from *stream*, using its `ios` formatting settings.

istream& operator>> (*istream&* **stream**, *mpq_t* **rop**)   [Function]
An integer like '123' will be read, or a fraction like '5/9'. No whitespace is allowed around the '/'. If the fraction is not in canonical form then `mpq_canonicalize` must be called (see Chapter 6 [Rational Number Functions], page 46) before operating on it.

As per integer input, an '0' or '0x' base indicator is read when none of `ios::dec`, `ios::oct` or `ios::hex` are set. This is done separately for numerator and denominator, so that for instance '0x10/11' is 16/11 and '0x10/0x11' is 16/17.

istream& operator>> (*istream&* **stream**, *mpf_t* **rop**)   [Function]
Read *rop* from *stream*, using its `ios` formatting settings.

Hex or octal floats are not supported, but might be in the future, or perhaps it's best to accept only what the standard float `operator>>` does.

Note that digit grouping specified by the `istream` locale is currently not accepted. Perhaps this will change in the future.

These operators mean that GMP types can be read in the usual C++ way, for example,

```
mpz_t  z;
...
cin >> z;
```

But note that `istream` input (and `ostream` output, see Section 10.3 [C++ Formatted Output], page 74) is the only overloading available for the GMP types and that for instance using + with an `mpz_t` will have unpredictable results. For classes with overloading, see Chapter 12 [C++ Class Interface], page 80.

12 C++ Class Interface

This chapter describes the C++ class based interface to GMP.

All GMP C language types and functions can be used in C++ programs, since `gmp.h` has `extern "C"` qualifiers, but the class interface offers overloaded functions and operators which may be more convenient.

Due to the implementation of this interface, a reasonably recent C++ compiler is required, one supporting namespaces, partial specialization of templates and member templates.

Everything described in this chapter is to be considered preliminary and might be subject to incompatible changes if some unforeseen difficulty reveals itself.

12.1 C++ Interface General

All the C++ classes and functions are available with

```
#include <gmpxx.h>
```

Programs should be linked with the `libgmpxx` and `libgmp` libraries. For example,

```
g++ mycxxprog.cc -lgmpxx -lgmp
```

The classes defined are

`mpz_class`	[Class]
`mpq_class`	[Class]
`mpf_class`	[Class]

The standard operators and various standard functions are overloaded to allow arithmetic with these classes. For example,

```
int
main (void)
{
  mpz_class a, b, c;

  a = 1234;
  b = "-5678";
  c = a+b;
  cout << "sum is " << c << "\n";
  cout << "absolute value is " << abs(c) << "\n";

  return 0;
}
```

An important feature of the implementation is that an expression like a=b+c results in a single call to the corresponding `mpz_add`, without using a temporary for the b+c part. Expressions which by their nature imply intermediate values, like a=b*c+d*e, still use temporaries though.

The classes can be freely intermixed in expressions, as can the classes and the standard types `long`, `unsigned long` and `double`. Smaller types like `int` or `float` can also be intermixed, since C++ will promote them.

Note that `bool` is not accepted directly, but must be explicitly cast to an `int` first. This is because C++ will automatically convert any pointer to a `bool`, so if GMP accepted `bool` it would make all sorts of invalid class and pointer combinations compile but almost certainly not do anything sensible.

Conversions back from the classes to standard C++ types aren't done automatically, instead member functions like `get_si` are provided (see the following sections for details).

Also there are no automatic conversions from the classes to the corresponding GMP C types, instead a reference to the underlying C object can be obtained with the following functions,

`mpz_t mpz_class::get_mpz_t ()`	[Function]
`mpq_t mpq_class::get_mpq_t ()`	[Function]
`mpf_t mpf_class::get_mpf_t ()`	[Function]

These can be used to call a C function which doesn't have a C++ class interface. For example to set `a` to the GCD of `b` and `c`,

```
mpz_class a, b, c;
...
mpz_gcd (a.get_mpz_t(), b.get_mpz_t(), c.get_mpz_t());
```

In the other direction, a class can be initialized from the corresponding GMP C type, or assigned to if an explicit constructor is used. In both cases this makes a copy of the value, it doesn't create any sort of association. For example,

```
mpz_t z;
// ... init and calculate z ...
mpz_class x(z);
mpz_class y;
y = mpz_class (z);
```

There are no namespace setups in `gmpxx.h`, all types and functions are simply put into the global namespace. This is what `gmp.h` has done in the past, and continues to do for compatibility. The extras provided by `gmpxx.h` follow GMP naming conventions and are unlikely to clash with anything.

12.2 C++ Interface Integers

`mpz_class::mpz_class (type n)`   [Function]
> Construct an `mpz_class`. All the standard C++ types may be used, except `long long` and `long double`, and all the GMP C++ classes can be used, although conversions from `mpq_class` and `mpf_class` are explicit. Any necessary conversion follows the corresponding C function, for example `double` follows `mpz_set_d` (see Section 5.2 [Assigning Integers], page 31).

`explicit mpz_class::mpz_class (const mpz_t z)`   [Function]
> Construct an `mpz_class` from an `mpz_t`. The value in `z` is copied into the new `mpz_class`, there won't be any permanent association between it and `z`.

`explicit mpz_class::mpz_class (const char *s, int base = 0)`   [Function]
`explicit mpz_class::mpz_class (const string& s, int base = 0)`   [Function]
> Construct an `mpz_class` converted from a string using `mpz_set_str` (see Section 5.2 [Assigning Integers], page 31).
>
> If the string is not a valid integer, an `std::invalid_argument` exception is thrown. The same applies to `operator=`.

`mpz_class operator"" _mpz (const char *str)`   [Function]
    With C++11 compilers, integers can be constructed with the syntax `123_mpz` which is equivalent to `mpz_class("123")`.

`mpz_class operator/ (mpz_class a, mpz_class d)`   [Function]
`mpz_class operator% (mpz_class a, mpz_class d)`   [Function]
    Divisions involving `mpz_class` round towards zero, as per the `mpz_tdiv_q` and `mpz_tdiv_r` functions (see Section 5.6 [Integer Division], page 33). This is the same as the C99 / and % operators.

    The `mpz_fdiv...` or `mpz_cdiv...` functions can always be called directly if desired. For example,

```
mpz_class q, a, d;
...
mpz_fdiv_q (q.get_mpz_t(), a.get_mpz_t(), d.get_mpz_t());
```

`mpz_class abs (mpz_class op)`   [Function]
`int cmp (mpz_class op1, type op2)`   [Function]
`int cmp (type op1, mpz_class op2)`   [Function]
`bool mpz_class::fits_sint_p (void)`   [Function]
`bool mpz_class::fits_slong_p (void)`   [Function]
`bool mpz_class::fits_sshort_p (void)`   [Function]
`bool mpz_class::fits_uint_p (void)`   [Function]
`bool mpz_class::fits_ulong_p (void)`   [Function]
`bool mpz_class::fits_ushort_p (void)`   [Function]
`double mpz_class::get_d (void)`   [Function]
`long mpz_class::get_si (void)`   [Function]
`string mpz_class::get_str (int base = 10)`   [Function]
`unsigned long mpz_class::get_ui (void)`   [Function]
`int mpz_class::set_str (const char *str, int base)`   [Function]
`int mpz_class::set_str (const string& str, int base)`   [Function]
`int sgn (mpz_class op)`   [Function]
`mpz_class sqrt (mpz_class op)`   [Function]
`void mpz_class::swap (mpz_class& op)`   [Function]
`void swap (mpz_class& op1, mpz_class& op2)`   [Function]
    These functions provide a C++ class interface to the corresponding GMP C routines.

    `cmp` can be used with any of the classes or the standard C++ types, except `long long` and `long double`.

Overloaded operators for combinations of `mpz_class` and `double` are provided for completeness, but it should be noted that if the given `double` is not an integer then the way any rounding is done is currently unspecified. The rounding might take place at the start, in the middle, or at the end of the operation, and it might change in the future.

Conversions between `mpz_class` and `double`, however, are defined to follow the corresponding C functions `mpz_get_d` and `mpz_set_d`. And comparisons are always made exactly, as per `mpz_cmp_d`.

12.3 C++ Interface Rationals

In all the following constructors, if a fraction is given then it should be in canonical form, or if not then `mpq_class::canonicalize` called.

`mpq_class::mpq_class` (*type op*)   [Function]

`mpq_class::mpq_class` (*integer* **num**, *integer* **den**)   [Function]

Construct an `mpq_class`. The initial value can be a single value of any type (conversion from `mpf_class` is explicit), or a pair of integers (`mpz_class` or standard C++ integer types) representing a fraction, except that `long long` and `long double` are not supported. For example,

```
mpq_class q (99);
mpq_class q (1.75);
mpq_class q (1, 3);
```

`explicit mpq_class::mpq_class` (*const mpq_t* **q**)   [Function]

Construct an `mpq_class` from an `mpq_t`. The value in *q* is copied into the new `mpq_class`, there won't be any permanent association between it and *q*.

`explicit mpq_class::mpq_class` (*const char *s, int* **base** = *0*)   [Function]

`explicit mpq_class::mpq_class` (*const string&* **s**, *int* **base** = *0*) [Function]

Construct an `mpq_class` converted from a string using `mpq_set_str` (see Section 6.1 [Initializing Rationals], page 46).

If the string is not a valid rational, an `std::invalid_argument` exception is thrown. The same applies to `operator=`.

`mpq_class operator"" _mpq` (*const char *str*)   [Function]

With C++11 compilers, integral rationals can be constructed with the syntax `123_mpq` which is equivalent to `mpq_class(123_mpz)`. Other rationals can be built as `-1_mpq/2` or `0xb_mpq/123456_mpz`.

`void mpq_class::canonicalize` ()   [Function]

Put an `mpq_class` into canonical form, as per Chapter 6 [Rational Number Functions], page 46. All arithmetic operators require their operands in canonical form, and will return results in canonical form.

`mpq_class abs` (*mpq_class op*)   [Function]
`int cmp` (*mpq_class op1, type op2*)   [Function]
`int cmp` (*type op1, mpq_class op2*)   [Function]
`double mpq_class::get_d` (*void*)   [Function]
`string mpq_class::get_str` (*int* **base** = *10*)   [Function]
`int mpq_class::set_str` (*const char *str, int* **base**)   [Function]
`int mpq_class::set_str` (*const string&* **str**, *int* **base**)   [Function]
`int sgn` (*mpq_class op*)   [Function]
`void mpq_class::swap` (*mpq_class& op*)   [Function]
`void swap` (*mpq_class& op1, mpq_class& op2*)   [Function]

These functions provide a C++ class interface to the corresponding GMP C routines.

`cmp` can be used with any of the classes or the standard C++ types, except `long long` and `long double`.

`mpz_class& mpq_class::get_num` ()   [Function]
`mpz_class& mpq_class::get_den` ()   [Function]

Get a reference to an `mpz_class` which is the numerator or denominator of an `mpq_class`. This can be used both for read and write access. If the object returned is modified, it modifies the original `mpq_class`.

If direct manipulation might produce a non-canonical value, then `mpq_class::canonicalize` must be called before further operations.

`mpz_t mpq_class::get_num_mpz_t ()`   [Function]
`mpz_t mpq_class::get_den_mpz_t ()`   [Function]
> Get a reference to the underlying `mpz_t` numerator or denominator of an `mpq_class`. This can be passed to C functions expecting an `mpz_t`. Any modifications made to the `mpz_t` will modify the original `mpq_class`.

> If direct manipulation might produce a non-canonical value, then `mpq_class::canonicalize` must be called before further operations.

`istream& operator>>` (*istream&* **stream**, *mpq_class&* **rop**)*;*   [Function]
> Read *rop* from *stream*, using its `ios` formatting settings, the same as `mpq_t operator>>` (see Section 11.3 [C++ Formatted Input], page 78).

> If the *rop* read might not be in canonical form then `mpq_class::canonicalize` must be called.

12.4 C++ Interface Floats

When an expression requires the use of temporary intermediate `mpf_class` values, like `f=g*h+x*y`, those temporaries will have the same precision as the destination `f`. Explicit constructors can be used if this doesn't suit.

`mpf_class::mpf_class` (*type* **op**)   [Function]
`mpf_class::mpf_class` (*type* **op**, *mp_bitcnt_t* **prec**)   [Function]
> Construct an `mpf_class`. Any standard C++ type can be used, except `long long` and `long double`, and any of the GMP C++ classes can be used.

> If *prec* is given, the initial precision is that value, in bits. If *prec* is not given, then the initial precision is determined by the type of *op* given. An `mpz_class`, `mpq_class`, or C++ builtin type will give the default `mpf` precision (see Section 7.1 [Initializing Floats], page 50). An `mpf_class` or expression will give the precision of that value. The precision of a binary expression is the higher of the two operands.

```
mpf_class f(1.5);         // default precision
mpf_class f(1.5, 500);    // 500 bits (at least)
mpf_class f(x);           // precision of x
mpf_class f(abs(x));      // precision of x
mpf_class f(-g, 1000);    // 1000 bits (at least)
mpf_class f(x+y);         // greater of precisions of x and y
```

`explicit mpf_class::mpf_class` (*const mpf_t* **f**)   [Function]
`mpf_class::mpf_class` (*const mpf_t* **f**, *mp_bitcnt_t* **prec**)   [Function]
> Construct an `mpf_class` from an `mpf_t`. The value in *f* is copied into the new `mpf_class`, there won't be any permanent association between it and *f*.

> If *prec* is given, the initial precision is that value, in bits. If *prec* is not given, then the initial precision is that of *f*.

`explicit mpf_class::mpf_class` (*const char* ***s**)   [Function]
`mpf_class::mpf_class` (*const char* ***s**, *mp_bitcnt_t* **prec**, *int* **base** = *0*)   [Function]
`explicit mpf_class::mpf_class` (*const string&* **s**)   [Function]

`mpf_class::mpf_class` (*const string&* **s**, *mp_bitcnt_t* **prec**, *int* **base** = *0*)   [Function]
  Construct an `mpf_class` converted from a string using `mpf_set_str` (see Section 7.2 [Assigning Floats], page 52). If *prec* is given, the initial precision is that value, in bits. If not, the default `mpf` precision (see Section 7.1 [Initializing Floats], page 50) is used.

  If the string is not a valid float, an `std::invalid_argument` exception is thrown. The same applies to `operator=`.

`mpf_class operator""` _mpf (*const char* ***str**)   [Function]
  With C++11 compilers, floats can be constructed with the syntax `1.23e-1_mpf` which is equivalent to `mpf_class("1.23e-1")`.

`mpf_class& mpf_class::operator=` (*type* **op**)   [Function]
  Convert and store the given *op* value to an `mpf_class` object. The same types are accepted as for the constructors above.

  Note that `operator=` only stores a new value, it doesn't copy or change the precision of the destination, instead the value is truncated if necessary. This is the same as `mpf_set` etc. Note in particular this means for `mpf_class` a copy constructor is not the same as a default constructor plus assignment.

```
mpf_class x (y);   // x created with precision of y

mpf_class x;       // x created with default precision
x = y;             // value truncated to that precision
```

  Applications using templated code may need to be careful about the assumptions the code makes in this area, when working with `mpf_class` values of various different or non-default precisions. For instance implementations of the standard `complex` template have been seen in both styles above, though of course `complex` is normally only actually specified for use with the builtin float types.

`mpf_class abs` (*mpf_class* **op**)	[Function]
`mpf_class ceil` (*mpf_class* **op**)	[Function]
`int cmp` (*mpf_class* **op1**, *type* **op2**)	[Function]
`int cmp` (*type* **op1**, *mpf_class* **op2**)	[Function]
`bool mpf_class::fits_sint_p` (*void*)	[Function]
`bool mpf_class::fits_slong_p` (*void*)	[Function]
`bool mpf_class::fits_sshort_p` (*void*)	[Function]
`bool mpf_class::fits_uint_p` (*void*)	[Function]
`bool mpf_class::fits_ulong_p` (*void*)	[Function]
`bool mpf_class::fits_ushort_p` (*void*)	[Function]
`mpf_class floor` (*mpf_class* **op**)	[Function]
`mpf_class hypot` (*mpf_class* **op1**, *mpf_class* **op2**)	[Function]
`double mpf_class::get_d` (*void*)	[Function]
`long mpf_class::get_si` (*void*)	[Function]
`string mpf_class::get_str` (*mp_exp_t&* **exp**, *int* **base** = *10*, *size_t* **digits** = *0*)	[Function]
`unsigned long mpf_class::get_ui` (*void*)	[Function]
`int mpf_class::set_str` (*const char* ***str**, *int* **base**)	[Function]
`int mpf_class::set_str` (*const string&* **str**, *int* **base**)	[Function]
`int sgn` (*mpf_class* **op**)	[Function]
`mpf_class sqrt` (*mpf_class* **op**)	[Function]
`void mpf_class::swap` (*mpf_class&* **op**)	[Function]

void swap (*mpf_class&* **op1**, *mpf_class&* **op2**)   [Function]
mpf_class trunc (*mpf_class* **op**)   [Function]
> These functions provide a C++ class interface to the corresponding GMP C routines.

> cmp can be used with any of the classes or the standard C++ types, except `long long` and `long double`.

> The accuracy provided by `hypot` is not currently guaranteed.

mp_bitcnt_t mpf_class::get_prec ()   [Function]
void mpf_class::set_prec (*mp_bitcnt_t* **prec**)   [Function]
void mpf_class::set_prec_raw (*mp_bitcnt_t* **prec**)   [Function]
> Get or set the current precision of an `mpf_class`.

> The restrictions described for `mpf_set_prec_raw` (see Section 7.1 [Initializing Floats], page 50) apply to `mpf_class::set_prec_raw`. Note in particular that the `mpf_class` must be restored to it's allocated precision before being destroyed. This must be done by application code, there's no automatic mechanism for it.

12.5 C++ Interface Random Numbers

gmp_randclass   [Class]
> The C++ class interface to the GMP random number functions uses `gmp_randclass` to hold an algorithm selection and current state, as per `gmp_randstate_t`.

gmp_randclass::gmp_randclass (*void (*randinit)* (*gmp_randstate_t,*   [Function]
    ...), ...)
> Construct a `gmp_randclass`, using a call to the given *randinit* function (see Section 9.1 [Random State Initialization], page 69). The arguments expected are the same as *randinit*, but with `mpz_class` instead of `mpz_t`. For example,

```
gmp_randclass r1 (gmp_randinit_default);
gmp_randclass r2 (gmp_randinit_lc_2exp_size, 32);
gmp_randclass r3 (gmp_randinit_lc_2exp, a, c, m2exp);
gmp_randclass r4 (gmp_randinit_mt);
```

> `gmp_randinit_lc_2exp_size` will fail if the size requested is too big, an `std::length_error` exception is thrown in that case.

gmp_randclass::gmp_randclass (*gmp_randalg_t* **alg**, ...)   [Function]
> Construct a `gmp_randclass` using the same parameters as `gmp_randinit` (see Section 9.1 [Random State Initialization], page 69). This function is obsolete and the above *randinit* style should be preferred.

void gmp_randclass::seed (*unsigned long int* **s**)   [Function]
void gmp_randclass::seed (*mpz_class* **s**)   [Function]
> Seed a random number generator. See see Chapter 9 [Random Number Functions], page 69, for how to choose a good seed.

mpz_class gmp_randclass::get_z_bits (*mp_bitcnt_t* **bits**)   [Function]
mpz_class gmp_randclass::get_z_bits (*mpz_class* **bits**)   [Function]
> Generate a random integer with a specified number of bits.

mpz_class gmp_randclass::get_z_range (*mpz_class* **n**)   [Function]
> Generate a random integer in the range 0 to $n - 1$ inclusive.

`mpf_class gmp_randclass::get_f ()` [Function]
`mpf_class gmp_randclass::get_f (`*mp_bitcnt_t* **prec**`)` [Function]

Generate a random float f in the range $0 <= f < 1$. f will be to *prec* bits precision, or if *prec* is not given then to the precision of the destination. For example,

```
gmp_randclass  r;
...
mpf_class  f (0, 512);   // 512 bits precision
f = r.get_f();           // random number, 512 bits
```

12.6 C++ Interface Limitations

`mpq_class` and Templated Reading

A generic piece of template code probably won't know that `mpq_class` requires a `canonicalize` call if inputs read with `operator>>` might be non-canonical. This can lead to incorrect results.

`operator>>` behaves as it does for reasons of efficiency. A canonicalize can be quite time consuming on large operands, and is best avoided if it's not necessary.

But this potential difficulty reduces the usefulness of `mpq_class`. Perhaps a mechanism to tell `operator>>` what to do will be adopted in the future, maybe a preprocessor define, a global flag, or an `ios` flag pressed into service. Or maybe, at the risk of inconsistency, the `mpq_class operator>>` could canonicalize and leave `mpq_t operator>>` not doing so, for use on those occasions when that's acceptable. Send feedback or alternate ideas to gmp-bugs@gmplib.org.

Subclassing

Subclassing the GMP C++ classes works, but is not currently recommended.

Expressions involving subclasses resolve correctly (or seem to), but in normal C++ fashion the subclass doesn't inherit constructors and assignments. There's many of those in the GMP classes, and a good way to reestablish them in a subclass is not yet provided.

Templated Expressions

A subtle difficulty exists when using expressions together with application-defined template functions. Consider the following, with `T` intended to be some numeric type,

```
template <class T>
T fun (const T &, const T &);
```

When used with, say, plain `mpz_class` variables, it works fine: `T` is resolved as `mpz_class`.

```
mpz_class f(1), g(2);
fun (f, g);    // Good
```

But when one of the arguments is an expression, it doesn't work.

```
mpz_class f(1), g(2), h(3);
fun (f, g+h);  // Bad
```

This is because `g+h` ends up being a certain expression template type internal to `gmpxx.h`, which the C++ template resolution rules are unable to automatically convert to `mpz_class`. The workaround is simply to add an explicit cast.

```
mpz_class f(1), g(2), h(3);
fun (f, mpz_class(g+h));  // Good
```

Similarly, within `fun` it may be necessary to cast an expression to type `T` when calling a templated `fun2`.

```
template <class T>
void fun (T f, T g)
{
  fun2 (f, f+g);      // Bad
}

template <class T>
void fun (T f, T g)
{
  fun2 (f, T(f+g));  // Good
}
```

C++11   C++11 provides several new ways in which types can be inferred: `auto`, `decltype`, etc. While they can be very convenient, they don't mix well with expression templates. In this example, the addition is performed twice, as if we had defined `sum` as a macro.

```
mpz_class z = 33;
auto sum = z + z;
mpz_class prod = sum * sum;
```

This other example may crash, though some compilers might make it look like it is working, because the expression `z+z` goes out of scope before it is evaluated.

```
mpz_class z = 33;
auto sum = z + z + z;
mpz_class prod = sum * 2;
```

It is thus strongly recommended to avoid `auto` anywhere a GMP C++ expression may appear.

13 Custom Allocation

By default GMP uses `malloc`, `realloc` and `free` for memory allocation, and if they fail GMP prints a message to the standard error output and terminates the program.

Alternate functions can be specified, to allocate memory in a different way or to have a different error action on running out of memory.

void mp_set_memory_functions ([Function]
        void *(*`alloc_func_ptr`)* (*size_t*),
        void *(*`realloc_func_ptr`)* (*void *, size_t, size_t*),
        void *(*`free_func_ptr`)* (*void *, size_t*))
>   Replace the current allocation functions from the arguments. If an argument is `NULL`, the corresponding default function is used.
>
>   These functions will be used for all memory allocation done by GMP, apart from temporary space from `alloca` if that function is available and GMP is configured to use it (see Section 2.1 [Build Options], page 3).
>
>   **Be sure to call `mp_set_memory_functions` only when there are no active GMP objects allocated using the previous memory functions! Usually that means calling it before any other GMP function.**

The functions supplied should fit the following declarations:

void * allocate_function (*size_t* `alloc_size`)   [Function]
>   Return a pointer to newly allocated space with at least *alloc_size* bytes.

void * reallocate_function (*void *`ptr`, size_t* `old_size`*, size_t*   [Function]
        `new_size`)
>   Resize a previously allocated block *ptr* of *old_size* bytes to be *new_size* bytes.
>
>   The block may be moved if necessary or if desired, and in that case the smaller of *old_size* and *new_size* bytes must be copied to the new location. The return value is a pointer to the resized block, that being the new location if moved or just *ptr* if not.
>
>   *ptr* is never `NULL`, it's always a previously allocated block. *new_size* may be bigger or smaller than *old_size*.

void free_function (*void *`ptr`, size_t* `size`)   [Function]
>   De-allocate the space pointed to by *ptr*.
>
>   *ptr* is never `NULL`, it's always a previously allocated block of *size* bytes.

A *byte* here means the unit used by the `sizeof` operator.

The *reallocate_function* parameter *old_size* and the *free_function* parameter *size* are passed for convenience, but of course they can be ignored if not needed by an implementation. The default functions using `malloc` and friends for instance don't use them.

No error return is allowed from any of these functions, if they return then they must have performed the specified operation. In particular note that *allocate_function* or *reallocate_function* mustn't return `NULL`.

Getting a different fatal error action is a good use for custom allocation functions, for example giving a graphical dialog rather than the default print to `stderr`. How much is possible when genuinely out of memory is another question though.

There's currently no defined way for the allocation functions to recover from an error such as out of memory, they must terminate program execution. A `longjmp` or throwing a C++ exception will have undefined results. This may change in the future.

GMP may use allocated blocks to hold pointers to other allocated blocks. This will limit the assumptions a conservative garbage collection scheme can make.

Since the default GMP allocation uses `malloc` and friends, those functions will be linked in even if the first thing a program does is an `mp_set_memory_functions`. It's necessary to change the GMP sources if this is a problem.

void **mp_get_memory_functions** ([Function]
        *void *(**alloc_func_ptr*) (*size_t*),
        *void *(**realloc_func_ptr*) (*void *, size_t, size_t*),
        void (**free_func_ptr) (*void *, size_t*))
Get the current allocation functions, storing function pointers to the locations given by the arguments. If an argument is `NULL`, that function pointer is not stored.

For example, to get just the current free function,

```
void (*freefunc) (void *, size_t);

mp_get_memory_functions (NULL, NULL, &freefunc);
```

14 Language Bindings

The following packages and projects offer access to GMP from languages other than C, though perhaps with varying levels of functionality and efficiency.

C++

- GMP C++ class interface, see Chapter 12 [C++ Class Interface], page 80
  Straightforward interface, expression templates to eliminate temporaries.
- ALP `https://www-sop.inria.fr/saga/logiciels/ALP/`
  Linear algebra and polynomials using templates.
- Arithmos `http://cant.ua.ac.be/old/arithmos/`
  Rationals with infinities and square roots.
- CLN `http://www.ginac.de/CLN/`
  High level classes for arithmetic.
- Linbox `http://www.linalg.org/`
  Sparse vectors and matrices.
- NTL `http://www.shoup.net/ntl/`
  A C++ number theory library.

Eiffel

- Eiffelroom `http://www.eiffelroom.org/node/442`

Haskell

- Glasgow Haskell Compiler `https://www.haskell.org/ghc/`

Java

- Kaffe `https://github.com/kaffe/kaffe`

Lisp

- GNU Common Lisp `https://www.gnu.org/software/gcl/gcl.html`
- Librep `http://librep.sourceforge.net/`
- XEmacs (21.5.18 beta and up) `http://www.xemacs.org`
  Optional big integers, rationals and floats using GMP.

M4

- GNU m4 betas `http://www.seindal.dk/rene/gnu/`
  Optionally provides an arbitrary precision `mpeval`.

ML

- MLton compiler `http://mlton.org/`

Objective Caml

- MLGMP `http://opam.ocamlpro.com/pkg/mlgmp.20120224.html`
- Numerix `http://pauillac.inria.fr/~quercia/`
  Optionally using GMP.

Oz

- Mozart `http://mozart.github.io/`

Pascal

- GNU Pascal Compiler `http://www.gnu-pascal.de/`
  GMP unit.

- Numerix `http://pauillac.inria.fr/~quercia/`
  For Free Pascal, optionally using GMP.

Perl

- GMP module, see `demos/perl` in the GMP sources (see Section 3.10 [Demonstration Programs], page 21).
- Math::GMP `http://www.cpan.org/`
  Compatible with Math::BigInt, but not as many functions as the GMP module above.
- Math::BigInt::GMP `http://www.cpan.org/`
  Plug Math::GMP into normal Math::BigInt operations.

Pike

- mpz module in the standard distribution, `http://pike.ida.liu.se/`

Prolog

- SWI Prolog `http://www.swi-prolog.org/`
  Arbitrary precision floats.

Python

- GMPY `https://code.google.com/p/gmpy/`

Ruby

- http://rubygems.org/gems/gmp

Scheme

- GNU Guile `https://www.gnu.org/software/guile/guile.html`
- RScheme `http://www.rscheme.org/`
- STklos `http://www.stklos.net/`

Smalltalk

- GNU Smalltalk `http://www.smalltalk.org/versions/GNUSmalltalk.html`

Other

- Axiom `https://savannah.nongnu.org/projects/axiom`
  Computer algebra using GCL.
- DrGenius `http://drgenius.seul.org/`
  Geometry system and mathematical programming language.
- GiNaC `http://www.ginac.de/`
  C++ computer algebra using CLN.
- GOO `https://www.eecs.berkeley.edu/~jrb/goo/`
  Dynamic object oriented language.
- Maxima `https://www.ma.utexas.edu/users/wfs/maxima.html`
  Macsyma computer algebra using GCL.
- Regina `http://regina.sourceforge.net/`
  Topological calculator.
- Yacas `http://yacas.sourceforge.net`
  Yet another computer algebra system.

15 Algorithms

This chapter is an introduction to some of the algorithms used for various GMP operations. The code is likely to be hard to understand without knowing something about the algorithms.

Some GMP internals are mentioned, but applications that expect to be compatible with future GMP releases should take care to use only the documented functions.

15.1 Multiplication

N×N limb multiplications and squares are done using one of seven algorithms, as the size N increases.

Algorithm	Threshold
Basecase	(none)
Karatsuba	`MUL_TOOM22_THRESHOLD`
Toom-3	`MUL_TOOM33_THRESHOLD`
Toom-4	`MUL_TOOM44_THRESHOLD`
Toom-6.5	`MUL_TOOM6H_THRESHOLD`
Toom-8.5	`MUL_TOOM8H_THRESHOLD`
FFT	`MUL_FFT_THRESHOLD`

Similarly for squaring, with the `SQR` thresholds.

N×M multiplications of operands with different sizes above `MUL_TOOM22_THRESHOLD` are currently done by special Toom-inspired algorithms or directly with FFT, depending on operand size (see Section 15.1.8 [Unbalanced Multiplication], page 99).

15.1.1 Basecase Multiplication

Basecase N×M multiplication is a straightforward rectangular set of cross-products, the same as long multiplication done by hand and for that reason sometimes known as the schoolbook or grammar school method. This is an $O(NM)$ algorithm. See Knuth section 4.3.1 algorithm M (see Appendix B [References], page 125), and the `mpn/generic/mul_basecase.c` code.

Assembly implementations of `mpn_mul_basecase` are essentially the same as the generic C code, but have all the usual assembly tricks and obscurities introduced for speed.

A square can be done in roughly half the time of a multiply, by using the fact that the cross products above and below the diagonal are the same. A triangle of products below the diagonal is formed, doubled (left shift by one bit), and then the products on the diagonal added. This can be seen in `mpn/generic/sqr_basecase.c`. Again the assembly implementations take essentially the same approach.

	u0	u1	u2	u3	u4
u0	d				
u1		d			
u2			d		
u3				d	
u4					d

In practice squaring isn't a full 2× faster than multiplying, it's usually around 1.5×. Less than 1.5× probably indicates `mpn_sqr_basecase` wants improving on that CPU.

On some CPUs `mpn_mul_basecase` can be faster than the generic C `mpn_sqr_basecase` on some small sizes. `SQR_BASECASE_THRESHOLD` is the size at which to use `mpn_sqr_basecase`, this will be zero if that routine should be used always.

15.1.2 Karatsuba Multiplication

The Karatsuba multiplication algorithm is described in Knuth section 4.3.3 part A, and various other textbooks. A brief description is given here.

The inputs x and y are treated as each split into two parts of equal length (or the most significant part one limb shorter if N is odd).

high   low

x_1	x_0
y_1	y_0

Let b be the power of 2 where the split occurs, i.e. if x_0 is k limbs (y_0 the same) then $b = 2^{k*\texttt{mp\_bits\_per\_limb}}$. With that $x = x_1 b + x_0$ and $y = y_1 b + y_0$, and the following holds,

$$xy = (b^2 + b)x_1 y_1 - b(x_1 - x_0)(y_1 - y_0) + (b + 1)x_0 y_0$$

This formula means doing only three multiplies of $(N/2) \times (N/2)$ limbs, whereas a basecase multiply of $N \times N$ limbs is equivalent to four multiplies of $(N/2) \times (N/2)$. The factors $(b^2 + b)$ etc represent the positions where the three products must be added.

high   low

	$x_1 y_1$		$x_0 y_0$	
+		$x_1 y_1$		
+		$x_0 y_0$		
−		$(x_1 - x_0)(y_1 - y_0)$		

The term $(x_1 - x_0)(y_1 - y_0)$ is best calculated as an absolute value, and the sign used to choose to add or subtract. Notice the sum $\text{high}(x_0 y_0) + \text{low}(x_1 y_1)$ occurs twice, so it's possible to do $5k$ limb additions, rather than $6k$, but in GMP extra function call overheads outweigh the saving.

Squaring is similar to multiplying, but with $x = y$ the formula reduces to an equivalent with three squares,

$$x^2 = (b^2 + b)x_1^2 - b(x_1 - x_0)^2 + (b + 1)x_0^2$$

The final result is accumulated from those three squares the same way as for the three multiplies above. The middle term $(x_1 - x_0)^2$ is now always positive.

A similar formula for both multiplying and squaring can be constructed with a middle term $(x_1 + x_0)(y_1 + y_0)$. But those sums can exceed k limbs, leading to more carry handling and additions than the form above.

Karatsuba multiplication is asymptotically an $O(N^{1.585})$ algorithm, the exponent being $\log 3/\log 2$, representing 3 multiplies each 1/2 the size of the inputs. This is a big improvement over the basecase multiply at $O(N^2)$ and the advantage soon overcomes the extra additions Karatsuba performs. `MUL_TOOM22_THRESHOLD` can be as little as 10 limbs. The `SQR` threshold is usually about twice the `MUL`.

The basecase algorithm will take a time of the form $M(N) = aN^2 + bN + c$ and the Karatsuba algorithm $K(N) = 3M(N/2) + dN + e$, which expands to $K(N) = \frac{3}{4}aN^2 + \frac{3}{2}bN + 3c + dN + e$. The factor $\frac{3}{4}$ for a means per-crossproduct speedups in the basecase code will increase the threshold since they benefit $M(N)$ more than $K(N)$. And conversely the $\frac{3}{2}$ for b means linear style speedups of b will increase the threshold since they benefit $K(N)$ more than $M(N)$. The latter can be seen for instance when adding an optimized `mpn_sqr_diagonal` to `mpn_sqr_basecase`. Of course all speedups reduce total time, and in that sense the algorithm thresholds are merely of academic interest.

15.1.3 Toom 3-Way Multiplication

The Karatsuba formula is the simplest case of a general approach to splitting inputs that leads to both Toom and FFT algorithms. A description of Toom can be found in Knuth section 4.3.3, with an example 3-way calculation after Theorem A. The 3-way form used in GMP is described here.

The operands are each considered split into 3 pieces of equal length (or the most significant part 1 or 2 limbs shorter than the other two).

high   low

x_2	x_1	x_0

y_2	y_1	y_0

These parts are treated as the coefficients of two polynomials

$$X(t) = x_2 t^2 + x_1 t + x_0$$
$$Y(t) = y_2 t^2 + y_1 t + y_0$$

Let b equal the power of 2 which is the size of the x_0, x_1, y_0 and y_1 pieces, i.e. if they're k limbs each then $b = 2^{k\,*\,\texttt{mp\_bits\_per\_limb}}$. With this $x = X(b)$ and $y = Y(b)$.

Let a polynomial $W(t) = X(t)Y(t)$ and suppose its coefficients are

$$W(t) = w_4 t^4 + w_3 t^3 + w_2 t^2 + w_1 t + w_0$$

The w_i are going to be determined, and when they are they'll give the final result using $w = W(b)$, since $xy = X(b)Y(b)$. The coefficients will be roughly b^2 each, and the final $W(b)$ will be an addition like,

high   low

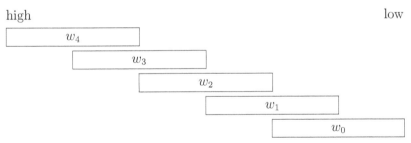

The w_i coefficients could be formed by a simple set of cross products, like $w_4 = x_2 y_2$, $w_3 = x_2 y_1 + x_1 y_2$, $w_2 = x_2 y_0 + x_1 y_1 + x_0 y_2$ etc, but this would need all nine $x_i y_j$ for $i, j = 0, 1, 2$, and would be equivalent merely to a basecase multiply. Instead the following approach is used.

$X(t)$ and $Y(t)$ are evaluated and multiplied at 5 points, giving values of $W(t)$ at those points. In GMP the following points are used,

Point	Value
$t = 0$	$x_0 y_0$, which gives w_0 immediately
$t = 1$	$(x_2 + x_1 + x_0)(y_2 + y_1 + y_0)$

$$
\begin{array}{ll}
t = -1 & (x_2 - x_1 + x_0)(y_2 - y_1 + y_0) \\
t = 2 & (4x_2 + 2x_1 + x_0)(4y_2 + 2y_1 + y_0) \\
t = \infty & x_2 y_2, \text{ which gives } w_4 \text{ immediately}
\end{array}
$$

At $t = -1$ the values can be negative and that's handled using the absolute values and tracking the sign separately. At $t = \infty$ the value is actually $\lim_{t \to \infty} \frac{X(t)Y(t)}{t^4}$, but it's much easier to think of as simply $x_2 y_2$ giving w_4 immediately (much like $x_0 y_0$ at $t = 0$ gives w_0 immediately).

Each of the points substituted into $W(t) = w_4 t^4 + \cdots + w_0$ gives a linear combination of the w_i coefficients, and the value of those combinations has just been calculated.

$$
\begin{array}{rclccccccccccc}
W(0) & = & & & & & & & & & & w_0 \\
W(1) & = & w_4 & + & w_3 & + & w_2 & + & w_1 & + & w_0 \\
W(-1) & = & w_4 & - & w_3 & + & w_2 & - & w_1 & + & w_0 \\
W(2) & = & 16w_4 & + & 8w_3 & + & 4w_2 & + & 2w_1 & + & w_0 \\
W(\infty) & = & w_4
\end{array}
$$

This is a set of five equations in five unknowns, and some elementary linear algebra quickly isolates each w_i. This involves adding or subtracting one $W(t)$ value from another, and a couple of divisions by powers of 2 and one division by 3, the latter using the special `mpn_divexact_by3` (see Section 15.2.5 [Exact Division], page 101).

The conversion of $W(t)$ values to the coefficients is interpolation. A polynomial of degree 4 like $W(t)$ is uniquely determined by values known at 5 different points. The points are arbitrary and can be chosen to make the linear equations come out with a convenient set of steps for quickly isolating the w_i.

Squaring follows the same procedure as multiplication, but there's only one $X(t)$ and it's evaluated at the 5 points, and those values squared to give values of $W(t)$. The interpolation is then identical, and in fact the same `toom_interpolate_5pts` subroutine is used for both squaring and multiplying.

Toom-3 is asymptotically $O(N^{1.465})$, the exponent being $\log 5 / \log 3$, representing 5 recursive multiplies of $1/3$ the original size each. This is an improvement over Karatsuba at $O(N^{1.585})$, though Toom does more work in the evaluation and interpolation and so it only realizes its advantage above a certain size.

Near the crossover between Toom-3 and Karatsuba there's generally a range of sizes where the difference between the two is small. `MUL_TOOM33_THRESHOLD` is a somewhat arbitrary point in that range and successive runs of the tune program can give different values due to small variations in measuring. A graph of time versus size for the two shows the effect, see `tune/README`.

At the fairly small sizes where the Toom-3 thresholds occur it's worth remembering that the asymptotic behaviour for Karatsuba and Toom-3 can't be expected to make accurate predictions, due of course to the big influence of all sorts of overheads, and the fact that only a few recursions of each are being performed. Even at large sizes there's a good chance machine dependent effects like cache architecture will mean actual performance deviates from what might be predicted.

The formula given for the Karatsuba algorithm (see Section 15.1.2 [Karatsuba Multiplication], page 94) has an equivalent for Toom-3 involving only five multiplies, but this would be complicated and unenlightening.

An alternate view of Toom-3 can be found in Zuras (see Appendix B [References], page 125), using a vector to represent the x and y splits and a matrix multiplication for the evaluation and interpolation stages. The matrix inverses are not meant to be actually used, and they have elements with values much greater than in fact arise in the interpolation steps. The diagram shown for the 3-way is attractive, but again doesn't have to be implemented that way and for example with a bit of rearrangement just one division by 6 can be done.

15.1.4 Toom 4-Way Multiplication

Karatsuba and Toom-3 split the operands into 2 and 3 coefficients, respectively. Toom-4 analogously splits the operands into 4 coefficients. Using the notation from the section on Toom-3 multiplication, we form two polynomials:

$$X(t) = x_3 t^3 + x_2 t^2 + x_1 t + x_0$$
$$Y(t) = y_3 t^3 + y_2 t^2 + y_1 t + y_0$$

$X(t)$ and $Y(t)$ are evaluated and multiplied at 7 points, giving values of $W(t)$ at those points. In GMP the following points are used,

Point	Value
$t = 0$	$x_0 y_0$, which gives w_0 immediately
$t = 1/2$	$(x_3 + 2x_2 + 4x_1 + 8x_0)(y_3 + 2y_2 + 4y_1 + 8y_0)$
$t = -1/2$	$(-x_3 + 2x_2 - 4x_1 + 8x_0)(-y_3 + 2y_2 - 4y_1 + 8y_0)$
$t = 1$	$(x_3 + x_2 + x_1 + x_0)(y_3 + y_2 + y_1 + y_0)$
$t = -1$	$(-x_3 + x_2 - x_1 + x_0)(-y_3 + y_2 - y_1 + y_0)$
$t = 2$	$(8x_3 + 4x_2 + 2x_1 + x_0)(8y_3 + 4y_2 + 2y_1 + y_0)$
$t = \infty$	$x_3 y_3$, which gives w_6 immediately

The number of additions and subtractions for Toom-4 is much larger than for Toom-3. But several subexpressions occur multiple times, for example $x_2 + x_0$, occurs for both $t = 1$ and $t = -1$.

Toom-4 is asymptotically $O(N^{1.404})$, the exponent being $\log 7 / \log 4$, representing 7 recursive multiplies of $1/4$ the original size each.

15.1.5 Higher degree Toom'n'half

The Toom algorithms described above (see Section 15.1.3 [Toom 3-Way Multiplication], page 95, see Section 15.1.4 [Toom 4-Way Multiplication], page 97) generalizes to split into an arbitrary number of pieces. In general a split of two equally long operands into r pieces leads to evaluations and pointwise multiplications done at $2r - 1$ points. To fully exploit symmetries it would be better to have a multiple of 4 points, that's why for higher degree Toom'n'half is used.

Toom'n'half means that the existence of one more piece is considered for a single operand. It can be virtual, i.e. zero, or real, when the two operand are not exactly balanced. By choosing an even r, Toom-$r\frac{1}{2}$ requires $2r$ points, a multiple of four.

The four-plets of points include 0, ∞, +1, -1 and $\pm 2^i$, $\pm 2^{-i}$. Each of them giving shortcuts for the evaluation phase and for some steps in the interpolation phase. Further tricks are used to reduce the memory footprint of the whole multiplication algorithm to a memory buffer equanl in size to the result of the product.

Current GMP uses both Toom-6'n'half and Toom-8'n'half.

15.1.6 FFT Multiplication

At large to very large sizes a Fermat style FFT multiplication is used, following Schönhage and Strassen (see Appendix B [References], page 125). Descriptions of FFTs in various forms can be found in many textbooks, for instance Knuth section 4.3.3 part C or Lipson chapter IX. A brief description of the form used in GMP is given here.

The multiplication done is $xy \bmod 2^N + 1$, for a given N. A full product xy is obtained by choosing $N \geq \mathrm{bits}(x) + \mathrm{bits}(y)$ and padding x and y with high zero limbs. The modular product is the native form for the algorithm, so padding to get a full product is unavoidable.

The algorithm follows a split, evaluate, pointwise multiply, interpolate and combine similar to that described above for Karatsuba and Toom-3. A k parameter controls the split, with an FFT-k splitting into 2^k pieces of $M = N/2^k$ bits each. N must be a multiple of $2^k \times$ `mp_bits_per_limb` so the split falls on limb boundaries, avoiding bit shifts in the split and combine stages.

The evaluations, pointwise multiplications, and interpolation, are all done modulo $2^{N'} + 1$ where N' is $2M + k + 3$ rounded up to a multiple of 2^k and of `mp_bits_per_limb`. The results of interpolation will be the following negacyclic convolution of the input pieces, and the choice of N' ensures these sums aren't truncated.

$$w_n = \sum_{\substack{i+j=b2^k+n \\ b=0,1}} (-1)^b x_i y_j$$

The points used for the evaluation are g^i for $i = 0$ to $2^k - 1$ where $g = 2^{2N'/2^k}$. g is a 2^kth root of unity mod $2^{N'} + 1$, which produces necessary cancellations at the interpolation stage, and it's also a power of 2 so the fast Fourier transforms used for the evaluation and interpolation do only shifts, adds and negations.

The pointwise multiplications are done modulo $2^{N'} + 1$ and either recurse into a further FFT or use a plain multiplication (Toom-3, Karatsuba or basecase), whichever is optimal at the size N'. The interpolation is an inverse fast Fourier transform. The resulting set of sums of $x_i y_j$ are added at appropriate offsets to give the final result.

Squaring is the same, but x is the only input so it's one transform at the evaluate stage and the pointwise multiplies are squares. The interpolation is the same.

For a mod $2^N + 1$ product, an FFT-k is an $O(N^{k/(k-1)})$ algorithm, the exponent representing 2^k recursed modular multiplies each $1/2^{k-1}$ the size of the original. Each successive k is an asymptotic improvement, but overheads mean each is only faster at bigger and bigger sizes. In the code, `MUL_FFT_TABLE` and `SQR_FFT_TABLE` are the thresholds where each k is used. Each new k effectively swaps some multiplying for some shifts, adds and overheads.

A mod $2^N + 1$ product can be formed with a normal $N \times N \rightarrow 2N$ bit multiply plus a subtraction, so an FFT and Toom-3 etc can be compared directly. A $k = 4$ FFT at $O(N^{1.333})$ can be expected to be the first faster than Toom-3 at $O(N^{1.465})$. In practice this is what's found, with `MUL_FFT_MODF_THRESHOLD` and `SQR_FFT_MODF_THRESHOLD` being between 300 and 1000 limbs, depending on the CPU. So far it's been found that only very large FFTs recurse into pointwise multiplies above these sizes.

When an FFT is to give a full product, the change of N to $2N$ doesn't alter the theoretical complexity for a given k, but for the purposes of considering where an FFT might be first used it can be assumed that the FFT is recursing into a normal multiply and that on that basis it's doing 2^k recursed multiplies each $1/2^{k-2}$ the size of the inputs, making it $O(N^{k/(k-2)})$. This would mean $k = 7$ at $O(N^{1.4})$ would be the first FFT faster than Toom-3. In practice `MUL_FFT_THRESHOLD` and `SQR_FFT_THRESHOLD` have been found to be in the $k = 8$ range, somewhere between 3000 and 10000 limbs.

The way N is split into 2^k pieces and then $2M + k + 3$ is rounded up to a multiple of 2^k and `mp_bits_per_limb` means that when $2^k \geq$ `mp_bits_per_limb` the effective N is a multiple of 2^{2k-1} bits. The $+k+3$ means some values of N just under such a multiple will be rounded to the next. The complexity calculations above assume that a favourable size is used, meaning one which isn't padded through rounding, and it's also assumed that the extra $+k+3$ bits are negligible at typical FFT sizes.

The practical effect of the 2^{2k-1} constraint is to introduce a step-effect into measured speeds. For example $k = 8$ will round N up to a multiple of 32768 bits, so for a 32-bit limb there'll be 512 limb groups of sizes for which `mpn_mul_n` runs at the same speed. Or for $k = 9$ groups of 2048 limbs, $k = 10$ groups of 8192 limbs, etc. In practice it's been found each k is used at quite small multiples of its size constraint and so the step effect is quite noticeable in a time versus size graph.

The threshold determinations currently measure at the mid-points of size steps, but this is sub-optimal since at the start of a new step it can happen that it's better to go back to the previous k for a while. Something more sophisticated for `MUL_FFT_TABLE` and `SQR_FFT_TABLE` will be needed.

15.1.7 Other Multiplication

The Toom algorithms described above (see Section 15.1.3 [Toom 3-Way Multiplication], page 95, see Section 15.1.4 [Toom 4-Way Multiplication], page 97) generalizes to split into an arbitrary number of pieces, as per Knuth section 4.3.3 algorithm C. This is not currently used. The notes here are merely for interest.

In general a split into $r + 1$ pieces is made, and evaluations and pointwise multiplications done at $2r + 1$ points. A 4-way split does 7 pointwise multiplies, 5-way does 9, etc. Asymptotically an $(r+1)$-way algorithm is $O(N^{log(2r+1)/log(r+1)})$. Only the pointwise multiplications count towards big-O complexity, but the time spent in the evaluate and interpolate stages grows with r and has a significant practical impact, with the asymptotic advantage of each r realized only at bigger and bigger sizes. The overheads grow as $O(Nr)$, whereas in an $r = 2^k$ FFT they grow only as $O(N \log r)$.

Knuth algorithm C evaluates at points $0,1,2,\ldots,2r$, but exercise 4 uses $-r,\ldots,0,\ldots,r$ and the latter saves some small multiplies in the evaluate stage (or rather trades them for additions), and has a further saving of nearly half the interpolate steps. The idea is to separate odd and even final coefficients and then perform algorithm C steps C7 and C8 on them separately. The divisors at step C7 become j^2 and the multipliers at C8 become $2tj - j^2$.

Splitting odd and even parts through positive and negative points can be thought of as using -1 as a square root of unity. If a 4th root of unity was available then a further split and speedup would be possible, but no such root exists for plain integers. Going to complex integers with $i = \sqrt{-1}$ doesn't help, essentially because in Cartesian form it takes three real multiplies to do a complex multiply. The existence of 2^kth roots of unity in a suitable ring or field lets the fast Fourier transform keep splitting and get to $O(N \log r)$.

Floating point FFTs use complex numbers approximating Nth roots of unity. Some processors have special support for such FFTs. But these are not used in GMP since it's very difficult to guarantee an exact result (to some number of bits). An occasional difference of 1 in the last bit might not matter to a typical signal processing algorithm, but is of course of vital importance to GMP.

15.1.8 Unbalanced Multiplication

Multiplication of operands with different sizes, both below `MUL_TOOM22_THRESHOLD` are done with plain schoolbook multiplication (see Section 15.1.1 [Basecase Multiplication], page 93).

For really large operands, we invoke FFT directly.

For operands between these sizes, we use Toom inspired algorithms suggested by Alberto Zanoni and Marco Bodrato. The idea is to split the operands into polynomials of different degree. GMP currently splits the smaller operand onto 2 coefficients, i.e., a polynomial of degree 1, but the larger operand can be split into 2, 3, or 4 coefficients, i.e., a polynomial of degree 1 to 3.

15.2 Division Algorithms

15.2.1 Single Limb Division

N×1 division is implemented using repeated 2×1 divisions from high to low, either with a hardware divide instruction or a multiplication by inverse, whichever is best on a given CPU.

The multiply by inverse follows "Improved division by invariant integers" by Möller and Granlund (see Appendix B [References], page 125) and is implemented as `udiv_qrnnd_preinv` in `gmp-impl.h`. The idea is to have a fixed-point approximation to $1/d$ (see `invert_limb`) and then multiply by the high limb (plus one bit) of the dividend to get a quotient q. With d normalized (high bit set), q is no more than 1 too small. Subtracting qd from the dividend gives a remainder, and reveals whether q or $q-1$ is correct.

The result is a division done with two multiplications and four or five arithmetic operations. On CPUs with low latency multipliers this can be much faster than a hardware divide, though the cost of calculating the inverse at the start may mean it's only better on inputs bigger than say 4 or 5 limbs.

When a divisor must be normalized, either for the generic C `__udiv_qrnnd_c` or the multiply by inverse, the division performed is actually $a2^k$ by $d2^k$ where a is the dividend and k is the power necessary to have the high bit of $d2^k$ set. The bit shifts for the dividend are usually accomplished "on the fly" meaning by extracting the appropriate bits at each step. Done this way the quotient limbs come out aligned ready to store. When only the remainder is wanted, an alternative is to take the dividend limbs unshifted and calculate $r = a \bmod d2^k$ followed by an extra final step $r2^k \bmod d2^k$. This can help on CPUs with poor bit shifts or few registers.

The multiply by inverse can be done two limbs at a time. The calculation is basically the same, but the inverse is two limbs and the divisor treated as if padded with a low zero limb. This means more work, since the inverse will need a 2×2 multiply, but the four 1×1s to do that are independent and can therefore be done partly or wholly in parallel. Likewise for a 2×1 calculating qd. The net effect is to process two limbs with roughly the same two multiplies worth of latency that one limb at a time gives. This extends to 3 or 4 limbs at a time, though the extra work to apply the inverse will almost certainly soon reach the limits of multiplier throughput.

A similar approach in reverse can be taken to process just half a limb at a time if the divisor is only a half limb. In this case the 1×1 multiply for the inverse effectively becomes two $\frac{1}{2} \times 1$ for each limb, which can be a saving on CPUs with a fast half limb multiply, or in fact if the only multiply is a half limb, and especially if it's not pipelined.

15.2.2 Basecase Division

Basecase N×M division is like long division done by hand, but in base $2^{\texttt{mp\_bits\_per\_limb}}$. See Knuth section 4.3.1 algorithm D, and `mpn/generic/sb_divrem_mn.c`.

Briefly stated, while the dividend remains larger than the divisor, a high quotient limb is formed and the N×1 product qd subtracted at the top end of the dividend. With a normalized divisor (most significant bit set), each quotient limb can be formed with a 2×1 division and a 1×1 multiplication plus some subtractions. The 2×1 division is by the high limb of the divisor and is done either with a hardware divide or a multiply by inverse (the same as in Section 15.2.1 [Single Limb Division], page 100) whichever is faster. Such a quotient is sometimes one too big, requiring an addback of the divisor, but that happens rarely.

With Q=N−M being the number of quotient limbs, this is an $O(QM)$ algorithm and will run at a speed similar to a basecase Q×M multiplication, differing in fact only in the extra multiply and divide for each of the Q quotient limbs.

15.2.3 Divide and Conquer Division

For divisors larger than `DC_DIV_QR_THRESHOLD`, division is done by dividing. Or to be precise by a recursive divide and conquer algorithm based on work by Moenck and Borodin, Jebelean, and Burnikel and Ziegler (see Appendix B [References], page 125).

The algorithm consists essentially of recognising that a 2N×N division can be done with the basecase division algorithm (see Section 15.2.2 [Basecase Division], page 100), but using N/2 limbs as a base, not just a single limb. This way the multiplications that arise are (N/2)×(N/2) and can take advantage of Karatsuba and higher multiplication algorithms (see Section 15.1 [Multiplication Algorithms], page 93). The two "digits" of the quotient are formed by recursive N×(N/2) divisions.

If the (N/2)×(N/2) multiplies are done with a basecase multiplication then the work is about the same as a basecase division, but with more function call overheads and with some subtractions separated from the multiplies. These overheads mean that it's only when N/2 is above `MUL_TOOM22_THRESHOLD` that divide and conquer is of use.

`DC_DIV_QR_THRESHOLD` is based on the divisor size N, so it will be somewhere above twice `MUL_TOOM22_THRESHOLD`, but how much above depends on the CPU. An optimized `mpn_mul_basecase` can lower `DC_DIV_QR_THRESHOLD` a little by offering a ready-made advantage over repeated `mpn_submul_1` calls.

Divide and conquer is asymptotically $O(M(N) \log N)$ where $M(N)$ is the time for an N×N multiplication done with FFTs. The actual time is a sum over multiplications of the recursed sizes, as can be seen near the end of section 2.2 of Burnikel and Ziegler. For example, within the Toom-3 range, divide and conquer is $2.63M(N)$. With higher algorithms the $M(N)$ term improves and the multiplier tends to $\log N$. In practice, at moderate to large sizes, a 2N×N division is about 2 to 4 times slower than an N×N multiplication.

15.2.4 Block-Wise Barrett Division

For the largest divisions, a block-wise Barrett division algorithm is used. Here, the divisor is inverted to a precision determined by the relative size of the dividend and divisor. Blocks of quotient limbs are then generated by multiplying blocks from the dividend by the inverse.

Our block-wise algorithm computes a smaller inverse than in the plain Barrett algorithm. For a $2n/n$ division, the inverse will be just $\lceil n/2 \rceil$ limbs.

15.2.5 Exact Division

A so-called exact division is when the dividend is known to be an exact multiple of the divisor. Jebelean's exact division algorithm uses this knowledge to make some significant optimizations (see Appendix B [References], page 125).

The idea can be illustrated in decimal for example with 368154 divided by 543. Because the low digit of the dividend is 4, the low digit of the quotient must be 8. This is arrived at from 4×7 mod 10, using the fact 7 is the modular inverse of 3 (the low digit of the divisor), since 3×7 ≡ 1 mod 10. So 8×543 = 4344 can be subtracted from the dividend leaving 363810. Notice the low digit has become zero.

The procedure is repeated at the second digit, with the next quotient digit 7 (1×7 mod 10), subtracting 7×543 = 3801, leaving 325800. And finally at the third digit with quotient digit 6 (8×7 mod 10), subtracting 6×543 = 3258 leaving 0. So the quotient is 678.

Notice however that the multiplies and subtractions don't need to extend past the low three digits of the dividend, since that's enough to determine the three quotient digits. For the last quotient digit no subtraction is needed at all. On a 2N×N division like this one, only about half the work of a normal basecase division is necessary.

For an N×M exact division producing Q=N−M quotient limbs, the saving over a normal basecase division is in two parts. Firstly, each of the Q quotient limbs needs only one multiply, not a 2×1 divide and multiply. Secondly, the crossproducts are reduced when $Q > M$ to $QM - M(M+1)/2$, or when $Q \leq M$ to $Q(Q-1)/2$. Notice the savings are complementary. If Q is big then many divisions are saved, or if Q is small then the crossproducts reduce to a small number.

The modular inverse used is calculated efficiently by `binvert_limb` in `gmp-impl.h`. This does four multiplies for a 32-bit limb, or six for a 64-bit limb. `tune/modlinv.c` has some alternate implementations that might suit processors better at bit twiddling than multiplying.

The sub-quadratic exact division described by Jebelean in "Exact Division with Karatsuba Complexity" is not currently implemented. It uses a rearrangement similar to the divide and conquer for normal division (see Section 15.2.3 [Divide and Conquer Division], page 101), but operating from low to high. A further possibility not currently implemented is "Bidirectional Exact Integer Division" by Krandick and Jebelean which forms quotient limbs from both the high and low ends of the dividend, and can halve once more the number of crossproducts needed in a 2N×N division.

A special case exact division by 3 exists in `mpn_divexact_by3`, supporting Toom-3 multiplication and `mpq` canonicalizations. It forms quotient digits with a multiply by the modular inverse of 3 (which is `0xAA..AAB`) and uses two comparisons to determine a borrow for the next limb. The multiplications don't need to be on the dependent chain, as long as the effect of the borrows is applied, which can help chips with pipelined multipliers.

15.2.6 Exact Remainder

If the exact division algorithm is done with a full subtraction at each stage and the dividend isn't a multiple of the divisor, then low zero limbs are produced but with a remainder in the high limbs. For dividend a, divisor d, quotient q, and $b = 2^{\texttt{mp-bits-per-limb}}$, this remainder r is of the form

$$a = qd + rb^n$$

n represents the number of zero limbs produced by the subtractions, that being the number of limbs produced for q. r will be in the range $0 \leq r < d$ and can be viewed as a remainder, but one shifted up by a factor of b^n.

Carrying out full subtractions at each stage means the same number of cross products must be done as a normal division, but there's still some single limb divisions saved. When d is a single limb some simplifications arise, providing good speedups on a number of processors.

The functions `mpn_divexact_by3`, `mpn_modexact_1_odd` and the internal `mpn_redc_X` functions differ subtly in how they return r, leading to some negations in the above formula, but all are essentially the same.

Clearly r is zero when a is a multiple of d, and this leads to divisibility or congruence tests which are potentially more efficient than a normal division.

The factor of b^n on r can be ignored in a GCD when d is odd, hence the use of `mpn_modexact_1_odd` by `mpn_gcd_1` and `mpz_kronecker_ui` etc (see Section 15.3 [Greatest Common Divisor Algorithms], page 103).

Montgomery's REDC method for modular multiplications uses operands of the form of xb^{-n} and yb^{-n} and on calculating $(xb^{-n})(yb^{-n})$ uses the factor of b^n in the exact remainder to reach a product in the same form $(xy)b^{-n}$ (see Section 15.4.2 [Modular Powering Algorithm], page 106).

Notice that r generally gives no useful information about the ordinary remainder $a \bmod d$ since $b^n \bmod d$ could be anything. If however $b^n \equiv 1 \bmod d$, then r is the negative of the ordinary remainder. This occurs whenever d is a factor of $b^n - 1$, as for example with 3 in `mpn_divexact_by3`. For a 32 or 64 bit limb other such factors include 5, 17 and 257, but no particular use has been found for this.

15.2.7 Small Quotient Division

An N×M division where the number of quotient limbs Q=N−M is small can be optimized somewhat.

An ordinary basecase division normalizes the divisor by shifting it to make the high bit set, shifting the dividend accordingly, and shifting the remainder back down at the end of the calculation. This is wasteful if only a few quotient limbs are to be formed. Instead a division of just the top 2Q limbs of the dividend by the top Q limbs of the divisor can be used to form a trial quotient. This requires only those limbs normalized, not the whole of the divisor and dividend.

A multiply and subtract then applies the trial quotient to the M−Q unused limbs of the divisor and N−Q dividend limbs (which includes Q limbs remaining from the trial quotient division). The starting trial quotient can be 1 or 2 too big, but all cases of 2 too big and most cases of 1 too big are detected by first comparing the most significant limbs that will arise from the subtraction. An addback is done if the quotient still turns out to be 1 too big.

This whole procedure is essentially the same as one step of the basecase algorithm done in a Q limb base, though with the trial quotient test done only with the high limbs, not an entire Q limb "digit" product. The correctness of this weaker test can be established by following the argument of Knuth section 4.3.1 exercise 20 but with the $v_2 \hat{q} > b\hat{r} + u_2$ condition appropriately relaxed.

15.3 Greatest Common Divisor

15.3.1 Binary GCD

At small sizes GMP uses an $O(N^2)$ binary style GCD. This is described in many textbooks, for example Knuth section 4.5.2 algorithm B. It simply consists of successively reducing odd operands a and b using

$a, b = \mathrm{abs}\,(a - b), \min\,(a, b)$
strip factors of 2 from a

The Euclidean GCD algorithm, as per Knuth algorithms E and A, repeatedly computes the quotient $q = \lfloor a/b \rfloor$ and replaces a, b by $v, u - qv$. The binary algorithm has so far been found to be faster than the Euclidean algorithm everywhere. One reason the binary method does well is that the implied quotient at each step is usually small, so often only one or two subtractions are needed to get the same effect as a division. Quotients 1, 2 and 3 for example occur 67.7% of the time, see Knuth section 4.5.3 Theorem E.

When the implied quotient is large, meaning b is much smaller than a, then a division is worthwhile. This is the basis for the initial $a \bmod b$ reductions in `mpn_gcd` and `mpn_gcd_1` (the latter for both N×1 and 1×1 cases). But after that initial reduction, big quotients occur too rarely to make it worth checking for them.

The final 1×1 GCD in `mpn_gcd_1` is done in the generic C code as described above. For two N-bit operands, the algorithm takes about 0.68 iterations per bit. For optimum performance some attention needs to be paid to the way the factors of 2 are stripped from a.

Firstly it may be noted that in twos complement the number of low zero bits on $a - b$ is the same as $b - a$, so counting or testing can begin on $a - b$ without waiting for $\mathrm{abs}\,(a - b)$ to be determined.

A loop stripping low zero bits tends not to branch predict well, since the condition is data dependent. But on average there's only a few low zeros, so an option is to strip one or two bits arithmetically then loop for more (as done for AMD K6). Or use a lookup table to get a count for several bits then loop for more (as done for AMD K7). An alternative approach is to keep just one of a or b odd and iterate

$$a, b = \mathrm{abs}\,(a - b), \min\,(a, b)$$
$$a = a/2 \text{ if even}$$
$$b = b/2 \text{ if even}$$

This requires about 1.25 iterations per bit, but stripping of a single bit at each step avoids any branching. Repeating the bit strip reduces to about 0.9 iterations per bit, which may be a worthwhile tradeoff.

Generally with the above approaches a speed of perhaps 6 cycles per bit can be achieved, which is still not terribly fast with for instance a 64-bit GCD taking nearly 400 cycles. It's this sort of time which means it's not usually advantageous to combine a set of divisibility tests into a GCD.

Currently, the binary algorithm is used for GCD only when $N < 3$.

15.3.2 Lehmer's algorithm

Lehmer's improvement of the Euclidean algorithms is based on the observation that the initial part of the quotient sequence depends only on the most significant parts of the inputs. The variant of Lehmer's algorithm used in GMP splits off the most significant two limbs, as suggested, e.g., in "A Double-Digit Lehmer-Euclid Algorithm" by Jebelean (see Appendix B [References], page 125). The quotients of two double-limb inputs are collected as a 2 by 2 matrix with single-limb elements. This is done by the function `mpn_hgcd2`. The resulting matrix is applied to the inputs using `mpn_mul_1` and `mpn_submul_1`. Each iteration usually reduces the inputs by almost one limb. In the rare case of a large quotient, no progress can be made by examining just the most significant two limbs, and the quotient is computed using plain division.

The resulting algorithm is asymptotically $O(N^2)$, just as the Euclidean algorithm and the binary algorithm. The quadratic part of the work are the calls to `mpn_mul_1` and `mpn_submul_1`. For small sizes, the linear work is also significant. There are roughly N calls to the `mpn_hgcd2` function. This function uses a couple of important optimizations:

- It uses the same relaxed notion of correctness as `mpn_hgcd` (see next section). This means that when called with the most significant two limbs of two large numbers, the returned matrix does not always correspond exactly to the initial quotient sequence for the two large numbers; the final quotient may sometimes be one off.
- It takes advantage of the fact the quotients are usually small. The division operator is not used, since the corresponding assembler instruction is very slow on most architectures. (This code could probably be improved further, it uses many branches that are unfriendly to prediction).
- It switches from double-limb calculations to single-limb calculations half-way through, when the input numbers have been reduced in size from two limbs to one and a half.

15.3.3 Subquadratic GCD

For inputs larger than `GCD_DC_THRESHOLD`, GCD is computed via the HGCD (Half GCD) function, as a generalization to Lehmer's algorithm.

Let the inputs a, b be of size N limbs each. Put $S = \lfloor N/2 \rfloor + 1$. Then HGCD(a,b) returns a transformation matrix T with non-negative elements, and reduced numbers $(c; d) = T^{-1}(a; b)$. The reduced numbers c, d must be larger than S limbs, while their difference $abs(c - d)$ must fit in S limbs. The matrix elements will also be of size roughly $N/2$.

The HGCD base case uses Lehmer's algorithm, but with the above stop condition that returns reduced numbers and the corresponding transformation matrix half-way through. For inputs larger than `HGCD_THRESHOLD`, HGCD is computed recursively, using the divide and conquer algorithm in "On Schönhage's algorithm and subquadratic integer GCD computation" by Möller (see Appendix B [References], page 125). The recursive algorithm consists of these main steps.

- Call HGCD recursively, on the most significant $N/2$ limbs. Apply the resulting matrix T_1 to the full numbers, reducing them to a size just above $3N/2$.
- Perform a small number of division or subtraction steps to reduce the numbers to size below $3N/2$. This is essential mainly for the unlikely case of large quotients.
- Call HGCD recursively, on the most significant $N/2$ limbs of the reduced numbers. Apply the resulting matrix T_2 to the full numbers, reducing them to a size just above $N/2$.
- Compute $T = T_1 T_2$.
- Perform a small number of division and subtraction steps to satisfy the requirements, and return.

GCD is then implemented as a loop around HGCD, similarly to Lehmer's algorithm. Where Lehmer repeatedly chops off the top two limbs, calls `mpn_hgcd2`, and applies the resulting matrix to the full numbers, the subquadratic GCD chops off the most significant third of the limbs (the proportion is a tuning parameter, and 1/3 seems to be more efficient than, e.g, 1/2), calls `mpn_hgcd`, and applies the resulting matrix. Once the input numbers are reduced to size below `GCD_DC_THRESHOLD`, Lehmer's algorithm is used for the rest of the work.

The asymptotic running time of both HGCD and GCD is $O(M(N) \log N)$, where $M(N)$ is the time for multiplying two N-limb numbers.

15.3.4 Extended GCD

The extended GCD function, or GCDEXT, calculates $\gcd(a, b)$ and also cofactors x and y satisfying $ax + by = \gcd(a, b)$. All the algorithms used for plain GCD are extended to handle this case. The binary algorithm is used only for single-limb GCDEXT. Lehmer's algorithm is used for sizes up to `GCDEXT_DC_THRESHOLD`. Above this threshold, GCDEXT is implemented as a loop around HGCD, but with more book-keeping to keep track of the cofactors. This gives the same asymptotic running time as for GCD and HGCD, $O(M(N) \log N)$

One difference to plain GCD is that while the inputs a and b are reduced as the algorithm proceeds, the cofactors x and y grow in size. This makes the tuning of the chopping-point more difficult. The current code chops off the most significant half of the inputs for the call to HGCD in the first iteration, and the most significant two thirds for the remaining calls. This strategy could surely be improved. Also the stop condition for the loop, where Lehmer's algorithm is invoked once the inputs are reduced below `GCDEXT_DC_THRESHOLD`, could maybe be improved by taking into account the current size of the cofactors.

15.3.5 Jacobi Symbol

[This section is obsolete. The current Jacobi code actually uses a very efficient algorithm.]

`mpz_jacobi` and `mpz_kronecker` are currently implemented with a simple binary algorithm similar to that described for the GCDs (see Section 15.3.1 [Binary GCD], page 103). They're not very fast when both inputs are large. Lehmer's multi-step improvement or a binary based multi-step algorithm is likely to be better.

When one operand fits a single limb, and that includes `mpz_kronecker_ui` and friends, an initial reduction is done with either `mpn_mod_1` or `mpn_modexact_1_odd`, followed by the binary algorithm on a single limb. The binary algorithm is well suited to a single limb, and the whole calculation in this case is quite efficient.

In all the routines sign changes for the result are accumulated using some bit twiddling, avoiding table lookups or conditional jumps.

15.4 Powering Algorithms

15.4.1 Normal Powering

Normal `mpz` or `mpf` powering uses a simple binary algorithm, successively squaring and then multiplying by the base when a 1 bit is seen in the exponent, as per Knuth section 4.6.3. The "left to right" variant described there is used rather than algorithm A, since it's just as easy and can be done with somewhat less temporary memory.

15.4.2 Modular Powering

Modular powering is implemented using a 2^k-ary sliding window algorithm, as per "Handbook of Applied Cryptography" algorithm 14.85 (see Appendix B [References], page 125). k is chosen according to the size of the exponent. Larger exponents use larger values of k, the choice being made to minimize the average number of multiplications that must supplement the squaring.

The modular multiplies and squarings use either a simple division or the REDC method by Montgomery (see Appendix B [References], page 125). REDC is a little faster, essentially saving N single limb divisions in a fashion similar to an exact remainder (see Section 15.2.6 [Exact Remainder], page 102).

15.5 Root Extraction Algorithms

15.5.1 Square Root

Square roots are taken using the "Karatsuba Square Root" algorithm by Paul Zimmermann (see Appendix B [References], page 125).

An input n is split into four parts of k bits each, so with $b = 2^k$ we have $n = a_3b^3 + a_2b^2 + a_1b + a_0$. Part a_3 must be "normalized" so that either the high or second highest bit is set. In GMP, k is kept on a limb boundary and the input is left shifted (by an even number of bits) to normalize.

The square root of the high two parts is taken, by recursive application of the algorithm (bottoming out in a one-limb Newton's method),

$$s', r' = \text{sqrtrem}\,(a_3b + a_2)$$

This is an approximation to the desired root and is extended by a division to give s,r,

$$q, u = \text{divrem}\,(r'b + a_1, 2s')$$
$$s = s'b + q$$
$$r = ub + a_0 - q^2$$

The normalization requirement on a_3 means at this point s is either correct or 1 too big. r is negative in the latter case, so

$$\text{if } r < 0 \text{ then}$$
$$r \leftarrow r + 2s - 1$$
$$s \leftarrow s - 1$$

The algorithm is expressed in a divide and conquer form, but as noted in the paper it can also be viewed as a discrete variant of Newton's method, or as a variation on the schoolboy method (no longer taught) for square roots two digits at a time.

If the remainder r is not required then usually only a few high limbs of r and u need to be calculated to determine whether an adjustment to s is required. This optimization is not currently implemented.

In the Karatsuba multiplication range this algorithm is $O(\frac{3}{2}M(N/2))$, where $M(n)$ is the time to multiply two numbers of n limbs. In the FFT multiplication range this grows to a bound of $O(6M(N/2))$. In practice a factor of about 1.5 to 1.8 is found in the Karatsuba and Toom-3 ranges, growing to 2 or 3 in the FFT range.

The algorithm does all its calculations in integers and the resulting `mpn_sqrtrem` is used for both `mpz_sqrt` and `mpf_sqrt`. The extended precision given by `mpf_sqrt_ui` is obtained by padding with zero limbs.

15.5.2 Nth Root

Integer Nth roots are taken using Newton's method with the following iteration, where A is the input and n is the root to be taken.

$$a_{i+1} = \frac{1}{n}\left(\frac{A}{a_i^{n-1}} + (n-1)a_i\right)$$

The initial approximation a_1 is generated bitwise by successively powering a trial root with or without new 1 bits, aiming to be just above the true root. The iteration converges quadratically when started from a good approximation. When n is large more initial bits are needed to get good convergence. The current implementation is not particularly well optimized.

15.5.3 Perfect Square

A significant fraction of non-squares can be quickly identified by checking whether the input is a quadratic residue modulo small integers.

`mpz_perfect_square_p` first tests the input mod 256, which means just examining the low byte. Only 44 different values occur for squares mod 256, so 82.8% of inputs can be immediately identified as non-squares.

On a 32-bit system similar tests are done mod 9, 5, 7, 13 and 17, for a total 99.25% of inputs identified as non-squares. On a 64-bit system 97 is tested too, for a total 99.62%.

These moduli are chosen because they're factors of $2^{24} - 1$ (or $2^{48} - 1$ for 64-bits), and such a remainder can be quickly taken just using additions (see `mpn_mod_34lsub1`).

When nails are in use moduli are instead selected by the `gen-psqr.c` program and applied with an `mpn_mod_1`. The same $2^{24} - 1$ or $2^{48} - 1$ could be done with nails using some extra bit shifts, but this is not currently implemented.

In any case each modulus is applied to the `mpn_mod_34lsub1` or `mpn_mod_1` remainder and a table lookup identifies non-squares. By using a "modexact" style calculation, and suitably permuted tables, just one multiply each is required, see the code for details. Moduli are also combined to save operations, so long as the lookup tables don't become too big. `gen-psqr.c` does all the pre-calculations.

A square root must still be taken for any value that passes these tests, to verify it's really a square and not one of the small fraction of non-squares that get through (i.e. a pseudo-square to all the tested bases).

Clearly more residue tests could be done, `mpz_perfect_square_p` only uses a compact and efficient set. Big inputs would probably benefit from more residue testing, small inputs might be better off with less. The assumed distribution of squares versus non-squares in the input would affect such considerations.

15.5.4 Perfect Power

Detecting perfect powers is required by some factorization algorithms. Currently `mpz_perfect_power_p` is implemented using repeated Nth root extractions, though naturally only prime roots need to be considered. (See Section 15.5.2 [Nth Root Algorithm], page 107.)

If a prime divisor p with multiplicity e can be found, then only roots which are divisors of e need to be considered, much reducing the work necessary. To this end divisibility by a set of small primes is checked.

15.6 Radix Conversion

Radix conversions are less important than other algorithms. A program dominated by conversions should probably use a different data representation.

15.6.1 Binary to Radix

Conversions from binary to a power-of-2 radix use a simple and fast $O(N)$ bit extraction algorithm.

Conversions from binary to other radices use one of two algorithms. Sizes below `GET_STR_PRECOMPUTE_THRESHOLD` use a basic $O(N^2)$ method. Repeated divisions by b^n are made, where b is the radix and n is the biggest power that fits in a limb. But instead of simply using the remainder r from such divisions, an extra divide step is done to give a fractional limb representing r/b^n. The digits of r can then be extracted using multiplications by b rather than divisions. Special case code is provided for decimal, allowing multiplications by 10 to optimize to shifts and adds.

Above `GET_STR_PRECOMPUTE_THRESHOLD` a sub-quadratic algorithm is used. For an input t, powers b^{n2^i} of the radix are calculated, until a power between t and $\sqrt{t}$ is reached. t is then divided by that largest power, giving a quotient which is the digits above that power, and a remainder which is those below. These two parts are in turn divided by the second highest power, and so on recursively. When a piece has been divided down to less than `GET_STR_DC_THRESHOLD` limbs, the basecase algorithm described above is used.

The advantage of this algorithm is that big divisions can make use of the sub-quadratic divide and conquer division (see Section 15.2.3 [Divide and Conquer Division], page 101), and big divisions tend to have less overheads than lots of separate single limb divisions anyway. But in any case the cost of calculating the powers b^{n2^i} must first be overcome.

`GET_STR_PRECOMPUTE_THRESHOLD` and `GET_STR_DC_THRESHOLD` represent the same basic thing, the point where it becomes worth doing a big division to cut the input in half. `GET_STR_PRECOMPUTE_THRESHOLD` includes the cost of calculating the radix power required, whereas `GET_STR_DC_THRESHOLD` assumes that's already available, which is the case when recursing.

Since the base case produces digits from least to most significant but they want to be stored from most to least, it's necessary to calculate in advance how many digits there will be, or at least be sure not to underestimate that. For GMP the number of input bits is multiplied by `chars_per_bit_exactly` from `mp_bases`, rounding up. The result is either correct or one too big.

Examining some of the high bits of the input could increase the chance of getting the exact number of digits, but an exact result every time would not be practical, since in general the difference between numbers 100... and 99... is only in the last few bits and the work to identify 99... might well be almost as much as a full conversion.

`mpf_get_str` doesn't currently use the algorithm described here, it multiplies or divides by a power of b to move the radix point to the just above the highest non-zero digit (or at worst one above that location), then multiplies by b^n to bring out digits. This is $O(N^2)$ and is certainly not optimal.

The r/b^n scheme described above for using multiplications to bring out digits might be useful for more than a single limb. Some brief experiments with it on the base case when recursing didn't give a noticeable improvement, but perhaps that was only due to the implementation. Something similar would work for the sub-quadratic divisions too, though there would be the cost of calculating a bigger radix power.

Another possible improvement for the sub-quadratic part would be to arrange for radix powers that balanced the sizes of quotient and remainder produced, i.e. the highest power would be an b^{nk} approximately equal to $\sqrt{t}$, not restricted to a 2^i factor. That ought to smooth out a graph of times against sizes, but may or may not be a net speedup.

15.6.2 Radix to Binary

This section needs to be rewritten, it currently describes the algorithms used before GMP 4.3.

Conversions from a power-of-2 radix into binary use a simple and fast $O(N)$ bitwise concatenation algorithm.

Conversions from other radices use one of two algorithms. Sizes below `SET_STR_PRECOMPUTE_THRESHOLD` use a basic $O(N^2)$ method. Groups of n digits are converted to limbs, where n is the biggest power of the base b which will fit in a limb, then those groups are accumulated into the result by multiplying by b^n and adding. This saves multi-precision operations, as per Knuth section 4.4 part E (see Appendix B [References], page 125). Some special case code is provided for decimal, giving the compiler a chance to optimize multiplications by 10.

Above `SET_STR_PRECOMPUTE_THRESHOLD` a sub-quadratic algorithm is used. First groups of n digits are converted into limbs. Then adjacent limbs are combined into limb pairs with $xb^n + y$, where x and y are the limbs. Adjacent limb pairs are combined into quads similarly with $xb^{2n} + y$. This continues until a single block remains, that being the result.

The advantage of this method is that the multiplications for each x are big blocks, allowing Karatsuba and higher algorithms to be used. But the cost of calculating the powers b^{n2^i} must be overcome. `SET_STR_PRECOMPUTE_THRESHOLD` usually ends up quite big, around 5000 digits, and on some processors much bigger still.

`SET_STR_PRECOMPUTE_THRESHOLD` is based on the input digits (and tuned for decimal), though it might be better based on a limb count, so as to be independent of the base. But that sort of count isn't used by the base case and so would need some sort of initial calculation or estimate.

The main reason `SET_STR_PRECOMPUTE_THRESHOLD` is so much bigger than the corresponding `GET_STR_PRECOMPUTE_THRESHOLD` is that `mpn_mul_1` is much faster than `mpn_divrem_1` (often by a factor of 5, or more).

15.7 Other Algorithms

15.7.1 Prime Testing

The primality testing in `mpz_probab_prime_p` (see Section 5.9 [Number Theoretic Functions], page 37) first does some trial division by small factors and then uses the Miller-Rabin probabilistic primality testing algorithm, as described in Knuth section 4.5.4 algorithm P (see Appendix B [References], page 125).

For an odd input n, and with $n = q2^k + 1$ where q is odd, this algorithm selects a random base x and tests whether $x^q \bmod n$ is 1 or -1, or an $x^{q2^j} \bmod n$ is 1, for $1 \le j \le k$. If so then n is probably prime, if not then n is definitely composite.

Any prime n will pass the test, but some composites do too. Such composites are known as strong pseudoprimes to base x. No n is a strong pseudoprime to more than 1/4 of all bases (see Knuth exercise 22), hence with x chosen at random there's no more than a 1/4 chance a "probable prime" will in fact be composite.

In fact strong pseudoprimes are quite rare, making the test much more powerful than this analysis would suggest, but 1/4 is all that's proven for an arbitrary n.

15.7.2 Factorial

Factorials are calculated by a combination of two algorithms. An idea is shared among them: to compute the odd part of the factorial; a final step takes account of the power of 2 term, by shifting.

For small n, the odd factor of $n!$ is computed with the simple observation that it is equal to the product of all positive odd numbers smaller than n times the odd factor of $\lfloor n/2 \rfloor!$, where $\lfloor x \rfloor$ is the integer part of x, and so on recursively. The procedure can be best illustrated with an example,

$$23! = (23.21.19.17.15.13.11.9.7.5.3)(11.9.7.5.3)(5.3)2^{19}$$

Current code collects all the factors in a single list, with a loop and no recursion, and compute the product, with no special care for repeated chunks.

When n is larger, computation pass trough prime sieving. An helper function is used, as suggested by Peter Luschny:

$$\mathrm{msf}(n) = \frac{n!}{\lfloor n/2 \rfloor!^2 \cdot 2^k} = \prod_{p=3}^{n} p^{\mathrm{L}(p,n)}$$

Where p ranges on odd prime numbers. The exponent k is chosen to obtain an odd integer number: k is the number of 1 bits in the binary representation of $\lfloor n/2 \rfloor$. The function $\mathrm{L}(p, n)$ can be defined as zero when p is composite, and, for any prime p, it is computed with:

$$\mathrm{L}(p, n) = \sum_{i>0} \left\lfloor \frac{n}{p^i} \right\rfloor \bmod 2 \le \log_p(n)$$

With this helper function, we are able to compute the odd part of $n!$ using the recursion implied by $n! = \lfloor n/2 \rfloor!^2 \cdot \mathrm{msf}(n) \cdot 2^k$. The recursion stops using the small-n algorithm on some $\lfloor n/2^i \rfloor$.

Both the above algorithms use binary splitting to compute the product of many small factors. At first as many products as possible are accumulated in a single register, generating a list of factors that fit in a machine word. This list is then split into halves, and the product is computed recursively.

Such splitting is more efficient than repeated N×1 multiplies since it forms big multiplies, allowing Karatsuba and higher algorithms to be used. And even below the Karatsuba threshold a big block of work can be more efficient for the basecase algorithm.

15.7.3 Binomial Coefficients

Binomial coefficients $\binom{n}{k}$ are calculated by first arranging $k \leq n/2$ using $\binom{n}{k} = \binom{n}{n-k}$ if necessary, and then evaluating the following product simply from $i = 2$ to $i = k$.

$$\binom{n}{k} = (n - k + 1) \prod_{i=2}^{k} \frac{n - k + i}{i}$$

It's easy to show that each denominator i will divide the product so far, so the exact division algorithm is used (see Section 15.2.5 [Exact Division], page 101).

The numerators $n - k + i$ and denominators i are first accumulated into as many fit a limb, to save multi-precision operations, though for `mpz_bin_ui` this applies only to the divisors, since n is an `mpz_t` and $n - k + i$ in general won't fit in a limb at all.

15.7.4 Fibonacci Numbers

The Fibonacci functions `mpz_fib_ui` and `mpz_fib2_ui` are designed for calculating isolated F_n or F_n, F_{n-1} values efficiently.

For small n, a table of single limb values in `__gmp_fib_table` is used. On a 32-bit limb this goes up to F_{47}, or on a 64-bit limb up to F_{93}. For convenience the table starts at F_{-1}.

Beyond the table, values are generated with a binary powering algorithm, calculating a pair F_n and F_{n-1} working from high to low across the bits of n. The formulas used are

$$F_{2k+1} = 4F_k^2 - F_{k-1}^2 + 2(-1)^k$$
$$F_{2k-1} = F_k^2 + F_{k-1}^2$$
$$F_{2k} = F_{2k+1} - F_{2k-1}$$

At each step, k is the high b bits of n. If the next bit of n is 0 then F_{2k}, F_{2k-1} is used, or if it's a 1 then F_{2k+1}, F_{2k} is used, and the process repeated until all bits of n are incorporated. Notice these formulas require just two squares per bit of n.

It'd be possible to handle the first few n above the single limb table with simple additions, using the defining Fibonacci recurrence $F_{k+1} = F_k + F_{k-1}$, but this is not done since it usually turns out to be faster for only about 10 or 20 values of n, and including a block of code for just those doesn't seem worthwhile. If they really mattered it'd be better to extend the data table.

Using a table avoids lots of calculations on small numbers, and makes small n go fast. A bigger table would make more small n go fast, it's just a question of balancing size against desired speed. For GMP the code is kept compact, with the emphasis primarily on a good powering algorithm.

`mpz_fib2_ui` returns both F_n and F_{n-1}, but `mpz_fib_ui` is only interested in F_n. In this case the last step of the algorithm can become one multiply instead of two squares. One of the following two formulas is used, according as n is odd or even.

$$F_{2k} = F_k(F_k + 2F_{k-1})$$
$$F_{2k+1} = (2F_k + F_{k-1})(2F_k - F_{k-1}) + 2(-1)^k$$

F_{2k+1} here is the same as above, just rearranged to be a multiply. For interest, the $2(-1)^k$ term both here and above can be applied just to the low limb of the calculation, without a carry or borrow into further limbs, which saves some code size. See comments with `mpz_fib_ui` and the internal `mpn_fib2_ui` for how this is done.

15.7.5 Lucas Numbers

`mpz_lucnum2_ui` derives a pair of Lucas numbers from a pair of Fibonacci numbers with the following simple formulas.

$$L_k = F_k + 2F_{k-1}$$
$$L_{k-1} = 2F_k - F_{k-1}$$

`mpz_lucnum_ui` is only interested in L_n, and some work can be saved. Trailing zero bits on n can be handled with a single square each.

$$L_{2k} = L_k^2 - 2(-1)^k$$

And the lowest 1 bit can be handled with one multiply of a pair of Fibonacci numbers, similar to what `mpz_fib_ui` does.

$$L_{2k+1} = 5F_{k-1}(2F_k + F_{k-1}) - 4(-1)^k$$

15.7.6 Random Numbers

For the `urandomb` functions, random numbers are generated simply by concatenating bits produced by the generator. As long as the generator has good randomness properties this will produce well-distributed N bit numbers.

For the `urandomm` functions, random numbers in a range $0 \leq R < N$ are generated by taking values R of $\lceil \log_2 N \rceil$ bits each until one satisfies $R < N$. This will normally require only one or two attempts, but the attempts are limited in case the generator is somehow degenerate and produces only 1 bits or similar.

The Mersenne Twister generator is by Matsumoto and Nishimura (see Appendix B [References], page 125). It has a non-repeating period of $2^{19937} - 1$, which is a Mersenne prime, hence the name of the generator. The state is 624 words of 32-bits each, which is iterated with one XOR and shift for each 32-bit word generated, making the algorithm very fast. Randomness properties are also very good and this is the default algorithm used by GMP.

Linear congruential generators are described in many text books, for instance Knuth volume 2 (see Appendix B [References], page 125). With a modulus M and parameters A and C, an integer state S is iterated by the formula $S \leftarrow AS + C \bmod M$. At each step the new state is a linear function of the previous, mod M, hence the name of the generator.

In GMP only moduli of the form 2^N are supported, and the current implementation is not as well optimized as it could be. Overheads are significant when N is small, and when N is large clearly the multiply at each step will become slow. This is not a big concern, since the Mersenne Twister generator is better in every respect and is therefore recommended for all normal applications.

For both generators the current state can be deduced by observing enough output and applying some linear algebra (over GF(2) in the case of the Mersenne Twister). This generally means raw output is unsuitable for cryptographic applications without further hashing or the like.

15.8 Assembly Coding

The assembly subroutines in GMP are the most significant source of speed at small to moderate sizes. At larger sizes algorithm selection becomes more important, but of course speedups in low level routines will still speed up everything proportionally.

Carry handling and widening multiplies that are important for GMP can't be easily expressed in C. GCC `asm` blocks help a lot and are provided in `longlong.h`, but hand coding low level routines invariably offers a speedup over generic C by a factor of anything from 2 to 10.

15.8.1 Code Organisation

The various `mpn` subdirectories contain machine-dependent code, written in C or assembly. The `mpn/generic` subdirectory contains default code, used when there's no machine-specific version of a particular file.

Each `mpn` subdirectory is for an ISA family. Generally 32-bit and 64-bit variants in a family cannot share code and have separate directories. Within a family further subdirectories may exist for CPU variants.

In each directory a `nails` subdirectory may exist, holding code with nails support for that CPU variant. A `NAILS_SUPPORT` directive in each file indicates the nails values the code handles. Nails code only exists where it's faster, or promises to be faster, than plain code. There's no effort put into nails if they're not going to enhance a given CPU.

15.8.2 Assembly Basics

`mpn_addmul_1` and `mpn_submul_1` are the most important routines for overall GMP performance. All multiplications and divisions come down to repeated calls to these. `mpn_add_n`, `mpn_sub_n`, `mpn_lshift` and `mpn_rshift` are next most important.

On some CPUs assembly versions of the internal functions `mpn_mul_basecase` and `mpn_sqr_basecase` give significant speedups, mainly through avoiding function call overheads. They can also potentially make better use of a wide superscalar processor, as can bigger primitives like `mpn_addmul_2` or `mpn_addmul_4`.

The restrictions on overlaps between sources and destinations (see Chapter 8 [Low-level Functions], page 58) are designed to facilitate a variety of implementations. For example, knowing `mpn_add_n` won't have partly overlapping sources and destination means reading can be done far ahead of writing on superscalar processors, and loops can be vectorized on a vector processor, depending on the carry handling.

15.8.3 Carry Propagation

The problem that presents most challenges in GMP is propagating carries from one limb to the next. In functions like `mpn_addmul_1` and `mpn_add_n`, carries are the only dependencies between limb operations.

On processors with carry flags, a straightforward CISC style `adc` is generally best. AMD K6 `mpn_addmul_1` however is an example of an unusual set of circumstances where a branch works out better.

On RISC processors generally an add and compare for overflow is used. This sort of thing can be seen in `mpn/generic/aors_n.c`. Some carry propagation schemes require 4 instructions, meaning at least 4 cycles per limb, but other schemes may use just 1 or 2. On wide superscalar processors performance may be completely determined by the number of dependent instructions between carry-in and carry-out for each limb.

On vector processors good use can be made of the fact that a carry bit only very rarely propagates more than one limb. When adding a single bit to a limb, there's only a carry out if that limb was `0xFF...FF` which on random data will be only 1 in $2^{\texttt{mp\_bits\_per\_limb}}$. `mpn/cray/add_n.c` is an example of this, it adds all limbs in parallel, adds one set of carry bits in parallel and then only rarely needs to fall through to a loop propagating further carries.

On the x86s, GCC (as of version 2.95.2) doesn't generate particularly good code for the RISC style idioms that are necessary to handle carry bits in C. Often conditional jumps are generated where `adc` or `sbb` forms would be better. And so unfortunately almost any loop involving carry bits needs to be coded in assembly for best results.

15.8.4 Cache Handling

GMP aims to perform well both on operands that fit entirely in L1 cache and those which don't.

Basic routines like `mpn_add_n` or `mpn_lshift` are often used on large operands, so L2 and main memory performance is important for them. `mpn_mul_1` and `mpn_addmul_1` are mostly used for multiply and square basecases, so L1 performance matters most for them, unless assembly versions of `mpn_mul_basecase` and `mpn_sqr_basecase` exist, in which case the remaining uses are mostly for larger operands.

For L2 or main memory operands, memory access times will almost certainly be more than the calculation time. The aim therefore is to maximize memory throughput, by starting a load of the next cache line while processing the contents of the previous one. Clearly this is only possible if the chip has a lock-up free cache or some sort of prefetch instruction. Most current chips have both these features.

Prefetching sources combines well with loop unrolling, since a prefetch can be initiated once per unrolled loop (or more than once if the loop covers more than one cache line).

On CPUs without write-allocate caches, prefetching destinations will ensure individual stores don't go further down the cache hierarchy, limiting bandwidth. Of course for calculations which are slow anyway, like `mpn_divrem_1`, write-throughs might be fine.

The distance ahead to prefetch will be determined by memory latency versus throughput. The aim of course is to have data arriving continuously, at peak throughput. Some CPUs have limits on the number of fetches or prefetches in progress.

If a special prefetch instruction doesn't exist then a plain load can be used, but in that case care must be taken not to attempt to read past the end of an operand, since that might produce a segmentation violation.

Some CPUs or systems have hardware that detects sequential memory accesses and initiates suitable cache movements automatically, making life easy.

15.8.5 Functional Units

When choosing an approach for an assembly loop, consideration is given to what operations can execute simultaneously and what throughput can thereby be achieved. In some cases an algorithm can be tweaked to accommodate available resources.

Loop control will generally require a counter and pointer updates, costing as much as 5 instructions, plus any delays a branch introduces. CPU addressing modes might reduce pointer updates, perhaps by allowing just one updating pointer and others expressed as offsets from it, or on CISC chips with all addressing done with the loop counter as a scaled index.

The final loop control cost can be amortised by processing several limbs in each iteration (see Section 15.8.9 [Assembly Loop Unrolling], page 116). This at least ensures loop control isn't a big fraction the work done.

Memory throughput is always a limit. If perhaps only one load or one store can be done per cycle then 3 cycles/limb will the top speed for "binary" operations like `mpn_add_n`, and any code achieving that is optimal.

Integer resources can be freed up by having the loop counter in a float register, or by pressing the float units into use for some multiplying, perhaps doing every second limb on the float side (see Section 15.8.6 [Assembly Floating Point], page 115).

Float resources can be freed up by doing carry propagation on the integer side, or even by doing integer to float conversions in integers using bit twiddling.

15.8.6 Floating Point

Floating point arithmetic is used in GMP for multiplications on CPUs with poor integer multipliers. It's mostly useful for `mpn_mul_1`, `mpn_addmul_1` and `mpn_submul_1` on 64-bit machines, and `mpn_mul_basecase` on both 32-bit and 64-bit machines.

With IEEE 53-bit double precision floats, integer multiplications producing up to 53 bits will give exact results. Breaking a 64×64 multiplication into eight $16 \times 32 \rightarrow 48$ bit pieces is convenient. With some care though six $21 \times 32 \rightarrow 53$ bit products can be used, if one of the lower two 21-bit pieces also uses the sign bit.

For the `mpn_mul_1` family of functions on a 64-bit machine, the invariant single limb is split at the start, into 3 or 4 pieces. Inside the loop, the bignum operand is split into 32-bit pieces. Fast conversion of these unsigned 32-bit pieces to floating point is highly machine-dependent. In some cases, reading the data into the integer unit, zero-extending to 64-bits, then transferring to the floating point unit back via memory is the only option.

Converting partial products back to 64-bit limbs is usually best done as a signed conversion. Since all values are smaller than 2^{53}, signed and unsigned are the same, but most processors lack unsigned conversions.

Here is a diagram showing 16×32 bit products for an `mpn_mul_1` or `mpn_addmul_1` with a 64-bit limb. The single limb operand V is split into four 16-bit parts. The multi-limb operand U is split in the loop into two 32-bit parts.

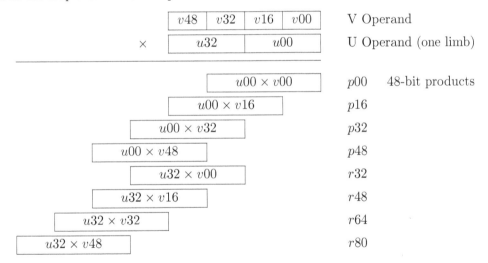

$p32$ and $r32$ can be summed using floating-point addition, and likewise $p48$ and $r48$. $p00$ and $p16$ can be summed with $r64$ and $r80$ from the previous iteration.

For each loop then, four 49-bit quantities are transferred to the integer unit, aligned as follows,

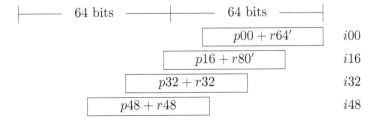

The challenge then is to sum these efficiently and add in a carry limb, generating a low 64-bit result limb and a high 33-bit carry limb ($i48$ extends 33 bits into the high half).

15.8.7 SIMD Instructions

The single-instruction multiple-data support in current microprocessors is aimed at signal processing algorithms where each data point can be treated more or less independently. There's generally not much support for propagating the sort of carries that arise in GMP.

SIMD multiplications of say four 16×16 bit multiplies only do as much work as one 32×32 from GMP's point of view, and need some shifts and adds besides. But of course if say the SIMD form is fully pipelined and uses less instruction decoding then it may still be worthwhile.

On the x86 chips, MMX has so far found a use in `mpn_rshift` and `mpn_lshift`, and is used in a special case for 16-bit multipliers in the P55 `mpn_mul_1`. SSE2 is used for Pentium 4 `mpn_mul_1`, `mpn_addmul_1`, and `mpn_submul_1`.

15.8.8 Software Pipelining

Software pipelining consists of scheduling instructions around the branch point in a loop. For example a loop might issue a load not for use in the present iteration but the next, thereby allowing extra cycles for the data to arrive from memory.

Naturally this is wanted only when doing things like loads or multiplies that take several cycles to complete, and only where a CPU has multiple functional units so that other work can be done in the meantime.

A pipeline with several stages will have a data value in progress at each stage and each loop iteration moves them along one stage. This is like juggling.

If the latency of some instruction is greater than the loop time then it will be necessary to unroll, so one register has a result ready to use while another (or multiple others) are still in progress. (see Section 15.8.9 [Assembly Loop Unrolling], page 116).

15.8.9 Loop Unrolling

Loop unrolling consists of replicating code so that several limbs are processed in each loop. At a minimum this reduces loop overheads by a corresponding factor, but it can also allow better register usage, for example alternately using one register combination and then another. Judicious use of `m4` macros can help avoid lots of duplication in the source code.

Any amount of unrolling can be handled with a loop counter that's decremented by N each time, stopping when the remaining count is less than the further N the loop will process. Or by subtracting N at the start, the termination condition becomes when the counter C is less than 0 (and the count of remaining limbs is $C + N$).

Alternately for a power of 2 unroll the loop count and remainder can be established with a shift and mask. This is convenient if also making a computed jump into the middle of a large loop.

The limbs not a multiple of the unrolling can be handled in various ways, for example

- A simple loop at the end (or the start) to process the excess. Care will be wanted that it isn't too much slower than the unrolled part.

- A set of binary tests, for example after an 8-limb unrolling, test for 4 more limbs to process, then a further 2 more or not, and finally 1 more or not. This will probably take more code space than a simple loop.

- A `switch` statement, providing separate code for each possible excess, for example an 8-limb unrolling would have separate code for 0 remaining, 1 remaining, etc, up to 7 remaining.

This might take a lot of code, but may be the best way to optimize all cases in combination with a deep pipelined loop.

- A computed jump into the middle of the loop, thus making the first iteration handle the excess. This should make times smoothly increase with size, which is attractive, but setups for the jump and adjustments for pointers can be tricky and could become quite difficult in combination with deep pipelining.

15.8.10 Writing Guide

This is a guide to writing software pipelined loops for processing limb vectors in assembly.

First determine the algorithm and which instructions are needed. Code it without unrolling or scheduling, to make sure it works. On a 3-operand CPU try to write each new value to a new register, this will greatly simplify later steps.

Then note for each instruction the functional unit and/or issue port requirements. If an instruction can use either of two units, like U0 or U1 then make a category "U0/U1". Count the total using each unit (or combined unit), and count all instructions.

Figure out from those counts the best possible loop time. The goal will be to find a perfect schedule where instruction latencies are completely hidden. The total instruction count might be the limiting factor, or perhaps a particular functional unit. It might be possible to tweak the instructions to help the limiting factor.

Suppose the loop time is N, then make N issue buckets, with the final loop branch at the end of the last. Now fill the buckets with dummy instructions using the functional units desired. Run this to make sure the intended speed is reached.

Now replace the dummy instructions with the real instructions from the slow but correct loop you started with. The first will typically be a load instruction. Then the instruction using that value is placed in a bucket an appropriate distance down. Run the loop again, to check it still runs at target speed.

Keep placing instructions, frequently measuring the loop. After a few you will need to wrap around from the last bucket back to the top of the loop. If you used the new-register for new-value strategy above then there will be no register conflicts. If not then take care not to clobber something already in use. Changing registers at this time is very error prone.

The loop will overlap two or more of the original loop iterations, and the computation of one vector element result will be started in one iteration of the new loop, and completed one or several iterations later.

The final step is to create feed-in and wind-down code for the loop. A good way to do this is to make a copy (or copies) of the loop at the start and delete those instructions which don't have valid antecedents, and at the end replicate and delete those whose results are unwanted (including any further loads).

The loop will have a minimum number of limbs loaded and processed, so the feed-in code must test if the request size is smaller and skip either to a suitable part of the wind-down or to special code for small sizes.

16 Internals

This chapter is provided only for informational purposes and the various internals described here may change in future GMP releases. Applications expecting to be compatible with future releases should use only the documented interfaces described in previous chapters.

16.1 Integer Internals

`mpz_t` variables represent integers using sign and magnitude, in space dynamically allocated and reallocated. The fields are as follows.

`_mp_size`   The number of limbs, or the negative of that when representing a negative integer. Zero is represented by `_mp_size` set to zero, in which case the `_mp_d` data is unused.

`_mp_d`   A pointer to an array of limbs which is the magnitude. These are stored "little endian" as per the `mpn` functions, so `_mp_d[0]` is the least significant limb and `_mp_d[ABS(_mp_size)-1]` is the most significant. Whenever `_mp_size` is non-zero, the most significant limb is non-zero.

Currently there's always at least one limb allocated, so for instance `mpz_set_ui` never needs to reallocate, and `mpz_get_ui` can fetch `_mp_d[0]` unconditionally (though its value is then only wanted if `_mp_size` is non-zero).

`_mp_alloc`

`_mp_alloc` is the number of limbs currently allocated at `_mp_d`, and naturally `_mp_alloc >= ABS(_mp_size)`. When an `mpz` routine is about to (or might be about to) increase `_mp_size`, it checks `_mp_alloc` to see whether there's enough space, and reallocates if not. `MPZ_REALLOC` is generally used for this.

The various bitwise logical functions like `mpz_and` behave as if negative values were twos complement. But sign and magnitude is always used internally, and necessary adjustments are made during the calculations. Sometimes this isn't pretty, but sign and magnitude are best for other routines.

Some internal temporary variables are setup with `MPZ_TMP_INIT` and these have `_mp_d` space obtained from `TMP_ALLOC` rather than the memory allocation functions. Care is taken to ensure that these are big enough that no reallocation is necessary (since it would have unpredictable consequences).

`_mp_size` and `_mp_alloc` are `int`, although `mp_size_t` is usually a `long`. This is done to make the fields just 32 bits on some 64 bits systems, thereby saving a few bytes of data space but still providing plenty of range.

16.2 Rational Internals

`mpq_t` variables represent rationals using an `mpz_t` numerator and denominator (see Section 16.1 [Integer Internals], page 118).

The canonical form adopted is denominator positive (and non-zero), no common factors between numerator and denominator, and zero uniquely represented as 0/1.

It's believed that casting out common factors at each stage of a calculation is best in general. A GCD is an $O(N^2)$ operation so it's better to do a few small ones immediately than to delay and have to do a big one later. Knowing the numerator and denominator have no common factors can be used for example in `mpq_mul` to make only two cross GCDs necessary, not four.

This general approach to common factors is badly sub-optimal in the presence of simple factorizations or little prospect for cancellation, but GMP has no way to know when this will occur.

As per Section 3.11 [Efficiency], page 22, that's left to applications. The mpq_t framework might still suit, with mpq_numref and mpq_denref for direct access to the numerator and denominator, or of course mpz_t variables can be used directly.

16.3 Float Internals

Efficient calculation is the primary aim of GMP floats and the use of whole limbs and simple rounding facilitates this.

mpf_t floats have a variable precision mantissa and a single machine word signed exponent. The mantissa is represented using sign and magnitude.

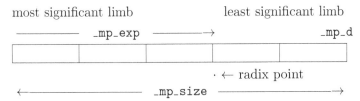

The fields are as follows.

_mp_size   The number of limbs currently in use, or the negative of that when representing a negative value. Zero is represented by _mp_size and _mp_exp both set to zero, and in that case the _mp_d data is unused. (In the future _mp_exp might be undefined when representing zero.)

_mp_prec   The precision of the mantissa, in limbs. In any calculation the aim is to produce _mp_prec limbs of result (the most significant being non-zero).

_mp_d   A pointer to the array of limbs which is the absolute value of the mantissa. These are stored "little endian" as per the mpn functions, so _mp_d[0] is the least significant limb and _mp_d[ABS(_mp_size)-1] the most significant.

           The most significant limb is always non-zero, but there are no other restrictions on its value, in particular the highest 1 bit can be anywhere within the limb.

           _mp_prec+1 limbs are allocated to _mp_d, the extra limb being for convenience (see below). There are no reallocations during a calculation, only in a change of precision with mpf_set_prec.

_mp_exp   The exponent, in limbs, determining the location of the implied radix point. Zero means the radix point is just above the most significant limb. Positive values mean a radix point offset towards the lower limbs and hence a value ≥ 1, as for example in the diagram above. Negative exponents mean a radix point further above the highest limb.

           Naturally the exponent can be any value, it doesn't have to fall within the limbs as the diagram shows, it can be a long way above or a long way below. Limbs other than those included in the {_mp_d,_mp_size} data are treated as zero.

The _mp_size and _mp_prec fields are int, although the mp_size_t type is usually a long. The _mp_exp field is usually long. This is done to make some fields just 32 bits on some 64 bits systems, thereby saving a few bytes of data space but still providing plenty of precision and a very large range.

The following various points should be noted.

Low Zeros   The least significant limbs _mp_d[0] etc can be zero, though such low zeros can always be ignored. Routines likely to produce low zeros check and avoid them to save time in subsequent calculations, but for most routines they're quite unlikely and aren't checked.

Mantissa Size Range

The _mp_size count of limbs in use can be less than _mp_prec if the value can be represented in less. This means low precision values or small integers stored in a high precision mpf_t can still be operated on efficiently.

_mp_size can also be greater than _mp_prec. Firstly a value is allowed to use all of the _mp_prec+1 limbs available at _mp_d, and secondly when mpf_set_prec_raw lowers _mp_prec it leaves _mp_size unchanged and so the size can be arbitrarily bigger than _mp_prec.

Rounding   All rounding is done on limb boundaries. Calculating _mp_prec limbs with the high non-zero will ensure the application requested minimum precision is obtained.

The use of simple "trunc" rounding towards zero is efficient, since there's no need to examine extra limbs and increment or decrement.

Bit Shifts   Since the exponent is in limbs, there are no bit shifts in basic operations like mpf_add and mpf_mul. When differing exponents are encountered all that's needed is to adjust pointers to line up the relevant limbs.

Of course mpf_mul_2exp and mpf_div_2exp will require bit shifts, but the choice is between an exponent in limbs which requires shifts there, or one in bits which requires them almost everywhere else.

Use of _mp_prec+1 Limbs

The extra limb on _mp_d (_mp_prec+1 rather than just _mp_prec) helps when an mpf routine might get a carry from its operation. mpf_add for instance will do an mpn_add of _mp_prec limbs. If there's no carry then that's the result, but if there is a carry then it's stored in the extra limb of space and _mp_size becomes _mp_prec+1.

Whenever _mp_prec+1 limbs are held in a variable, the low limb is not needed for the intended precision, only the _mp_prec high limbs. But zeroing it out or moving the rest down is unnecessary. Subsequent routines reading the value will simply take the high limbs they need, and this will be _mp_prec if their target has that same precision. This is no more than a pointer adjustment, and must be checked anyway since the destination precision can be different from the sources.

Copy functions like mpf_set will retain a full _mp_prec+1 limbs if available. This ensures that a variable which has _mp_size equal to _mp_prec+1 will get its full exact value copied. Strictly speaking this is unnecessary since only _mp_prec limbs are needed for the application's requested precision, but it's considered that an mpf_set from one variable into another of the same precision ought to produce an exact copy.

Application Precisions

__GMPF_BITS_TO_PREC converts an application requested precision to an _mp_prec. The value in bits is rounded up to a whole limb then an extra limb is added since the most significant limb of _mp_d is only non-zero and therefore might contain only one bit.

__GMPF_PREC_TO_BITS does the reverse conversion, and removes the extra limb from _mp_prec before converting to bits. The net effect of reading back with mpf_get_prec is simply the precision rounded up to a multiple of mp_bits_per_limb.

Note that the extra limb added here for the high only being non-zero is in addition to the extra limb allocated to _mp_d. For example with a 32-bit limb, an application request for 250 bits will be rounded up to 8 limbs, then an extra added for the high being only non-zero, giving an _mp_prec of 9. _mp_d then gets 10 limbs allocated.

Reading back with `mpf_get_prec` will take `_mp_prec` subtract 1 limb and multiply by 32, giving 256 bits.

Strictly speaking, the fact the high limb has at least one bit means that a float with, say, 3 limbs of 32-bits each will be holding at least 65 bits, but for the purposes of `mpf_t` it's considered simply to be 64 bits, a nice multiple of the limb size.

16.4 Raw Output Internals

`mpz_out_raw` uses the following format.

size	data bytes

The size is 4 bytes written most significant byte first, being the number of subsequent data bytes, or the twos complement negative of that when a negative integer is represented. The data bytes are the absolute value of the integer, written most significant byte first.

The most significant data byte is always non-zero, so the output is the same on all systems, irrespective of limb size.

In GMP 1, leading zero bytes were written to pad the data bytes to a multiple of the limb size. `mpz_inp_raw` will still accept this, for compatibility.

The use of "big endian" for both the size and data fields is deliberate, it makes the data easy to read in a hex dump of a file. Unfortunately it also means that the limb data must be reversed when reading or writing, so neither a big endian nor little endian system can just read and write `_mp_d`.

16.5 C++ Interface Internals

A system of expression templates is used to ensure something like `a=b+c` turns into a simple call to `mpz_add` etc. For `mpf_class` the scheme also ensures the precision of the final destination is used for any temporaries within a statement like `f=w*x+y*z`. These are important features which a naive implementation cannot provide.

A simplified description of the scheme follows. The true scheme is complicated by the fact that expressions have different return types. For detailed information, refer to the source code.

To perform an operation, say, addition, we first define a "function object" evaluating it,

```
struct __gmp_binary_plus
{
  static void eval(mpf_t f, const mpf_t g, const mpf_t h)
  {
    mpf_add(f, g, h);
  }
};
```

And an "additive expression" object,

```
__gmp_expr<__gmp_binary_expr<mpf_class, mpf_class, __gmp_binary_plus> >
operator+(const mpf_class &f, const mpf_class &g)
{
  return __gmp_expr
    <__gmp_binary_expr<mpf_class, mpf_class, __gmp_binary_plus> >(f, g);
}
```

The seemingly redundant `__gmp_expr<__gmp_binary_expr<...>>` is used to encapsulate any possible kind of expression into a single template type. In fact even `mpf_class` etc are `typedef` specializations of `__gmp_expr`.

Next we define assignment of `__gmp_expr` to `mpf_class`.

```
template <class T>
mpf_class & mpf_class::operator=(const __gmp_expr<T> &expr)
{
  expr.eval(this->get_mpf_t(), this->precision());
  return *this;
}

template <class Op>
void __gmp_expr<__gmp_binary_expr<mpf_class, mpf_class, Op> >::eval
(mpf_t f, mp_bitcnt_t precision)
{
  Op::eval(f, expr.val1.get_mpf_t(), expr.val2.get_mpf_t());
}
```

where `expr.val1` and `expr.val2` are references to the expression's operands (here `expr` is the `__gmp_binary_expr` stored within the `__gmp_expr`).

This way, the expression is actually evaluated only at the time of assignment, when the required precision (that of `f`) is known. Furthermore the target `mpf_t` is now available, thus we can call `mpf_add` directly with `f` as the output argument.

Compound expressions are handled by defining operators taking subexpressions as their arguments, like this:

```
template <class T, class U>
__gmp_expr
<__gmp_binary_expr<__gmp_expr<T>, __gmp_expr<U>, __gmp_binary_plus> >
operator+(const __gmp_expr<T> &expr1, const __gmp_expr<U> &expr2)
{
  return __gmp_expr
    <__gmp_binary_expr<__gmp_expr<T>, __gmp_expr<U>, __gmp_binary_plus> >
    (expr1, expr2);
}
```

And the corresponding specializations of `__gmp_expr::eval`:

```
template <class T, class U, class Op>
void __gmp_expr
<__gmp_binary_expr<__gmp_expr<T>, __gmp_expr<U>, Op> >::eval
(mpf_t f, mp_bitcnt_t precision)
{
  // declare two temporaries
  mpf_class temp1(expr.val1, precision), temp2(expr.val2, precision);
  Op::eval(f, temp1.get_mpf_t(), temp2.get_mpf_t());
}
```

The expression is thus recursively evaluated to any level of complexity and all subexpressions are evaluated to the precision of `f`.

Appendix A Contributors

Torbjörn Granlund wrote the original GMP library and is still the main developer. Code not explicitly attributed to others, was contributed by Torbjörn. Several other individuals and organizations have contributed GMP. Here is a list in chronological order on first contribution:

Gunnar Sjödin and Hans Riesel helped with mathematical problems in early versions of the library.

Richard Stallman helped with the interface design and revised the first version of this manual.

Brian Beuning and Doug Lea helped with testing of early versions of the library and made creative suggestions.

John Amanatides of York University in Canada contributed the function `mpz_probab_prime_p`.

Paul Zimmermann wrote the REDC-based mpz_powm code, the Schönhage-Strassen FFT multiply code, and the Karatsuba square root code. He also improved the Toom3 code for GMP 4.2. Paul sparked the development of GMP 2, with his comparisons between bignum packages. The ECMNET project Paul is organizing was a driving force behind many of the optimizations in GMP 3. Paul also wrote the new GMP 4.3 nth root code (with Torbjörn).

Ken Weber (Kent State University, Universidade Federal do Rio Grande do Sul) contributed now defunct versions of `mpz_gcd`, `mpz_divexact`, `mpn_gcd`, and `mpn_bdivmod`, partially supported by CNPq (Brazil) grant 301314194-2.

Per Bothner of Cygnus Support helped to set up GMP to use Cygnus' configure. He has also made valuable suggestions and tested numerous intermediary releases.

Joachim Hollman was involved in the design of the `mpf` interface, and in the `mpz` design revisions for version 2.

Bennet Yee contributed the initial versions of `mpz_jacobi` and `mpz_legendre`.

Andreas Schwab contributed the files `mpn/m68k/lshift.S` and `mpn/m68k/rshift.S` (now in `.asm` form).

Robert Harley of Inria, France and David Seal of ARM, England, suggested clever improvements for population count. Robert also wrote highly optimized Karatsuba and 3-way Toom multiplication functions for GMP 3, and contributed the ARM assembly code.

Torsten Ekedahl of the Mathematical department of Stockholm University provided significant inspiration during several phases of the GMP development. His mathematical expertise helped improve several algorithms.

Linus Nordberg wrote the new configure system based on autoconf and implemented the new random functions.

Kevin Ryde worked on a large number of things: optimized x86 code, m4 asm macros, parameter tuning, speed measuring, the configure system, function inlining, divisibility tests, bit scanning, Jacobi symbols, Fibonacci and Lucas number functions, printf and scanf functions, perl interface, demo expression parser, the algorithms chapter in the manual, `gmpasm-mode.el`, and various miscellaneous improvements elsewhere.

Kent Boortz made the Mac OS 9 port.

Steve Root helped write the optimized alpha 21264 assembly code.

Gerardo Ballabio wrote the `gmpxx.h` C++ class interface and the C++ `istream` input routines.

Jason Moxham rewrote `mpz_fac_ui`.

Pedro Gimeno implemented the Mersenne Twister and made other random number improvements.

Niels Möller wrote the sub-quadratic GCD, extended GCD and jacobi code, the quadratic Hensel division code, and (with Torbjörn) the new divide and conquer division code for GMP 4.3. Niels also helped implement the new Toom multiply code for GMP 4.3 and implemented helper functions to simplify Toom evaluations for GMP 5.0. He wrote the original version of mpn_mulmod_bnm1, and he is the main author of the mini-gmp package used for gmp bootstrapping.

Alberto Zanoni and Marco Bodrato suggested the unbalanced multiply strategy, and found the optimal strategies for evaluation and interpolation in Toom multiplication.

Marco Bodrato helped implement the new Toom multiply code for GMP 4.3 and implemented most of the new Toom multiply and squaring code for 5.0. He is the main author of the current mpn_mulmod_bnm1 and mpn_mullo_n. Marco also wrote the functions mpn_invert and mpn_invertappr. He is the author of the current combinatorial functions: binomial, factorial, multifactorial, primorial.

David Harvey suggested the internal function `mpn_bdiv_dbm1`, implementing division relevant to Toom multiplication. He also worked on fast assembly sequences, in particular on a fast AMD64 `mpn_mul_basecase`. He wrote the internal middle product functions `mpn_mulmid_basecase`, `mpn_toom42_mulmid`, `mpn_mulmid_n` and related helper routines.

Martin Boij wrote `mpn_perfect_power_p`.

Marc Glisse improved `gmpxx.h`: use fewer temporaries (faster), specializations of `numeric_limits` and `common_type`, C++11 features (move constructors, explicit bool conversion, UDL), make the conversion from `mpq_class` to `mpz_class` explicit, optimize operations where one argument is a small compile-time constant, replace some heap allocations by stack allocations. He also fixed the eofbit handling of C++ streams, and removed one division from `mpq/aors.c`.

David S Miller wrote assembly code for SPARC T3 and T4.

Mark Sofroniou cleaned up the types of mul_fft.c, letting it work for huge operands.

Ulrich Weigand ported GMP to the powerpc64le ABI.

(This list is chronological, not ordered after significance. If you have contributed to GMP but are not listed above, please tell `gmp-devel@gmplib.org` about the omission!)

The development of floating point functions of GNU MP 2, were supported in part by the ESPRIT-BRA (Basic Research Activities) 6846 project POSSO (POlynomial System SOlving).

The development of GMP 2, 3, and 4.0 was supported in part by the IDA Center for Computing Sciences.

The development of GMP 4.3, 5.0, and 5.1 was supported in part by the Swedish Foundation for Strategic Research.

Thanks go to Hans Thorsen for donating an SGI system for the GMP test system environment.

Appendix B References

B.1 Books

- Jonathan M. Borwein and Peter B. Borwein, "Pi and the AGM: A Study in Analytic Number Theory and Computational Complexity", Wiley, 1998.

- Richard Crandall and Carl Pomerance, "Prime Numbers: A Computational Perspective", 2nd edition, Springer-Verlag, 2005.
  `http://www.math.dartmouth.edu/~carlp/`

- Henri Cohen, "A Course in Computational Algebraic Number Theory", Graduate Texts in Mathematics number 138, Springer-Verlag, 1993.
  `http://www.math.u-bordeaux.fr/~cohen/`

- Donald E. Knuth, "The Art of Computer Programming", volume 2, "Seminumerical Algorithms", 3rd edition, Addison-Wesley, 1998.
  `http://www-cs-faculty.stanford.edu/~knuth/taocp.html`

- John D. Lipson, "Elements of Algebra and Algebraic Computing", The Benjamin Cummings Publishing Company Inc, 1981.

- Alfred J. Menezes, Paul C. van Oorschot and Scott A. Vanstone, "Handbook of Applied Cryptography", `http://www.cacr.math.uwaterloo.ca/hac/`

- Richard M. Stallman and the GCC Developer Community, "Using the GNU Compiler Collection", Free Software Foundation, 2008, available online `https://gcc.gnu.org/onlinedocs/`, and in the GCC package `https://ftp.gnu.org/gnu/gcc/`

B.2 Papers

- Yves Bertot, Nicolas Magaud and Paul Zimmermann, "A Proof of GMP Square Root", Journal of Automated Reasoning, volume 29, 2002, pp. 225-252. Also available online as INRIA Research Report 4475, June 2002, `http://hal.inria.fr/docs/00/07/21/13/PDF/RR-4475.pdf`

- Christoph Burnikel and Joachim Ziegler, "Fast Recursive Division", Max-Planck-Institut fuer Informatik Research Report MPI-I-98-1-022,
  `http://data.mpi-sb.mpg.de/internet/reports.nsf/NumberView/1998-1-022`

- Torbjörn Granlund and Peter L. Montgomery, "Division by Invariant Integers using Multiplication", in Proceedings of the SIGPLAN PLDI'94 Conference, June 1994. Also available `https://gmplib.org/~tege/divcnst-pldi94.pdf`.

- Niels Möller and Torbjörn Granlund, "Improved division by invariant integers", IEEE Transactions on Computers, 11 June 2010. `https://gmplib.org/~tege/division-paper.pdf`

- Torbjörn Granlund and Niels Möller, "Division of integers large and small", to appear.

- Tudor Jebelean, "An algorithm for exact division", Journal of Symbolic Computation, volume 15, 1993, pp. 169-180. Research report version available
  `ftp://ftp.risc.uni-linz.ac.at/pub/techreports/1992/92-35.ps.gz`

- Tudor Jebelean, "Exact Division with Karatsuba Complexity - Extended Abstract", RISC-Linz technical report 96-31,
  `ftp://ftp.risc.uni-linz.ac.at/pub/techreports/1996/96-31.ps.gz`

- Tudor Jebelean, "Practical Integer Division with Karatsuba Complexity", ISSAC 97, pp. 339-341. Technical report available
  `ftp://ftp.risc.uni-linz.ac.at/pub/techreports/1996/96-29.ps.gz`

- Tudor Jebelean, "A Generalization of the Binary GCD Algorithm", ISSAC 93, pp. 111-116. Technical report version available
  `ftp://ftp.risc.uni-linz.ac.at/pub/techreports/1993/93-01.ps.gz`

- Tudor Jebelean, "A Double-Digit Lehmer-Euclid Algorithm for Finding the GCD of Long Integers", Journal of Symbolic Computation, volume 19, 1995, pp. 145-157. Technical report version also available
  `ftp://ftp.risc.uni-linz.ac.at/pub/techreports/1992/92-69.ps.gz`

- Werner Krandick and Tudor Jebelean, "Bidirectional Exact Integer Division", Journal of Symbolic Computation, volume 21, 1996, pp. 441-455. Early technical report version also available `ftp://ftp.risc.uni-linz.ac.at/pub/techreports/1994/94-50.ps.gz`

- Makoto Matsumoto and Takuji Nishimura, "Mersenne Twister: A 623-dimensionally equidistributed uniform pseudorandom number generator", ACM Transactions on Modelling and Computer Simulation, volume 8, January 1998, pp. 3-30. Available online
  `http://www.math.sci.hiroshima-u.ac.jp/~m-mat/MT/ARTICLES/mt.ps.gz` (or .pdf)

- R. Moenck and A. Borodin, "Fast Modular Transforms via Division", Proceedings of the 13th Annual IEEE Symposium on Switching and Automata Theory, October 1972, pp. 90-96. Reprinted as "Fast Modular Transforms", Journal of Computer and System Sciences, volume 8, number 3, June 1974, pp. 366-386.

- Niels Möller, "On Schönhage's algorithm and subquadratic integer GCD computation", in Mathematics of Computation, volume 77, January 2008, pp. 589-607.

- Peter L. Montgomery, "Modular Multiplication Without Trial Division", in Mathematics of Computation, volume 44, number 170, April 1985.

- Arnold Schönhage and Volker Strassen, "Schnelle Multiplikation grosser Zahlen", Computing 7, 1971, pp. 281-292.

- Kenneth Weber, "The accelerated integer GCD algorithm", ACM Transactions on Mathematical Software, volume 21, number 1, March 1995, pp. 111-122.

- Paul Zimmermann, "Karatsuba Square Root", INRIA Research Report 3805, November 1999, `http://hal.inria.fr/inria-00072854/PDF/RR-3805.pdf`

- Paul Zimmermann, "A Proof of GMP Fast Division and Square Root Implementations",
  `http://www.loria.fr/~zimmerma/papers/proof-div-sqrt.ps.gz`

- Dan Zuras, "On Squaring and Multiplying Large Integers", ARITH-11: IEEE Symposium on Computer Arithmetic, 1993, pp. 260 to 271. Reprinted as "More on Multiplying and Squaring Large Integers", IEEE Transactions on Computers, volume 43, number 8, August 1994, pp. 899-908.

Appendix C GNU Free Documentation License

Version 1.3, 3 November 2008

Copyright © 2000-2002, 2007, 2008 Free Software Foundation, Inc.
http://fsf.org/

Everyone is permitted to copy and distribute verbatim copies
of this license document, but changing it is not allowed.

0. PREAMBLE

The purpose of this License is to make a manual, textbook, or other functional and useful document *free* in the sense of freedom: to assure everyone the effective freedom to copy and redistribute it, with or without modifying it, either commercially or noncommercially. Secondarily, this License preserves for the author and publisher a way to get credit for their work, while not being considered responsible for modifications made by others.

This License is a kind of "copyleft", which means that derivative works of the document must themselves be free in the same sense. It complements the GNU General Public License, which is a copyleft license designed for free software.

We have designed this License in order to use it for manuals for free software, because free software needs free documentation: a free program should come with manuals providing the same freedoms that the software does. But this License is not limited to software manuals; it can be used for any textual work, regardless of subject matter or whether it is published as a printed book. We recommend this License principally for works whose purpose is instruction or reference.

1. APPLICABILITY AND DEFINITIONS

This License applies to any manual or other work, in any medium, that contains a notice placed by the copyright holder saying it can be distributed under the terms of this License. Such a notice grants a world-wide, royalty-free license, unlimited in duration, to use that work under the conditions stated herein. The "Document", below, refers to any such manual or work. Any member of the public is a licensee, and is addressed as "you". You accept the license if you copy, modify or distribute the work in a way requiring permission under copyright law.

A "Modified Version" of the Document means any work containing the Document or a portion of it, either copied verbatim, or with modifications and/or translated into another language.

A "Secondary Section" is a named appendix or a front-matter section of the Document that deals exclusively with the relationship of the publishers or authors of the Document to the Document's overall subject (or to related matters) and contains nothing that could fall directly within that overall subject. (Thus, if the Document is in part a textbook of mathematics, a Secondary Section may not explain any mathematics.) The relationship could be a matter of historical connection with the subject or with related matters, or of legal, commercial, philosophical, ethical or political position regarding them.

The "Invariant Sections" are certain Secondary Sections whose titles are designated, as being those of Invariant Sections, in the notice that says that the Document is released under this License. If a section does not fit the above definition of Secondary then it is not allowed to be designated as Invariant. The Document may contain zero Invariant Sections. If the Document does not identify any Invariant Sections then there are none.

The "Cover Texts" are certain short passages of text that are listed, as Front-Cover Texts or Back-Cover Texts, in the notice that says that the Document is released under this License. A Front-Cover Text may be at most 5 words, and a Back-Cover Text may be at most 25 words.

A "Transparent" copy of the Document means a machine-readable copy, represented in a format whose specification is available to the general public, that is suitable for revising the document straightforwardly with generic text editors or (for images composed of pixels) generic paint programs or (for drawings) some widely available drawing editor, and that is suitable for input to text formatters or for automatic translation to a variety of formats suitable for input to text formatters. A copy made in an otherwise Transparent file format whose markup, or absence of markup, has been arranged to thwart or discourage subsequent modification by readers is not Transparent. An image format is not Transparent if used for any substantial amount of text. A copy that is not "Transparent" is called "Opaque".

Examples of suitable formats for Transparent copies include plain ASCII without markup, Texinfo input format, LaTeX input format, SGML or XML using a publicly available DTD, and standard-conforming simple HTML, PostScript or PDF designed for human modification. Examples of transparent image formats include PNG, XCF and JPG. Opaque formats include proprietary formats that can be read and edited only by proprietary word processors, SGML or XML for which the DTD and/or processing tools are not generally available, and the machine-generated HTML, PostScript or PDF produced by some word processors for output purposes only.

The "Title Page" means, for a printed book, the title page itself, plus such following pages as are needed to hold, legibly, the material this License requires to appear in the title page. For works in formats which do not have any title page as such, "Title Page" means the text near the most prominent appearance of the work's title, preceding the beginning of the body of the text.

The "publisher" means any person or entity that distributes copies of the Document to the public.

A section "Entitled XYZ" means a named subunit of the Document whose title either is precisely XYZ or contains XYZ in parentheses following text that translates XYZ in another language. (Here XYZ stands for a specific section name mentioned below, such as "Acknowledgements", "Dedications", "Endorsements", or "History".) To "Preserve the Title" of such a section when you modify the Document means that it remains a section "Entitled XYZ" according to this definition.

The Document may include Warranty Disclaimers next to the notice which states that this License applies to the Document. These Warranty Disclaimers are considered to be included by reference in this License, but only as regards disclaiming warranties: any other implication that these Warranty Disclaimers may have is void and has no effect on the meaning of this License.

2. VERBATIM COPYING

You may copy and distribute the Document in any medium, either commercially or noncommercially, provided that this License, the copyright notices, and the license notice saying this License applies to the Document are reproduced in all copies, and that you add no other conditions whatsoever to those of this License. You may not use technical measures to obstruct or control the reading or further copying of the copies you make or distribute. However, you may accept compensation in exchange for copies. If you distribute a large enough number of copies you must also follow the conditions in section 3.

You may also lend copies, under the same conditions stated above, and you may publicly display copies.

3. COPYING IN QUANTITY

If you publish printed copies (or copies in media that commonly have printed covers) of the Document, numbering more than 100, and the Document's license notice requires Cover Texts, you must enclose the copies in covers that carry, clearly and legibly, all these Cover Texts: Front-Cover Texts on the front cover, and Back-Cover Texts on the back cover. Both covers must also clearly and legibly identify you as the publisher of these copies. The front cover must present the full title with all words of the title equally prominent and visible. You may add other material on the covers in addition. Copying with changes limited to the covers, as long as they preserve the title of the Document and satisfy these conditions, can be treated as verbatim copying in other respects.

If the required texts for either cover are too voluminous to fit legibly, you should put the first ones listed (as many as fit reasonably) on the actual cover, and continue the rest onto adjacent pages.

If you publish or distribute Opaque copies of the Document numbering more than 100, you must either include a machine-readable Transparent copy along with each Opaque copy, or state in or with each Opaque copy a computer-network location from which the general network-using public has access to download using public-standard network protocols a complete Transparent copy of the Document, free of added material. If you use the latter option, you must take reasonably prudent steps, when you begin distribution of Opaque copies in quantity, to ensure that this Transparent copy will remain thus accessible at the stated location until at least one year after the last time you distribute an Opaque copy (directly or through your agents or retailers) of that edition to the public.

It is requested, but not required, that you contact the authors of the Document well before redistributing any large number of copies, to give them a chance to provide you with an updated version of the Document.

4. MODIFICATIONS

You may copy and distribute a Modified Version of the Document under the conditions of sections 2 and 3 above, provided that you release the Modified Version under precisely this License, with the Modified Version filling the role of the Document, thus licensing distribution and modification of the Modified Version to whoever possesses a copy of it. In addition, you must do these things in the Modified Version:

A. Use in the Title Page (and on the covers, if any) a title distinct from that of the Document, and from those of previous versions (which should, if there were any, be listed in the History section of the Document). You may use the same title as a previous version if the original publisher of that version gives permission.

B. List on the Title Page, as authors, one or more persons or entities responsible for authorship of the modifications in the Modified Version, together with at least five of the principal authors of the Document (all of its principal authors, if it has fewer than five), unless they release you from this requirement.

C. State on the Title page the name of the publisher of the Modified Version, as the publisher.

D. Preserve all the copyright notices of the Document.

E. Add an appropriate copyright notice for your modifications adjacent to the other copyright notices.

F. Include, immediately after the copyright notices, a license notice giving the public permission to use the Modified Version under the terms of this License, in the form shown in the Addendum below.

G. Preserve in that license notice the full lists of Invariant Sections and required Cover Texts given in the Document's license notice.

H. Include an unaltered copy of this License.

I. Preserve the section Entitled "History", Preserve its Title, and add to it an item stating at least the title, year, new authors, and publisher of the Modified Version as given on the Title Page. If there is no section Entitled "History" in the Document, create one stating the title, year, authors, and publisher of the Document as given on its

Title Page, then add an item describing the Modified Version as stated in the previous sentence.

J. Preserve the network location, if any, given in the Document for public access to a Transparent copy of the Document, and likewise the network locations given in the Document for previous versions it was based on. These may be placed in the "History" section. You may omit a network location for a work that was published at least four years before the Document itself, or if the original publisher of the version it refers to gives permission.

K. For any section Entitled "Acknowledgements" or "Dedications", Preserve the Title of the section, and preserve in the section all the substance and tone of each of the contributor acknowledgements and/or dedications given therein.

L. Preserve all the Invariant Sections of the Document, unaltered in their text and in their titles. Section numbers or the equivalent are not considered part of the section titles.

M. Delete any section Entitled "Endorsements". Such a section may not be included in the Modified Version.

N. Do not retitle any existing section to be Entitled "Endorsements" or to conflict in title with any Invariant Section.

O. Preserve any Warranty Disclaimers.

If the Modified Version includes new front-matter sections or appendices that qualify as Secondary Sections and contain no material copied from the Document, you may at your option designate some or all of these sections as invariant. To do this, add their titles to the list of Invariant Sections in the Modified Version's license notice. These titles must be distinct from any other section titles.

You may add a section Entitled "Endorsements", provided it contains nothing but endorsements of your Modified Version by various parties—for example, statements of peer review or that the text has been approved by an organization as the authoritative definition of a standard.

You may add a passage of up to five words as a Front-Cover Text, and a passage of up to 25 words as a Back-Cover Text, to the end of the list of Cover Texts in the Modified Version. Only one passage of Front-Cover Text and one of Back-Cover Text may be added by (or through arrangements made by) any one entity. If the Document already includes a cover text for the same cover, previously added by you or by arrangement made by the same entity you are acting on behalf of, you may not add another; but you may replace the old one, on explicit permission from the previous publisher that added the old one.

The author(s) and publisher(s) of the Document do not by this License give permission to use their names for publicity for or to assert or imply endorsement of any Modified Version.

5. COMBINING DOCUMENTS

You may combine the Document with other documents released under this License, under the terms defined in section 4 above for modified versions, provided that you include in the combination all of the Invariant Sections of all of the original documents, unmodified, and list them all as Invariant Sections of your combined work in its license notice, and that you preserve all their Warranty Disclaimers.

The combined work need only contain one copy of this License, and multiple identical Invariant Sections may be replaced with a single copy. If there are multiple Invariant Sections with the same name but different contents, make the title of each such section unique by adding at the end of it, in parentheses, the name of the original author or publisher of that section if known, or else a unique number. Make the same adjustment to the section titles in the list of Invariant Sections in the license notice of the combined work.

In the combination, you must combine any sections Entitled "History" in the various original documents, forming one section Entitled "History"; likewise combine any sections Entitled

"Acknowledgements", and any sections Entitled "Dedications". You must delete all sections Entitled "Endorsements."

6. COLLECTIONS OF DOCUMENTS

You may make a collection consisting of the Document and other documents released under this License, and replace the individual copies of this License in the various documents with a single copy that is included in the collection, provided that you follow the rules of this License for verbatim copying of each of the documents in all other respects.

You may extract a single document from such a collection, and distribute it individually under this License, provided you insert a copy of this License into the extracted document, and follow this License in all other respects regarding verbatim copying of that document.

7. AGGREGATION WITH INDEPENDENT WORKS

A compilation of the Document or its derivatives with other separate and independent documents or works, in or on a volume of a storage or distribution medium, is called an "aggregate" if the copyright resulting from the compilation is not used to limit the legal rights of the compilation's users beyond what the individual works permit. When the Document is included in an aggregate, this License does not apply to the other works in the aggregate which are not themselves derivative works of the Document.

If the Cover Text requirement of section 3 is applicable to these copies of the Document, then if the Document is less than one half of the entire aggregate, the Document's Cover Texts may be placed on covers that bracket the Document within the aggregate, or the electronic equivalent of covers if the Document is in electronic form. Otherwise they must appear on printed covers that bracket the whole aggregate.

8. TRANSLATION

Translation is considered a kind of modification, so you may distribute translations of the Document under the terms of section 4. Replacing Invariant Sections with translations requires special permission from their copyright holders, but you may include translations of some or all Invariant Sections in addition to the original versions of these Invariant Sections. You may include a translation of this License, and all the license notices in the Document, and any Warranty Disclaimers, provided that you also include the original English version of this License and the original versions of those notices and disclaimers. In case of a disagreement between the translation and the original version of this License or a notice or disclaimer, the original version will prevail.

If a section in the Document is Entitled "Acknowledgements", "Dedications", or "History", the requirement (section 4) to Preserve its Title (section 1) will typically require changing the actual title.

9. TERMINATION

You may not copy, modify, sublicense, or distribute the Document except as expressly provided under this License. Any attempt otherwise to copy, modify, sublicense, or distribute it is void, and will automatically terminate your rights under this License.

However, if you cease all violation of this License, then your license from a particular copyright holder is reinstated (a) provisionally, unless and until the copyright holder explicitly and finally terminates your license, and (b) permanently, if the copyright holder fails to notify you of the violation by some reasonable means prior to 60 days after the cessation.

Moreover, your license from a particular copyright holder is reinstated permanently if the copyright holder notifies you of the violation by some reasonable means, this is the first time you have received notice of violation of this License (for any work) from that copyright holder, and you cure the violation prior to 30 days after your receipt of the notice.

Termination of your rights under this section does not terminate the licenses of parties who have received copies or rights from you under this License. If your rights have been terminated and not permanently reinstated, receipt of a copy of some or all of the same material does not give you any rights to use it.

10. FUTURE REVISIONS OF THIS LICENSE

The Free Software Foundation may publish new, revised versions of the GNU Free Documentation License from time to time. Such new versions will be similar in spirit to the present version, but may differ in detail to address new problems or concerns. See `https://www.gnu.org/copyleft/`.

Each version of the License is given a distinguishing version number. If the Document specifies that a particular numbered version of this License "or any later version" applies to it, you have the option of following the terms and conditions either of that specified version or of any later version that has been published (not as a draft) by the Free Software Foundation. If the Document does not specify a version number of this License, you may choose any version ever published (not as a draft) by the Free Software Foundation. If the Document specifies that a proxy can decide which future versions of this License can be used, that proxy's public statement of acceptance of a version permanently authorizes you to choose that version for the Document.

11. RELICENSING

"Massive Multiauthor Collaboration Site" (or "MMC Site") means any World Wide Web server that publishes copyrightable works and also provides prominent facilities for anybody to edit those works. A public wiki that anybody can edit is an example of such a server. A "Massive Multiauthor Collaboration" (or "MMC") contained in the site means any set of copyrightable works thus published on the MMC site.

"CC-BY-SA" means the Creative Commons Attribution-Share Alike 3.0 license published by Creative Commons Corporation, a not-for-profit corporation with a principal place of business in San Francisco, California, as well as future copyleft versions of that license published by that same organization.

"Incorporate" means to publish or republish a Document, in whole or in part, as part of another Document.

An MMC is "eligible for relicensing" if it is licensed under this License, and if all works that were first published under this License somewhere other than this MMC, and subsequently incorporated in whole or in part into the MMC, (1) had no cover texts or invariant sections, and (2) were thus incorporated prior to November 1, 2008.

The operator of an MMC Site may republish an MMC contained in the site under CC-BY-SA on the same site at any time before August 1, 2009, provided the MMC is eligible for relicensing.

ADDENDUM: How to use this License for your documents

To use this License in a document you have written, include a copy of the License in the document and put the following copyright and license notices just after the title page:

```
Copyright (C)  year  your name.
Permission is granted to copy, distribute and/or modify this document
under the terms of the GNU Free Documentation License, Version 1.3
or any later version published by the Free Software Foundation;
with no Invariant Sections, no Front-Cover Texts, and no Back-Cover
Texts.  A copy of the license is included in the section entitled ''GNU
Free Documentation License''.
```

If you have Invariant Sections, Front-Cover Texts and Back-Cover Texts, replace the "with...Texts." line with this:

```
with the Invariant Sections being list their titles, with
the Front-Cover Texts being list, and with the Back-Cover Texts
being list.
```

If you have Invariant Sections without Cover Texts, or some other combination of the three, merge those two alternatives to suit the situation.

If your document contains nontrivial examples of program code, we recommend releasing these examples in parallel under your choice of free software license, such as the GNU General Public License, to permit their use in free software.

Concept Index

Function and Type Index

O

S

T